THIRD WORLD
AMERICA

THIRD WORLD
AMERICA

HOW OUR POLITICIANS ARE ABANDONING THE MIDDLE CLASS
AND BETRAYING THE AMERICAN DREAM

ARIANNA
HUFFINGTON

CROWN PUBLISHERS ★ NEW YORK

Library of Congress Cataloging-in-Publication Data
Huffington, Arianna Stassinopoulos
Third World America/Arianna Huffington. —1st ed.
p.   cm.
1. United States—Economic policy—2009–   2. United
States—Economic conditions—2009–   3. United States—Social
policy—1993–   4. United States—Politics and government—
2009–   I. Title.
HC106.84.H84 2010
330.973—dc22   2010026871

ISBN 978-0-307-71982-9

PRINTED IN THE UNITED STATES OF AMERICA

Design by Gretchen Achilles

7   9   10   8   6

For the millions of middle-class Americans fighting
to keep the American Dream alive

CONTENTS

PREFACE

Growing up, I remember walking to school in Athens past a statue of President Truman. The statue was a daily reminder of the magnificent nation responsible for, among other things, the Marshall Plan.

Everyone in Greece either had a family member, or, like my family, a friend, who'd left to find a better life in America. That was the phrase everyone associated with America: "a better life." America was a place you could go to work really hard, make a good living, and even send money back home—a better life.

I was sixteen when I first came to America as part of a program called the Experiment in International Living. I spent the summer in York, Pennsylvania, staying with four different families. I went back to Athens, and then soon went on to Cambridge and London. But part of me remained in America.

When I came back in 1980, I knew that this time it would be for good. Thirty years later, there's still no other place I'd rather live. Over that time, one of the characteristics I've come to love the most about my adopted country is its optimism. In fact, it melded perfectly with my own Greek temperament: Zorba the Greek meets the American spirit. The Italian journalist Luigi Barzini wrote that America "is alarmingly optimistic, compassionate, incredibly generous . . . It was a spiritual wind that drove

Americans irresistibly ahead from the beginning." The only downside of the optimistic spirit is that it can sometimes prevent us from seeing what is unfolding until it's too late.

In recent years, as the evidence mounted about the road we're on as a country—one that I was sure would prove disastrous if we failed to course-correct in time—I was conflicted. I wanted to believe everything would turn out okay, as it has so often in the past. But the stubborn facts kept nagging at me as the warning signs became more and more numerous. I had to choose whether to sound like Cassandra or fall back on a double dose of the congenital optimism of both my native and adopted countries and assume it was all just another speed bump on the road to a "more perfect union." It's never fun being Cassandra. But remember, Cassandra ended up being right. And the Trojans, who remained blissfully blind to her warnings, ended up being very wrong and very dead.

So, yes, as I look around at our great, sprawling country, we are obviously not yet a Third World nation. But we are well on our way. This is the unspoken fear of so many out-of-work Americans and those still at work but anxious about their futures and the futures of their children. My goal for this book is to sound the alarm so that we never do become "Third World America."

"America," Winston Churchill reportedly said, "can always be counted on to do the right thing, after it has exhausted all other possibilities." Well, we have exhausted a lot of possibilities, and for millions of the unemployed, the underemployed, the ones whose homes have been foreclosed, and the ones who've declared bankruptcy or can't pay their credit card bills, the process has already been very painful. It's time now to do the right things.

The book closes on an optimistic note. Part 5 is about many of those *right things* being done around the country. Because in the end, despite the acts of greed, cronyism, and disregard for the public interest committed by both business and political leaders, I am ultimately heartened by the resilience, creativity, and largely unheralded acts of compassion and empathy that I see among Americans everywhere. Turning our country around will take the concerted effort of citizens all across America, standing up for themselves, their families, and their communities—both demanding change and embodying it—and keeping the promise of the American Dream alive for future generations.

1

★

THIRD
WORLD AMERICA

★ ★ ★

"Third World America."

It's a jarring phrase, one that is deeply contrary to our national conviction that America is the greatest nation on Earth—as well as the richest, the most powerful, the most generous, and the most noble. It also doesn't match our day-to-day experience of the country we live in—where it seems there is, if not a chicken in every pot, then a flat-screen TV on every wall. And we're still the world's only military superpower, right?

So what, exactly, does it mean—"Third World America"?

For me, it's a warning: a shimmering foreshadowing of a possible future. It is the flip side of the American Dream—an American nightmare of our own making.

I use it to sum up the ugly facts we'd rather not know, to connect the uncomfortable dots we'd rather not connect, and to articulate one of our deepest fears as a people—that we are slipping as a nation. It's a harbinger, a clanging alarm telling us that if we don't correct our course, contrary to our history and to what has always seemed to be our destiny, we could indeed become a Third World nation—a place where there are only two classes: the rich . . . and everyone else. Think Mexico or Brazil, where the wealthy live behind fortified gates, with machine-gun-toting guards protecting their children from kidnapping.

A place that failed to keep up with history. A place not

taken down by a foreign enemy, but by the avarice of our corporate elite and the neglect of our elected leaders.

The warning lights on our national dashboard are flashing red: Our industrial base is vanishing, taking with it the kind of jobs that have formed the backbone of our economy for more than a century; our education system is in shambles, making it harder for tomorrow's workforce to acquire the information and training it needs to land good twenty-first-century jobs; our infrastructure—our roads, our bridges, our sewage and water and transportation and electrical systems—is crumbling.

And America's middle class, the driver of so much of our creative and economic success—the foundation of our democracy—is rapidly disappearing, taking with it a key component of the American Dream: the promise that, with hard work and discipline, our children will have the chance to do better than we did, just as we had the chance to do better than the generation before us.

Nothing better illustrates the ways in which we have begun to travel down this perilous road than the sorry state of America's middle class. So long as our middle class is thriving, it would be impossible for America to become a Third World nation. But the facts show a different trajectory. It's no longer an exaggeration to say that middle-class Americans are an endangered species.

"The middle class has been under assault for a long time," President Obama said early in 2010 while announcing a series of modest proposals to bolster what he called "the class that made the twentieth century the American century."

During the 2008 campaign, Barack Obama's guiding principle was that he "would not forget the middle class." Indeed, David Plouffe, Obama's campaign manager, told me after the election, "We held that North Star in our sights at all times. We made many mistakes along the way, but we always remembered that we were running because, as Barack put it, the dreams so many generations had fought for were slipping away." Well, you'd need a pretty powerful telescope to see that North Star these days.

According to Plouffe, Obama and his team decided that he should make a run for the White House because "the core leadership had turned rotten" and "the people were getting hosed." But the extent to which the people have continued to be hosed and the middle class assaulted becomes shockingly clear when the baby steps taken to bail out Main Street are compared to the all-hands-on-deck, no-expenses-spared bailout of Wall Street. In fact, the economic devastation of the middle class is a lot more threatening to the long-term stability of the country than the financial crisis that saw trillions of taxpayer dollars funneled—either directly or through government guarantees—to Wall Street.

The middle class is teetering on the brink of collapse just as surely as AIG was in the fall of 2009—only this time, it's not just one giant insurance company (and its banking counterparties) facing disaster, it's tens of millions of hardworking Americans who played by the rules. This country's middle class is going the way of Lehman Brothers—disappearing in front of our eyes. A decline that began decades ago has now become a plummeting free fall.

Just how bad things have gotten was succinctly—and bracingly—summed up by Elizabeth Warren, chair of the Congressional Oversight Panel charged with monitoring the Troubled Asset Relief Program (TARP): "One in five Americans is unemployed, underemployed or just plain out of work. One in nine families can't make the minimum payment on their credit cards. One in eight mortgages is in default or foreclosure. One in eight Americans is on food stamps. More than 120,000 families are filing for bankruptcy every month. The economic crisis has wiped more than $5 trillion from pensions and savings."

The Bush and Obama administrations bailed out America's big banks because it suddenly became imaginable that the financial system might collapse. When we take a hard look at what's happening to America's middle class, its disappearance suddenly becomes not only imaginable but, unless drastic action is taken, inevitable.

SHORTING THE MIDDLE CLASS

In April 2010, the shot heard around the country—or at least around Wall Street and Capitol Hill—was the Securities and Exchange Commission suing Goldman Sachs for fraud. It was big news in itself, as Goldman Sachs has become the poster child for the deep disconnect between Wall Street and Main Street. But much more important than the Goldman case in particular was the light it shed on what the financial and political elite had been doing to America for the last thirty years: shorting the middle class.

The American people have been sold on the very American idea that working hard and playing by the rules would ensure some modicum of prosperity and stability, while at the same time Wall Street has been overseeing a massive transfer of wealth from the middle class to the richest Americans. Ordinary working Americans were seen as the counterparty in a zero-sum bet—in Wall Street parlance, the proverbial "dumb money" at the table.

The results have been devastating: a disappearing middle class, a precipitous drop in economic and social mobility, and, ultimately, the undermining of the foundation of our democracy.

The human toll of the shorting of the middle class is tallied every day on websites such as Recessionwire.com, Layoff-SupportNetwork.com, and HowIGotLaidOff.com, where the casualties of Wall Street's systemic scam share their personal stories. One tale in particular struck me as emblematic of the place America's middle class finds itself these days. It feels like a dark reboot of the American Dream. Think Horatio Alger rewritten by O. Henry—or Rod Serling.

It's the story of Dean Blackburn of Alameda, California. The first part of his life was a classic American success story. Raised in Minnesota by a single mom who worked as a teacher, he was "middle class by default." Through a combination of smarts and hard work, he made his way to Yale, then, for seventeen years, he steadily progressed up the economic ladder, gaining skills as a project manager, analyst, and IT director.

Then came February 2009, when, at age thirty-five, he was laid off on the last day of the month. His boss chose that day because it meant the company would not have to pay for another month of his health coverage. "Looking back on it," he told me, "that hurt more than the layoff itself—just knowing that the president of the company was exactly that calculating and that unfeeling about my own and my family's well-being." The timing, Blackburn continued, "put those 'family days' and company picnics in a weird new light."

Fourteen months later, Blackburn was still looking for a

new job. His wife, who had taken a year off work when their daughter, Robin, was born, was eager to return to a full-time job. They faced the double challenge of finding an affordable preschool for their two-year-old as well as the jobs that would pay for it. Meanwhile, they tried to maintain their sanity by participating in life as they once had, "but we look at the numbers constantly now, and worry about what will happen when our savings run out," Blackburn told me. "Not if, but when."

As Blackburn dealt with the immediate financial struggles his extended unemployment brought, he became acutely aware of the broader implications of the shorting of the middle class. "Ultimately," he says, "it's not about a dip in corporate profits, but a change in corporate attitude—a change that means no one's job is safe, and never will be, ever again."

It's one of the reasons he decided to start his own company, NaviDate, a data-driven twist on online dating sites: "It's no longer a trade-off between doing what you love and having stability. Stability is long gone, so you better do something you love!"

Achieving middle-class stability has always been a big part of the American Dream, but, as Blackburn notes, mobility now is increasingly one way: "The plateaus of each step, which can be a great place to stop a bit and catch your breath, are gone. Now, it's climb, climb, climb, or start sliding back down immediately." The result: "The odds are you're going to wind up at the bottom eventually, unless you get lucky."

Luck. That's what the American Dream now rests on. It used to be about education, hard work, and perseverance, but today the system is rigged to such an extent that the middle-class life is the prize on a scratch-off lottery ticket. The revelation of the corruption behind the financial crisis has put the very idea of the middle class and the American Dream, as Blackburn put it, "in a weird new light."

A lot of people at the top of the economic food chain have done very well shorting the middle class. But the losers in those bets weren't Goldman Sachs investors—they were millions of Americans whose sole crime was to optimistically buy into the American Dream, only to find it had been replaced by a sophisticated scam.

In November 2008, as the initial aftershocks of the economic earthquake were being felt, *New York Times* columnist David Brooks predicted the rise of a new social class—"the formerly middle class"—made up of those who had just joined the middle class at the end of the boom, only to fall back when the recession began. "To them," he wrote, "the gap between where they are and where they used to be will seem wide and daunting." But, in the time since Brooks wrote this, the ranks of the formerly middle class have swelled far beyond those who joined at the tail end of the boom. And for millions of Americans, that "wide and daunting" gap is also beginning to look permanent.

The evidence that the middle class has been consistently shorted is so overwhelming—and the results so potentially damaging to our society—that even bastions of establishment thinking are on alert. In a 2010 strategy paper, the Hamilton Project—the economic think tank founded in 2006 by former U.S. Treasury secretary Robert Rubin (a big beneficiary of the shorting of the middle class)—argued "that the American tradition of expanding opportunity from one generation to the next is at risk because we are failing to make the necessary investments in human, physical, and environmental capital."

Of course, it's even worse than that. Beyond failing to make necessary investments for the future, we are actually cutting back on our current investment in people, with massive budget cuts in education, health care, and social services in state after state after state, all across America.

At least forty-five states have imposed budget cuts that hurt families and reduce vital services to their most vulnerable residents. Those affected include children, the elderly, the disabled, the sick, the homeless, and the mentally ill, as well as college students and faculty.

According to a report by the Center on Budget and Policy Priorities, at least twenty-nine states have made cuts to public health programs, twenty-four states have cut programs for the elderly and disabled, twenty-nine states have cut aid to K–12 education, and thirty-nine states have cut assistance to public colleges and universities.

America's states faced a cumulative budget gap of $166 billion for fiscal 2010. Total shortfalls through fiscal 2011 are estimated at $380 billion—and could be even higher depending on what happens to unemployment.

These are massive numbers. But when you remember that we spent $182 billion to bail out AIG ($12.9 billion of which went straight to Goldman Sachs), you realize that this amount alone would be more than enough to close the 2010 budget gap in every state in the Union. Toss in the $45 billion we gave to now-making-a-profit Bank of America and the $45 billion we gave to now-making-a-profit Citigroup, and we would be well on the way to ensuring that no state's vital services are cut through 2011.

But instead that money has gone to the banks without any fundamental reform of the system, without any strings attached or edicts about how much they have to lend to help the real economy recover—or, indeed, without even having to tell us what they did with our money.

All across the country, the fiscal ax is falling. The devastation is in the details:

- California is eliminating CalWORKS, a financial assistance program for families in need, a cut that will affect 1.4 million people, two-thirds of whom are children. This plan would also cut state subsidies for child care, affecting 142,000 children.

- Minnesota has eliminated a program that provides health care to 21,500 low-income employed adults with no children.

- Rhode Island has cut health insurance for 1,000 low-income families.

- Maine has cut education grants and funding for homeless shelters.

- Utah has cut Medicaid for physical and occupational therapies, as well as for speech and hearing services.

- Michigan, Nevada, California, and Utah have eliminated coverage of dental and vision services for those receiving Medicaid.

- Alabama has canceled services that allow 1,100 seniors to stay in their own homes instead of being sent to nursing facilities.

- Georgia has cut $112 million from an initiative designed to reduce the gap in funding between wealthy and poor school districts.

- Arizona has cut cash assistance grants for 38,500 low-income families.

- Virginia has decreased payments for people with mental retardation, mental health issues, and problems with substance abuse.

- Illinois has cut funding for child welfare and youth services programs.

- Connecticut has cut programs that help prevent child abuse and provide legal services for foster children.

- Massachusetts is making cuts in Head Start, universal pre-K programs, and services to prepare special-needs children for school.

Keep in mind, all these services are being cut at a time when more and more people are finding themselves in need of them. It's a perfect storm of middle-class suffering.

And yet the human consequences of the financial collapse are largely missing from our national debate. I'm referring especially to the people who had steady jobs; people with college degrees; people who were paying their bills, saving for retirement, doing the right thing—and who have, in many instances, lost everything. The daily miseries being visited upon them are unfolding across the country.

So why is there no sense of urgency coming out of Washington?

Perhaps the reason can be found in the stunning results of a study conducted by Northeastern University's Center for Labor Market Studies that broke down the unemployment rate by household income. Unemployment for those making $150,000 a year, the study found, was only 3 percent in the last quarter of 2009. The rate for those in the middle income range was 9 percent—not far off the national average. The rate for those in the bottom 10 percent of income was a staggering 31 percent.

These numbers, according to the *Wall Street Journal's* Robert Frank, "raise questions about the theory behind what is informally known as 'trickle down' economics, since full employment at the top doesn't seem to be translating into more jobs below."

In fact, these numbers do more than raise questions—they also supply the answers.

Does anyone believe that the sense of urgency coming out of Washington wouldn't be wildly different if the unemployment rate for the top 10 percent of income earners was 31 percent? If one-third of television news producers, pundits, bankers, and lobbyists were unemployed, would the measures proposed by the White House and Congress still be as anemic? Of course not—the sense of national emergency would be so great you'd hear air-raid sirens howling.

Instead we get policy Band-Aids—timid moves that will do little to abate a crisis that threatens to change the very fabric of our society. For much of our history, America was known for its promise of upward mobility. That promise has been called into question over the past three decades, and an extended run of high unemployment could be its death knell.

"These are the kinds of jobless rates that push families already struggling on meager incomes into destitution," wrote *New York Times* columnist Bob Herbert. "And such gruesome gaps in the condition of groups at the top and bottom of the economic ladder are unmistakable signs of impending societal instability. This is dangerous stuff."

The lack of urgency we are seeing in Washington—and the lack of focus on real people—is stunning considering that the consequences of our failed financial system are everywhere you look. Putting flesh and blood on the cold, hard statistics means putting the spotlight on the people whose lives were turned upside down as a result of our out-of-control financial system.

Ron Bednar and Mary McCurnin of Rancho Cordova, California, are a loving couple that got divorced last year, not because their relationship wasn't working but because it was the only way to make ends meet. Due to unemployment and a bankruptcy caused by a prolonged illness, they found themselves with only $300 in the bank. By getting divorced, McCurnin was able to collect Social Security widow's benefits from her first husband, who died in 1989. "We literally live from week to week," she says.

Kimberly Rios of North East, Maryland, sold her wedding ring on Craigslist so she could pay her utility bills. "This is no joke, please be a serious buyer," her ad read. "It is too cold for us to be without electric and heat so if you have been looking consider my deal." After selling her ring, she locked herself in her bathroom, pretending to take a shower, so she could cry without upsetting her family. "I just felt like it was the last piece of what little I had left," she says. "I came out smiling as usual and tried to get my husband and daughter excited that this was a good thing."

Faye Harris was laid off from her accounting job at Emory University Hospital in Atlanta last year. She had been diagnosed with cancer and was fighting it successfully. But as soon as the time off she was guaranteed by the Family and Medical Leave Act expired, she received a letter of termination and her health insurance was canceled. "Do I just lie down and die? Am I not worthy anymore?" she asked herself. "I've worked all my life. Put myself through school, raised four children, played by the rules, saved money, and this one illness has just wiped me out."

Ricky Macoy of Quinlan, Texas, is a fifty-two-year-old electrician who found himself among the long-term unemployed. With little work since late 2008, he began pawning his possessions, including his tools, and holding yard sales to get enough money to feed his family. "The thing that hurt the most was we had to hock my son's PlayStation 3, his Wii, his electric guitar," Macoy says. "We lived a good life. Middle-income America, man. I'm used to construction, the booms and the busts . . . [but] I was not expecting to be laid off this long."

Heather Tanner of Pacifica, California, put herself through law school, working during the day and attending classes at night—dreaming of one day being able to move her family out of their apartment and buy a house. In August, she was laid off from her $100,000-a-year job as an attorney—and then struggled to find a new position. "I applied for jobs at Target, Macy's, as a camp counselor," she says. "I've been on many interviews, but the comments I get at nonlegal jobs are, 'Why do you need this kind of job?' I mean, I have a family to support." She and her husband cashed in their 401(k)s and used their savings to pay off bills. "The kids don't understand," she says, explaining that the thing that hurt the most was having to disappoint her children when it came to things such as birthday visits to Disneyland the family could no longer afford. "I'd love to make their dreams come true, but right now we just have to focus on getting by."

There are, sadly, millions of these stories. Stories crying

out to be told. Stories that, if told often enough, will bring the human element to the fore of the debate—and grab the public's imagination.

In the last chapter of Michael Herr's *Dispatches,* he speaks of conventional journalism's inability to "reveal" the Vietnam War: "The press got all the facts (more or less). . . . But it never found a way to report meaningfully about death, which of course was really what it was all about." And Tom Wolfe, in "The Birth of 'The New Journalism': Eyewitness Report," discusses conventional journalism's inability to capture the turbulence of the 1960s: "You can't imagine what a positive word 'understatement' was among both journalists and literati. . . . The trouble was that by the early 1960s understatement had become an absolute pall." Well, it's happening again—we are failing to capture the turbulence of our times with narratives that allow the public, and force our leaders, to connect with the pain and suffering that should be fueling the fight to change direction while there's still time.

WORKING-CLASS SUFFERING MEETS REALITY TV

Before becoming prime minister of England, Benjamin Disraeli wanted to issue a wake-up call about the horrible state of the British working class. So, in 1845, he wrote a novel, *Sybil,* which warned of the danger of England disintegrating into "two nations between whom there is no sympathy . . . as if they were inhabitants of different planets." The book became a sensation, and the outrage it provoked propelled fundamental social reforms.

In the nineteenth century, one of the most effective ways to convey the quiet desperation of the working class to a wide audience was via a realistic novel. In 2010, it's through reality TV.

Now, I realize that most of what we are served up under that rubric is actually the farthest thing from reality. The exploits of Snooki, Jake the Bachelor, and all those Real Housewives hardly reflect life as most of America knows it and lives it.

The real America is hurting—not jetting off to an exotic location for "fantasy suite" canoodling. But no matter how sobering the statistics we are getting on a regular basis (and I'll offer up some bracing ones in a moment), the hardships and suffering tens of millions of Americans are experiencing are almost entirely absent from our popular culture. This is a shame, because drama and narrative have the ability to move people's perceptions in a way that raw numbers never can.

Enter *Undercover Boss,* the CBS reality show in which corporate CEOs don disguises and spend a few days experiencing what it's like to be a low-level worker at their companies. It's the kind of popular entertainment that can start out as one thing— a fun, high-concept reality show—but morph into something that affects the zeitgeist by shining a spotlight on just how out of touch America's corporate chiefs are. And their cluelessness is not just about the jobs their workers do—it's about the lives their workers lead.

Ever since *Roseanne* went off the air, the stories of working-class Americans have been all but invisible on network TV. But now, week in and week out, millions can see what downsizing and Wall Street's demands for ever-greater productivity and earnings margins did to the lives of so many Americans, even before the economic crisis.

The chasm between America's classes has reached Grand Canyon–esque proportions. Forty years ago, top executives at

S&P 500 companies made an average of thirty times what their workers did—now they make three hundred times what their workers make. That's the kind of statistic a show like *Undercover Boss* can bring to life. Here are a few others:

- Between 2007 and 2008, more than 800,000 additional American households found themselves trying to make do on under $25,000 a year, bringing the total to nearly 29 million.

- In 2005, households in the bottom 20 percent had an average income of $10,655, while the top 20 percent made $159,583—a disparity of 1,500 percent, the highest gap ever recorded.

- In 2007, the top 10 percent pocketed almost half of all the money earned in America—the highest percentage recorded since 1917 (including, as Business Insider editor Henry Blodget noted, in 1928, the peak of the stock market bubble in the "roaring 1920s").

- Between 2000 and 2008, the poverty rate in the suburbs of the largest metro areas in the United States grew by 25 percent—making the suburbs home to the country's biggest and most rapidly expanding segment of the poor.

Making matters even worse is the fact that while the classes are moving farther apart—with the middle class in real danger of disappearing entirely—mobility across the classes has declined. The American Dream is defined by the promise of economic and social mobility—but the American Reality proves just how elusive that dream has become. Indeed, Canada, Germany, Denmark, Norway, Finland, Sweden, and even the often-reviled France have greater upward mobility than we do.

Here are the numbers:

- Almost one hundred million Americans are in families that make less in real income than their parents did at the same age.

- The percentage of Americans born to parents in the bottom fifth of income who will climb to the top fifth as adults is now only 7 percent.

- If you were born to wealthy parents but didn't go to college, you're more likely to be wealthy than if you did go to college but had poor parents.

In other words, as the middle class is squeezed and more and more people are being pushed down, it's becoming harder than ever to move up. In a study of economic mobility, Isabel Sawhill of the Brookings Institution and John E. Morton of the Pew Charitable Trusts wrote, "The inherent promise of America is undermined if economic status is—or is seen as—merely a game of chance, with some having the good fortune to live in the best of times and some the bad luck to live in the worst of times. That is not the America heralded in lore and experienced in reality by millions of our predecessors."

And yet it's certainly the reality being experienced now, and, at least in part, the reality being shown on *Undercover Boss*. Now, I'm not suggesting that the show is going to foment a working-class rebellion or directly lead to a raft of social reforms. But it might lead to a conversation we, as a nation, desperately need to have—especially in Washington.

Maybe if our elected representatives went undercover for a little while and experienced the reality of millions of American families that are measurably worse off because of Washington's actions and inactions, we might get some real change.

MIDDLE-CLASS JOBS AND "THAT GIANT SUCKING SOUND"

Since the recession began in late 2007, we've lost more than 8.4 million jobs. Over 2 million of those were manufacturing jobs, the kind of jobs that have traditionally delivered American families into the middle class—and kept them there. We lost 1.2 million manufacturing jobs in 2009 alone. And while job numbers go up and down, the loss of these blue-collar jobs has been going on for decades.

In 1950, manufacturing accounted for more than 30 percent of nonfarm employment. As of last year, it's down to 10 percent. Indeed, one-third of all our manufacturing jobs have disappeared since 2000. This devastating downward trend has contributed greatly to the erosion of the middle class.

There have been a number of recessions over the past few decades, and our economy has rebounded after each one. But each time it has bounced back in a way that made it harder for those in the middle class to stay there—and even harder for those aspiring to become middle class to get there.

The way that the useful section of our economy is being replaced by the useless section of our economy is rarely talked about in Washington. But the numbers don't lie: The share of our economy devoted to making things of value is shrinking, while the share devoted to valuing made-up things (credit-swap derivatives, anyone?) is expanding. It's the financialization of our economy.

According to Thomas Philippon, professor at New York University's Stern School of Business, the financial industry made up 2.5 percent of America's GDP in 1947. By 1970, it had grown to 4 percent. By 2006, just before the meltdown, it was 8.3 percent.

The trend is even starker when you look at the financial sector's share of U.S. business profits. As MIT professor Simon Johnson recounted in the *Atlantic*, between 1973 and 1985, the financial industry's share of domestic corporate profits topped out at 16 percent. In the 1990s, it spanned between 21 percent and 30 percent. Just before the financial crisis hit, it stood at 41 percent.

That's right—over 40 percent of the profits of the entire U.S. corporate sector went to the financial industry. James Kwak, coauthor of the Baseline Scenario, a leading blog on economics and public policy, explains why this is a problem: "Remember that financial services are an intermediate product—that is, we don't eat them, or live in them, or put them on in the morning. They are supposed to enable a more efficient allocation of capital, so that the nonfinancial economy is more productive. But what we saw since the 1980s was the unmooring of the financial sector from the rest of the economy."

In other words—it's supposed to serve our economy, not *become* our economy.

The expansion of the financial industry has come at a significant cost to the rest of us. And those who have paid the highest price are the members—and former members—of America's middle class. According to *New York Times* columnist Paul

Krugman, "A growing body of analysis suggests that an over-sized financial industry is hurting the broader economy. Shrinking that oversized industry won't make Wall Street happy, but what's bad for Wall Street would be good for America."

It's no wonder that Wall Street breathed a deep sigh of relief when the Senate passed the Restoring American Financial Stability Act in May 2010. It was considered mission accomplished for financial reform.

Unfortunately, it was more of a Bush 43 mission accomplished than an *Apollo 13* mission accomplished. That's because the bill passed by the Senate, like Bush's ship-deck ceremony, was more notable for what it left undone.

First, it didn't do enough to rein in Wall Street. It didn't end too-big-to-fail banks, didn't create a Glass-Steagall-style firewall between commercial and investment banking, kept taxpayers on the hook for future bailouts, and left open dangerous loopholes in the regulation of derivatives. In D.C., crafting a bill without loopholes would be like baking bread without yeast. Though you can't see them, they're what makes a Washington bill rise.

Despite its name, this bill will not be restoring financial stability to the tens of millions of Americans whose lives have been turned upside down by the economic crisis.

On nearly every front in the real economy—from jobs to consumer spending to foreclosures—we've made virtually no progress. While Washington and the media were consumed with the titanic debate over this reform bill, talk of the actual suffering by actual people in the actual economy was virtually a taboo subject, at least judging by how rarely it made the front pages or led the TV news.

But the data points are all around us. In a speech, Sandra

Pianalto, president of the Cleveland Fed, surveyed the land-scape and described an economy facing serious and long-term challenges, partly because of the huge loss of skills that is being suffered by the long-term unemployed. "Research . . . tells us that workers lose valuable skills during long spells of unemployment, and that some jobs simply don't return," she said. "Multiply this effect millions of times over, and it has the potential to dampen overall economic productivity for years."

Her conclusion: "Many people are now just aiming for 'financial security' as their American Dream." In other words, the core idea of the American Dream—work hard and advance up the ladder—has been gutted. Now the American Dream is try to not fall, or do all you can to slow your rate of decline.

And forget about having enough in the bank to give your kids a leg up on doing better than you've done. It's hard enough just to keep a job until you retire—if that's even going to be an option. At a D.C. jobs fair for older workers in May 2010, more than 3,000 job seekers showed up for the event, entitled "Promoting Yourself at 50+." Not surprising given that, at the time, the average jobless stint for those unemployed who are fifty-five and over was around forty-three weeks. (Quick note to struggling politicians out there: want a huge crowd at your campaign rally? Call it a "jobs fair" and you'll have people lined up around the corner.)

Their children and grandchildren who recently graduated from college aren't faring any better. According to *BusinessWeek*, the 1.6 million new grads hitting the job market with their expensive degrees are confronting a youth unemployment rate of almost 20 percent—"the highest level since the Labor Department began tracking the data in 1948."

And many workers who have managed to hold on to their jobs are increasingly doing so only by accepting less pay and taking on a higher share of their health-care costs. "My company didn't eliminate my job, they just eliminated my salary," said marketing director Mike Cheaure. "I was back at work as a freelancer the next day working at one-fourth of the pay and no benefits." The experience has made him very familiar with the new reality. "For us, the American Dream is gone," he said. "Now it's just getting by."

Adding insult to injury, a growing number of working mothers are having to give up their jobs and rely on welfare because states are cutting back on child-care services that allowed them to keep working. And kids were left scrambling to find something to do this past summer when a number of states made deep cuts to summer school programs.

This spring saw a surge in consumer spending that spawned talk of "green shoots." But it turned out the spending surge was economically imbalanced. As the *Los Angeles Times*'s Don Lee put it, the "little-noticed reality" behind the "encouraging numbers" was that "much of the new spending [had] come not from America's broad middle class but from a small slice of affluent people at the top." In fact, according to the Labor Department, the richest 20 percent of American households accounted for 40 percent of all spending.

The news in consumer lending has been similarly dismal—especially among the banks that got the most help from taxpayers. According to the Federal Reserve, from June 2009 to June 2010, the largest banks cut business lending by over $148 billion—yet more evidence of the schism between the Wall Street economy and the real economy. Of course, the two economies aren't entirely separate—the Wall Street economy is happy to accept massive transfusions of cash from the fading middle class.

This isn't to say that there were no provisions considered that would help Main Street as part of the Restoring American Financial Stability Act. There were plenty—it's just that almost all of them were either voted down or taken out and never even put up for a vote. Even something as simple and sensible as putting a cap on credit card interest rates. Senator Sheldon Whitehouse's amendment to do just that was voted down 60 to 35. So much for "financial stability." Though I suppose it depends on whose financial stability you care about—the banks' or the taxpayers'.

Or how about payday lending—the largely unregulated advances on a paycheck that can carry interest rates in the triple digits? In Missouri, for example, rates can top 600 percent. Yes, you read that right. Not exactly a recipe for "financial stability." North Carolina's Kay Hagan offered an amendment that would have clamped down on the $40 billion industry. It was killed without a vote.

Then there is the Merkley-Levin amendment that would have prohibited banks from making risky proprietary trades— a version of the Volcker Rule. It also never even made it to a vote. This wasn't because it wouldn't have passed. On the contrary, anger from those mired in the real economy had reached enough lawmakers that the amendment had a real shot. Which is why, as Simon Johnson put it, "the big banks were forced into overdrive to stop it."

We've been told time and time again over the last two years that right after Washington deals with what's on its plate, "jobs is next." Well, it's been "next" for quite some time now, but it never seems to come to the floor. I often have a nightmare—a common sort—in which I'm stuck in a forest and I can't find my way out. I have a friend whose version is that her feet are stuck to the ground and she can't move. Not a bad description of our leaders' approach to the massive suffering that's going on across America.

A recent study by Duha Tore Altindag and Naci H. Mocan for the National Bureau of Economic Research found that the effects of unemployment can have troubling implications for a political system. The authors studied data from 130,000 people in 69 countries. Their conclusion: "We find that personal joblessness experience translates into negative opinions about the effectiveness of democracy."

No shock there. But it should frighten anyone genuinely concerned about our stability, financial and otherwise—especially since one out of every six blue-collar workers has lost his or her job in the latest recession, a number commensurate with what happened during the Great Depression. Andrew Sum, director of the Center for Labor Market Studies at Northeastern University in Boston, says, "Our ability to maintain a healthy middle class is very dependent on being able to get a lot of these individuals back into the workplace and back into jobs to keep the rest of the economy going. . . . There are very high multiplier effects from many manufacturing activities. So the loss of jobs spills over into the rest of the economy."

But isn't wringing our hands over the loss of manufacturing jobs the twenty-first-century equivalent to nineteenth-century concerns about America turning from an agrarian society into an industrial one? Isn't America's future to be found in newer, better, more modern service industry jobs?

Economist Jeff Madrick doesn't think so—for a number of reasons.

For starters, it turns out that manufacturing jobs aren't just more productive and valuable than jobs in the Wall Street casino—they're also more valuable than service jobs: "Making goods is on balance—with exceptions—more productive than providing services, and rising productivity is the fundamental source of prosperity," says Madrick. "A major nation must be able to maintain a balanced current account (and trade balance) over time, and goods are far more tradable than services. Without something to export, a nation will either become over-indebted or forced to reduce its standard of living."

In other words, in the absence of manufacturing, the only way to compete with Third World nations is to *become* a Third World nation, which is exactly what will happen if we allow our middle class to disappear.

What's more, it's not just manufacturing and lower skilled service jobs that are disappearing. According to the Hackett Group, a business and technology consultancy, companies with revenues of $5 billion and over are expected to take an estimated 350,000 jobs offshore in the next two years alone—nearly half in information technology, and the rest in finance, procurement, and human resources.

Linda Levine of the Congressional Research Service says that some see "perhaps a total of 3.4 million service sector jobs moving overseas by 2015 in a range of fairly well paid white-collar occupations." And in a 2006 study, consulting firm Booz Allen Hamilton found that white-collar outsourcing is no longer just about call center and credit card transactions. Now "companies are offshoring high-end work that has traditionally been considered 'core' to the business, including chip design, financial and legal research, clinical trials management, and book editing."

Do you hear that? It's Ross Perot's giant sucking sound being cranked up to a deafening roar—and it's about a lot more than NAFTA. Accenture now employs more people in India than in America. IBM is headed in the same direction. And the horizon looks even darker. A June 2008 Harvard Business School study found that up to 42 percent of U.S. jobs—more than fifty million of them—are vulnerable to being sent offshore.

Even more troubling is the reason so many of these jobs are being sent overseas. It's not just about cost control. "What used to be a tactical labor cost-saving exercise," the Booz Allen Hamilton study says, "is now a strategic imperative of competing for talent globally." In other words, America's talent pool—especially when it comes to professions such as engineers and computer scientists—is drying up. At the same time the demand for these highly skilled workers is growing, the number of Americans earning master's degrees and PhDs in engineering has fallen.

We are continuing to feel the sting of our lack of investment in our people—particularly when it comes to education, the other primary pillar (along with a good job) of a healthy middle class.

This is what happens when a country is willing to spend trillions of dollars fighting unnecessary wars while allowing college tuition to rise out of the reach of so many of its citizens. And it's what happens when a country turns its economy over to the casino of Wall Street.

It's not too late to change course. The financialization of our economy didn't just happen. Decisions were made that made it possible—and decisions can be unmade. But first we need to decide, as a country, what kind of economy we want to have: one that's good for middle-class families or one that's built to enrich Wall Street.

"The financial sector," wrote Martin Wolf of the *Financial Times,* "seems to be a machine to transfer income and wealth from outsiders to insiders, while increasing the fragility of the economy as a whole." When the chief economics commentator at the *Financial Times* is sounding like the second coming of Karl Marx, you know things have gotten way out of hand.

THE ECONOMIC CORONARY AROUND THE CORNER

Another potentially catastrophic problem headed our way is our mounting debt. And no, I'm not joining forces with those who use the debt explosion as a backdoor way of cutting or killing Social Security or Medicare. But ceding this issue to such retro-thinkers makes it that much harder to seriously tackle the problem.

America is like a patient in danger of suffering a massive heart attack. We may be able to postpone things with a bit of outpatient surgery, but we won't be able to avoid it without some serious lifestyle changes. The economic coronary isn't quite here yet, but it's on the way. Here are just a couple of the symptoms of big-time trouble ahead:

By 2020, interest alone on the total U.S. debt will reach $900 billion per year.

That same year, five segments of government spending—Medicare, Medicaid, Social Security, net interest, and defense spending—will account for an estimated 77 percent of all government expenditures. All other federal spending will have to come out of the remaining 23 percent.

A recent report by the Bank for International Settlements (BIS) shows that this is a worldwide phenomenon. Financial adviser John Mauldin distills the report's bottom line: "Everyone and their brother intuitively knows that the current government fiscal deficits in the developed world are unsustainable."

The numbers in the BIS study make this clear. For instance, in Greece, the problem child of the moment that everyone is looking at with horror, government debt could reach 130 percent of gross domestic product in 2011. But Greece is far from alone. In the United Kingdom, it is expected to hit 94 percent, jumping more than 10 percentage points in one year. And in the United States, we could approach nearly 100 percent. As a Greek American, I'm enthusiastic about all the shared traits of my two countries, but I'd prefer not to add crippling debt to the list.

"While fiscal problems need to be tackled soon," says the BIS report, "how to do that without seriously jeopardizing the incipient economic recovery is the current key challenge for fiscal authorities."

Exactly. And those fiscal authorities need to remember that there is more to tackling the deficit crisis than just cutting spending. We need to think bigger—we need to reorient our economy so that it's once more an engine for production and productivity, not a vehicle for gambling and speculation. As Mauldin says of the old—and still dominant—order on Wall Street: "Let's be very clear. This was purely gambling. No money was invested in mortgages or any productive enterprise. This was one group betting against another, and a *lot* of these deals were done all over New York and London."

Mauldin goes on to question why large institutional investors were even gambling on such things as synthetic collateralized debt obligations in the first place: "This is an investment that had no productive capital at work and no remotely socially redeeming value. It did not go to fund mortgages or buy capital equipment or build malls or office buildings."

Commenting on our looming debt crisis, Princeton economist Alan Blinder noted that "in 1980 [policymakers] knew about the year 2010 but that was really far away." Well, it's not anymore, and given that much of our deficit problem is about huge numbers of workers born decades ago now hitting retirement age, Blinder quipped, "The long run is now the short run and they're combining."

The needs of the past and the demands of the present exert a powerful pull on our attention, while the future doesn't have many advocates—it's always something we can get to later. There once was a time when we could get away with pushing our problems down the road, secure that our reserves would always bail us out. There was a strong safety net to catch those who fell through the cracks. Well, those reserves are gone now and the safety net is frayed and full of holes.

PERVERTED PRIORITIES

Another warning sign that we are on the way to becoming a Third World nation is the trillions of dollars we continue to spend fighting unnecessary wars and building ever more powerful weaponry while our people here at home do without.

You want Third World thinking? How about North Korea joining the nuclear club while its people starve? Since the fall of the Roman Empire, one of the hallmarks of nations in decline has been increased military spending at the expense of other essential priorities. Think of the Soviets trying to match America, nuclear warhead for nuclear warhead.

Historian Arnold Toynbee believed that civilizations almost always die from suicide, not by murder. That is, our future is dependent on the choices we make and the things we decide to value.

Partisanship pop quiz time. See if you can identify the bleeding-heart liberal who said this: "Every gun that is made, every warship launched, every rocket fired signifies, in the final sense, a theft from those who hunger and are not fed, those who are cold and not clothed. This world in arms is not spending money alone. It is spending the sweat of its laborers, the genius of its scientists, the hopes of its children."

Noam Chomsky? Michael Moore? Bernie Sanders?

No, it was that unrepentant lefty five-star general Dwight Eisenhower, in 1953, just a few months after taking office—a time when the economy was booming and unemployment was at 2.7 percent. Yet today, while America's economy sputters down the road to recovery and the middle class struggles to make ends meet—with more than twenty-six million people unemployed or underemployed and record numbers of homes being lost to foreclosure—the "guns versus butter" argument isn't even part of the national debate. Of course, today, the argument might be more accurately framed as "ICBM nukes, predator drones, and missile-defense shields versus jobs, affordable college, decent schools, foreclosure prevention, and fixing the gaping holes in our social safety net."

We hear endless talk in Washington about belt tightening

and deficit reduction, but hardly a word about whether the $161 billion being spent in 2010 alone to fight wars of choice in Afghanistan and Iraq might be better spent helping embattled Americans here at home.

Indeed, during his State of the Union speech in January 2010, President Obama proposed freezing all discretionary government spending for three years—but exempted military spending, even though the defense budget has ballooned over the last ten years. According to defense analyst Lawrence Korb, who served as assistant secretary of defense in the Reagan administration, the baseline defense budget has increased by 50 percent since 2000. Over that same period, nondefense discretionary spending increased less than half that much.

In fact, as Katherine McIntire Peters reported on GovernmentExecutive.com, President Obama is "on track to spend more on defense, in real dollars, than any other president has in one term of office since World War II." In that time we've had Korea, Vietnam, the massive military buildup under Reagan, and Bush's funded-by-tax-cuts invasions of Afghanistan and Iraq, but in the most trying economic times since the Great Depression, Obama's outgunning them all.

This is not about ignoring the threats to our national security. And it's certainly not about pacifism. To quote then Illinois state senator Barack Obama in 2002, "I don't oppose all wars. . . . What I am opposed to is a dumb war." Iraq was never about making us safer. And the original rationale for going to war in Afghanistan—taking on al-Qaeda—has been accomplished, with fewer than one hundred members of the group still operating in the country. The irrationality of continuing to spend precious resources on wars we shouldn't be fighting is all the more galling when juxtaposed with our urgent and growing needs at home.

According to the *Los Angeles Times,* before the summer 2010 surge in Kandahar (cost: $33 billion)—a surge the military claimed was as important to Afghanistan as securing Baghdad was to Iraq—Joint Chiefs of Staff chairman Admiral Michael Mullen told an Afghan leader that the goals of the surge, as well as defeating the Taliban, included, in the words of the *Times,* "reducing corruption, making local government work and, eventually, providing jobs." Talk about "mission creep"!

Is that why we are still fighting a war there nine years later, spending American blood and treasure—to provide jobs for the people of Kandahar? It's like a very bad joke: "The good news is, the Obama administration is ramping up a multibillion-dollar program that will create a host of new jobs. The bad news is, you have to move to Kandahar to apply."

The Bush-era rationale for these overseas misadventures was always "We'll fight 'em over there, so we don't have to fight 'em over here." Today, it seems, we're fighting to create jobs for 'em over there, while we don't have enough jobs for our people over here. At a time when so many middle-class families are reeling from the economic crisis—and our country is facing the harsh one-two punch of more people in need at the exact moment social services are being slashed to the bone—that seems like the most perverted of priorities.

Berkeley professor Ananya Roy defines the troubled state of America not so much as a fiscal crisis as "a crisis of priorities." And Representative Barney Frank, who has been one of the few in Washington arguing for the need to cut military spending, says that our military overcommitments have "devastated our ability to improve our quality of life through government programs." Looking at the money we've spent on Iraq and Afghanistan, Frank says, "We would have had $1 trillion now to help fix the economy and do the things for our people that they deserve."

The National Priorities Project (NPP) provides a useful online tool that brings this budget trade-off to life by showing—specifically—all the things that could have been done with the money spent on Afghanistan and Iraq. For example, according to the NPP, since 2003, more than $747 billion of taxpayer money has been spent in Iraq. That could have provided:

- 115 million people with low-income health care for a year;

- or 98 million places in a Head Start program;

- or funding for more than 11 million elementary school teachers;

- or 11 million police officers;

- or 13 million firefighters;

- or 94.7 million college scholarships.

While unaffordable college tuition prevents many qualified young people from achieving the American Dream, we are continuing to spend billions on outdated and redundant military defense programs, including pricey relics of the Cold War, such as the F-22 fighter, the Osprey transport helicopter, and America's hugely expensive nuclear triad—bombers, submarines, and intercontinental ballistic missiles—designed to annihilate a Soviet empire that no longer exists.

If we don't come to our senses and get our deeply misguided priorities back in order, America could find itself a superpower turned Third World nation—dead from our own hand.

BRENDA CARTER

I was a manager of information systems at the same company for thirteen years. I thought my job was secure. All the purchasing approval and budget monitoring went through me. I attended weekly board meetings. I was well liked.

One day the chief operating officer gave me a high-priority project. I never suspected I would be laid off the next day. When I arrived and said my "good mornings," my co-workers in finance and administration looked a little sad and they did not respond to my greeting in the normal fashion. I shrugged it off, went to my office, and put down my briefcase.

My phone rang. It was my boss. He told me to come to his office. He told me I was being laid off due to budget constraints. He said he was sorry but his hands were tied. He told me that since I was a longtime employee I would not be escorted immediately out of the building, and I could take as much time as I needed to remove my belongings.

Since I was at my office most hours of the day, I'd made it feel like home, with plants, pictures, and other personal items. As the manager of information systems, I was the one called to terminate employee user names and passwords. To allow me to clear my office knowing I had access to that information told me my boss trusted me and didn't want me to be humiliated in front of my co-workers.

Imagine getting up every day for thirteen years to go to the same job and suddenly that part of your life just ceases. I cried and cried and cried. I just could not believe it. I did the jobs of three people. How will they make it without me? Some days I did not get out of bed. I wondered why I wasn't given the option of demotion. My seniority should have counted for something.

Now I spend my days searching for work. It's hard to compete for jobs at my age. I hate putting my previous salary and age on applications. They are red flags. I developed a wall of rejection letters. I took it down because it started to depress me.

To broaden my opportunities and keep my mind fresh, I began taking technology courses in college. I also passed the real estate exam. I'm trying to make it by any means necessary, even selling my homemade candy door-to-door. The candy sold well, but it takes gas to travel. I have had only good feedback about the candy so I'll continue to pursue this dream, moving my sales online.

I applied for unemployment, and am back in the role of housewife. My children are adults now. They think the world of me. They cannot believe I have been out of work for so long. In their minds I was the one who was going to be a millionaire. I sometimes feel that I let them down.

I have been out of work since 2007. After all the years I have worked and raised a family, I'm now dealing with threats to turn off my utilities and repossess my car.

What have I learned from being unemployed? That it's frustrating and demoralizing. I have learned that I don't want to be dependent on a Congress that obviously does not have America's best interests at heart. I have learned to have more compassion for people who are in this situation.

I know there are many stories out there and mine is not the worst, but at times it feels like it is. It's like waking up in the same nightmare every day with no way out. There is a scripture I hold on to and say to myself when I open my eyes in the morning: "Ask, and it will be given to you; seek, and you will find; knock, and it will be opened to you." My response is, "Lord, I am asking for Your help, knocking on the door, asking you to open it and find favor on my family this day."

2

★

NIGHTMARE ON
MAIN STREET

★ ★ ★

America has long been known as the land of opportunity. So what happens when that opportunity vanishes, when the jobs that served as the gateway to the American Dream disappear, never to return? What happens when educational opportunities and the historical underpinning of our vision of ourselves as a nation give way? What steps into the void?

In a word: fear.

The fear that America is in decline—that our greatest triumphs are behind us. The fear that the jobs we have lost are gone forever. The fear that the middle class is on an extended death march—and that the American Dream of a secure, comfortable standard of living has become as outdated as an Edsel with an eight-track player.

We look at our obliterated 401(k)s and dwindling pensions, and hear the whispers about Social Security going broke, and we wonder if we will ever be able to retire—let alone maintain our standard of living into our sunset years. Golden visions of post-work leisure time have been replaced by dark, fevered flashes of deprivation—of having to decide between eating and paying for the medicine we need. Of letting our homes go into foreclosure to scrape together the money to live on.

The void is filled by the fear that America is becoming a nation of haves and have-nots—and that millions are in danger of becoming permanent members of the have-nots. Forget Freddy Krueger. The real nightmare is not happening on Elm Street. It's happening on Main Street. And it's not scantily clad teens being slashed—it's jobs and incomes and stability and quality of life. It's our future.

And we're afraid—very afraid—that the worst may not be over, and that the real economy, as opposed to the one on Wall Street, is still melting down. The housing crisis is still raging. The first run of foreclosures was because of subprime loans; the second run is because of people thrown out of work. And the government's loan modification programs won't be of any help with this round of foreclosures. As *Newsweek*'s Nancy Cook pointed out, "If you're unemployed, you don't qualify for a loan modification." And then there is the coming commercial property crisis and a potential credit card meltdown.

So we look at the suffering all around us, at the shuttered factories and stores, and worry that it is just the tip of the iceberg—or the tip of the tip of the iceberg. We try to fight off the fear that if things don't change—and in a big way—we may find ourselves working at Walmart or McDonald's or Dunkin' Donuts for minimum wage.

We are fast becoming a nation collectively waiting for the next shoe to drop.

Washington is filled with talk about national security: troop levels, airport screenings, Pentagon budgets, and terrorist threats. But there is another kind of national security: the one that keeps us feeling confident that the economic rug isn't going to suddenly be pulled out from under us, and that our way of life isn't going to suddenly implode—the kind of national security that gives us hope for the future. For that national security, especially when it comes to America's middle class, the threat level has definitely moved from yellow ("elevated") to orange ("high")—and we are afraid that red ("severe") is looming up ahead.

For more and more of its citizens, America has become a national insecurity state.

THE BROKEN BACKBONE OF AMERICA

In 1835, Alexis de Tocqueville published *Democracy in America,* his observations on the nature of our country. The opening line speaks volumes: "Amongst the novel objects that attracted my attention during my stay in the United States, nothing struck me more forcibly than the general equality of condition among the people."

Looking across the vast expanse of this developing country, the thing that most drew his attention was a vision of America as a level playing field, a place where the same rules applied to everyone. "Democratic laws," he noted, "generally tend to promote the welfare of the greatest possible number; for they emanate from the majority of the citizens, who are subject to error, but who cannot have an interest opposed to their own advantage."

America's enlightened elites have always understood that their long-term well-being and security depended on the middle and lower classes having an equal stake in the nation's prosperity and political institutions. They knew that this great democratic experiment would be defined not by breeding or religion or language, but by a unifying idea—"All men are created equal"—and by an ideal: the good of the many outweighs the good of the few. *E pluribus unum*. Out of many, one. In the infancy of our nation, Tocqueville saw the power of this idea and its centrality to the American experiment.

He traveled across America before the industrial revolution transformed the country. Once it did, manufacturing jobs helped turn the working poor into middle-class Americans, liberating them from the shackles of a hand-to-mouth existence and moving them closer to enjoying a "general equality of condition."

So, is America still a nation where its citizens enjoy a "general equality of condition"? Are we still promoting "the welfare of the greatest possible number"? It's hard to imagine a modern Tocqueville taking in the grand sweep of our current political and economic landscape—with its shrinking middle class, disappearing jobs, growing economic disparity, banking oligarchy, and public policy sold to the highest bidder—and reaching the same conclusions.

Tocqueville's words are deeply at odds with the reality of modern America. For decades our political leaders have systematically squeezed the nation's middle class in order to promote the corporate interests paying for their reelection. America's middle class has been the country's economic backbone. It is our vast, energized middle class that has done the heavy lifting and inspired the most innovation. Where the middle class heads, the rest of the country follows. So when the middle class is systematically worn down—when too many of its members become downwardly mobile, unable to keep their jobs or their homes or buy as many goods and services and drive market innovations—can a diminished America, a Third World America, be far behind?

MIDDLE CLASS: I KNOW IT WHEN I SEE IT

The crippling of America's middle class didn't happen overnight—and it wasn't the result of the bad bets made by the game-fixing gamblers on Wall Street (although they sure did their part). It's actually been decades in the making. But before we look at who set the roadside explosives along the middle class's road to the American Dream, it might help to define exactly what the term means.

What makes someone middle class? Is there a base income level (fall below it and you are officially poor), or a top line figure above which you instantly ascend to the upper class (with a quick rest stop at upper middle class)? Does it depend on the size of your house (do you even need a house—can renters be middle class?), the kind of car you drive, the amount of rainy-day savings you have squirreled away in the bank?

In truth, pinning down a hard-and-fast definition of "middle class" is tricky business. It's a lot like Supreme Court justice Potter Stewart's famous assessment of what constitutes pornography: "I know it when I see it." (Indeed, with both porn and the modern middle class, someone is usually getting screwed.)

There is no tidy formula. Paul Taylor, executive vice president of the Pew Research Center, asked during his testimony to the Senate Finance Committee: "Is a $30,000-a-year doctor doing his residency in brain surgery lower class? Is a $100,000-a-year plumber upper middle class?" Or are they both part of the great middle class?

According to the Pew Research Center, more than half of American adults (53 percent) define themselves as middle class. But behind this assertion, Pew discovered a host of caveats: "Four-in-ten (41%) adults with $100,000 or more in annual household income say they are middle class"—as do 46 percent of those with incomes below $40,000. At the same time, a third of those with incomes between $40,000 and $100,000 don't believe they are middle class.

For purposes of its research, Pew defined the middle class as those adults "who live in a household where the annual income falls within 75% and 150% of the median" gross income for a family of three in 2006 (the latest year data was available). In dollars and cents, that meant an income of between $45,000 and $90,000 made you middle class.

But, in the end, in a very American way, it all comes down to self-definition: If you consider yourself middle class, you *are* middle class.

THE MIDDLE CLASS'S LONG MARCH
TO THE EDGE OF THE CLIFF

From 1945 to the 1970s, a period characterized by widespread economic prosperity, the wealthiest Americans grew richer at a rate almost identical to that of America's lower and middle classes. From factory employees to chief executives, Americans experienced a doubling of income. By the end of the 1980s, however, things had changed drastically, with the income of the wealthy skyrocketing while the rest of the country lagged far behind.

What happened? Did middle-class Americans lose their mojo? Or had rich Americans unexpectedly come upon the economic equivalent of the Fountain of Youth—a Fountain of Wealth? They had, but rather than Ponce de León, it was Ronald

Reagan who led the income-boosting expedition, marching into Washington under the banner of lowering the taxes of America's moneyed elite.

But, the Reagan Revolution of the 1980s was about more than shifting the tax burden—it was about shifting the way America looked at itself. In short order, government was no longer seen as a solution—it was fingered as the problem. Tocqueville's "welfare of the greatest possible number" was replaced by the notion that the invisible hand of the free market could best determine society's winners and losers—until, that is, the winners got into trouble in 2008 and the government rushed to the rescue in the name of preventing Armageddon.

In books such as *The Virtue of Selfishness* and *Atlas Shrugged*, Ayn Rand, the high priestess of free-marketeers such as Alan Greenspan, championed the notion that by doing what is best for yourself, you end up doing what is best for everyone. But, as put into practice by corporate America over the past thirty years, that equation has been flipped upside down. It turns out that an unregulated free market is sooner or later corrupted by fraud and excess. In other words, it isn't free at all. In fact, it's as fixed as a street-corner game of three-card monte. And the interests of the elites have become disconnected from the public interest.

In the three decades since the Reagan Revolution, Americans have been preached to from pulpits far and wide the holy word of unregulated markets as the true path to a higher standard of living. As part of the new religion, we were converted from citizens to consumers and taught a catechism about how the market—not "equality of conditions"—was the foundation of our country. Along the way, the social contract—especially the subsections protecting workers, poor people, and our air, water, and oceans—was fed into a shredder. Starting with the New Deal, we began constructing a social safety net to help the most vulnerable among us. But who needed a safety net when the laws of supply and demand were there to protect us, when the trickle-down theory would provide sustenance for us all?

The missing tenet in this new free-market fundamentalism was the recognition, central to capitalism, that businessmen have responsibilities above and beyond the bottom line. Alfred Marshall, one of the founding fathers of modern capitalism, in an address to the British Economics Association in 1890, called it "economic chivalry." He explained that "the desire of men for approval of their own conscience and for the esteem of others is an economic force of the first order of importance." There is a reason Adam Smith's free-market gospel, *The Wealth of Nations,* was preceded by his *Theory of Moral Sentiments.* He knew that economic freedom could not flourish without a firm moral foundation.

But that moral foundation is by no means inevitable. The "approval of their own conscience" and "the esteem of others" have gotten a lot cheaper in recent years. We see the results of capitalism without a conscience all around us: the pollution of our environment, workers being injured or killed, the sale of dangerous products, the shameless promotion of risky mortgages for overvalued homes, and the wholesale loss of millions of jobs and trillions in savings.

The collapse of communism as a political system sounded the death knell for Marxism as an ideology. But while unregulated, laissez-faire capitalism has been a monumental failure in practice, the ideology is still alive and kicking. You can find all manner of free-market fundamentalists still on the Senate floor or in governors' mansions or showing up on TV trying to peddle deregulation snake oil.

Given how close we were in 2008 to the complete collapse of our economic and financial system, anyone who continues to make the case that markets do best when left alone should be laughed off his bully pulpit.

Despite the fact that many banks, car companies, and so on would be defunct without government intervention, the free-market fundamentalists continue to live in denial, trying to convince the world that if only left alone, free markets would right themselves.

Free-market fundamentalism didn't fail because our leaders didn't execute it well enough. In fact, during his time in office (until the economic house of cards finally collapsed at the end of his presidency), President George W. Bush and his team did a bang-up job executing a defective theory. The problem isn't just the bathwater; the baby itself is rotten.

William Seidman, the longtime GOP economic adviser who oversaw the savings and loan bailout in 1991, cuts to the chase: "[The Bush] administration made decisions that allowed the free market to operate as a barroom brawl instead of a prize fight. To make the market work well, you have to have a lot of rules." Even Alan Greenspan, whose owl-eyed visage could adorn a Mount Rushmore of free-market capitalists, finally saw the light, telling a House committee in October 2008 that he "made a mistake in presuming that the self-interests of organizations, specifically banks and others, were such that they were best capable of protecting their own shareholders and their equity in the firms."

Many, including Bush 43, lay the blame on a few rotten apples: "Wall Street got drunk," he said. Maybe so, but who made the Bush years a nonstop happy hour and kept serving up the drinks?

Of course, Republican leaders were not the only ones drinking the free-market Kool-Aid. It was also chugged by New Democrats such as Bill Clinton. He came into office knowing it was the economy, stupid, then proceeded to oversee a presidency focused on the soaring Dow Jones industrial average, even as the number of Americans living in poverty stubbornly refused to dip below thirty-two million, and the number of Americans unable to make ends meet without the aid of a soup kitchen or food bank hit twenty-six million—with more homeless children than at any time since the Great Depression. Yet the Clinton White House's messaging was like a twenty-four-hour Boom Channel: All Prosperity, All The Time.

In those go-go years, even being downsized could, in the eyes of the free-market evangelists, be turned to your advantage. In early 1996, after forty thousand AT&T workers were pink-slipped, future *Mad Money* host (and Jon Stewart whipping boy) Jim Cramer, then still a hedge-fund manager, wrote a piece that landed on the cover of the *New Republic*. Headlined "Let Them Eat Stocks," the article found a silver lining in the dark cloud of the massive layoff, proposing that the fired workers be given stock options. "Let them participate in the stock appreciation that their firings caused," Cramer gushed. Cue Eric Idle's "Always Look on the Bright Side of Life."

Four years later, *Bush v. Gore* ushered in the CEO president and his CEO VP. They promptly threw open the White House doors to their corporate cronies from Enron and Halliburton and declared open season on the interests of the average American. The Enronization of our economy was under way.

THE RICH GET RICHER

The Reagan years ushered in the era of the widening income gap. The rich grew considerably richer while the real income of everyone else, from the poor to the middle class, either slid back or, at best, leveled off.

In their paper on long-term change in the U.S. wage structure, economists Claudia Goldin and Lawrence Katz of Harvard and the National Bureau of Economic Research reported, "From 1980 to around 1987, wage inequality increased in a rapid and monotonic [i.e. steady] fashion. Those at the top grew most rapidly, those in the middle less rapidly, and the bottom the least of all. . . . [These] wage structure changes have been associated with a 'polarization' of the labor market with employment shifting into high- and low-wage jobs at the expense of middle-wage positions."

By the late 1980s, due to changes in technology, outsourcing, and the loss of manufacturing jobs, the middle class was sputtering. Even as productivity rose, the wages of the average worker remained flat.

In 1995, the midway point between the Reagan Revolution and today, John Cassidy penned an article in the *New Yorker* entitled "Who Killed the Middle Class?" Cassidy had his readers imagine a lineup composed of every American, arranged from poorest to richest. The individual exactly in the middle—

the median—was arguably the most middle-class person in the nation. That man or woman, in September 1979, was earning (in constant, inflation-adjusted dollars) $25,896 a year. In September 1995, that same man or woman was earning $24,700 a year—a 5 percent cut in salary over the intervening decade and a half.

In contrast, the nation's top 5 percent saw their pay rise 29 percent over the same period, up to $177,518. And the top 1 percent did best of all. In fact, between 1977 and 1989 the richest Americans' average income rose from $323,942 to $576,553—a whopping 78 percent increase in real terms.

The trend continued into the first decade of the twenty-first century. According to a report compiled by Elizabeth Warren, the average middle-class income between 2000 and 2007 fell $1,175, while expenses rose $4,655. Over the same period, the top 1 percent—which had pocketed 45 percent of the nation's income growth under Clinton—captured 65 percent of all income growth under Bush.

And according to a report released in May 2010 by the Brookings Institution, between 1999 and 2008 the median household income fell $2,241 to $52,029, while the share of households earning middle-class incomes dropped from 30 to 28.2 percent.

So it's clear: Well before the economic crisis hit in the fall of 2008, the once-envied American middle class was already being driven to its knees. Indeed, in a 2008 Pew survey, 56 percent of middle-class Americans said they had either fallen back or merely managed to tread water over the previous five years. It was, according to Pew, "the most downbeat short-term assessment of personal progress in nearly half a century of polling. Fewer Americans now than at any time in the past half century believe they're moving forward in life."

And that was just as the Great Recession was *beginning* to ravage the economy. Since then, life for the middle class has gone from bad to worse. In a revised take on the original Misery Index—the measure developed by the late economist Arthur Okun that combined the unemployment rate with the consumer price index to condense the state of the economy into one neat, digestible number—the Huffington Post created the Real Misery Index. Incorporating a more extensive host of metrics, including the most accurate unemployment figures; inflation rates for essentials such as food, gas, and medical costs; and data on credit card delinquencies, housing prices, home loan defaults, and food stamp participation, the Real Misery Index is a much more accurate estimate of economic hardship. In April 2010, as the unemployment rate remained stubbornly high and the number of Americans on food stamps grew to forty million, the Real Misery Index, which charts data from 1984 to today, hit the highest level on record. And the bull rally that sent the stock market up an impressive 56 percent from March 2009 to April 2010 surged in tandem with the Real Misery Index, which climbed 16 percent in the same period—reflecting what Lynn Reaser, the incoming president of the National Association of Business Economists, called a "two-tier economy."

THE MIDDLE CLASS PAYS ITS UNFAIR SHARE

This two-tier economy comes with two sets of rules—one for the corporate class and another for the middle class.

The middle class, by and large, plays by the rules, then watches as its jobs disappear. The corporate class games the system—making sure its license to break the rules is built into the rules themselves.

One of the most glaring examples of this continues to be the ability of corporations to cheat the public out of tens of billions of dollars a year by using offshore tax havens. Indeed, it's estimated that companies and wealthy individuals funneling money through offshore tax havens are evading around $100 billion a year in taxes—leaving the rest of us to pick up the tab. And with cash-strapped states all across the country cutting vital services to the bone, it's not like we don't need the money.

Here is Exhibit A of two sets of rules: According to the White House, in 2004, the last year data on this was compiled, U.S. multinational corporations paid roughly $16 billion in taxes on $700 billion in foreign active earnings—putting their tax rate at around 2.3 percent. Know many middle-class Americans getting off that easy at tax time?

In December 2008, the Government Accountability Office reported that 83 of the 100 largest publicly traded companies in the country—including AT&T, Chevron, IBM, American Express, GE, Boeing, Dow, and AIG—had subsidiaries in tax havens, or, as the corporate class comically calls them, "financial privacy jurisdictions."

Even more egregiously, of those 83 companies, 74 received government contracts in 2007. GM, for instance, got more than $517 million from the government—i.e. the taxpayers—that year, while shielding profits in tax-friendly places like Bermuda and the Cayman Islands. And Boeing, which received over $23 billion in federal contracts that year, had 38 subsidiaries in tax havens, including six in Bermuda.

It's as easy as opening up an island P.O. box, which is why

another GAO study found that more than 18,000 companies are registered at a single address in the Cayman Islands, a country with no corporate or capital gains taxes.

America's big banks—including those that pocketed billions from the taxpayers in bailout dollars—seem particularly fond of the Cayman Islands. At the time of the GAO report, Morgan Stanley had 273 subsidiaries in tax havens, 158 of them in the Caymans. Citigroup had 427, with 90 in the Caymans. Bank of America had 115, with 59 in the Caymans. Goldman Sachs had 29 offshore havens, including 15 in the Caymans. JPMorgan had 50, with seven in the Caymans. And Wells Fargo had 18, with nine in the Caymans.

Perhaps no company exemplifies the corporate class/middle class double standard more than KBR/Halliburton. The company got billions from U.S. taxpayers, then turned around and used a Cayman Islands address to reduce its expenses. As the *Boston Globe*'s Farah Stockman reported, KBR, until 2007 a unit of Halliburton, "has avoided paying hundreds of millions of dollars in federal Medicare and Social Security taxes by hiring workers through shell companies based in this tropical tax haven."

In 2008, KBR listed 10,500 Americans as being officially employed by two companies that, as Stockman wrote, "exist in a computer file on the fourth floor of a building on a palm-studded boulevard here in the Caribbean." Aside from the tax advantages, Stockman points out another benefit of this dodge: Americans who officially work for a company whose headquarters is a computer file in the Caymans are not eligible for unemployment insurance or other benefits when they get laid off—something many of them found out the hard way.

This kind of sun-kissed thievery is nothing new. Indeed, back in 2002, to call attention to the outrage of the sleazy accounting trick, I published a tongue-in-cheek newspaper column announcing I was thinking of moving my syndicated newspaper column to Bermuda. "I'll still live in America," I wrote, "earn my living here, and enjoy the protection, technology, infrastructure, and all the other myriad benefits of the land of the free and the home of the brave. I'm just changing my business address. Because if I do that, I won't have to pay for those benefits—I'll get them for free!"

Washington has been trying to address the issue for close to fifty years—JFK gave it a go in 1961. But time and again corporate America's game fixers—a.k.a. lobbyists—and water carriers in Congress have managed to keep the loopholes open.

The battle is once again afoot. While Congress considers legislation that would clamp down on some of the ways corporations hide their income offshore to avoid paying U.S. taxes, corporate lobbyists are furiously fighting to make sure America's corporate class can continue to enjoy the largesse of government services and contracts without the responsibility of paying its fair share.

The latest tax-reform bills are far from perfect—they leave open a number of loopholes and would only recoup a very small fraction of the $100 billion that corporations and wealthy individuals are siphoning off from the U.S. Treasury. And they wouldn't ban companies using offshore tax havens from receiving government contracts, which is stunning given the hard times we are in and the populist groundswell against the way average Americans are getting the short end of the stick.

But the bills would end one of the more egregious examples of the tax policy double standard, finally forcing hedge-fund managers to pay taxes at the same rate as everybody else. As the law stands now, their income is considered "carried interest," and is accordingly taxed at the capital gains rate of 15 percent.

According to former labor secretary Robert Reich, in 2009 "the 25 most successful hedge-fund managers earned a billion dollars each." The top earner clocked in at $4 billion. Closing this outrageous loophole would bring in close to $20 billion in revenue—money desperately needed at a time when teachers and nurses and firemen are being laid off all around the country.

But the two sets of rules—and the clout of corporate lobbyists—leave even commonsense, who-could-argue-with-that proposals in doubt, and leave the middle class shouldering an unfair share of a very taxing burden.

Indeed, the double standard was famously ridiculed by Warren Buffett in 2007 when he noted that his receptionist paid 30 percent of her income in taxes, while he paid only 17.7 percent on his taxable income of $46 million.

HOMER SIMPSON HAS IT TOO GOOD: SNAPSHOTS FROM THE MIDDLE-CLASS BATTLEFIELD

The numbers don't lie: We increasingly live in a "winner take all" economy. Indeed, we've arrived at a point where even Homer Simpson—created as a classic American Everyman character—is now living a middle-class fantasy. After all, how many American middle-class families do you know where the family's sole breadwinner, a safety inspector at a nuclear power plant, can still comfortably support a family of five on a single income?

A more accurate snapshot of a modern middle-class family

can be found in Nan Mooney's book *(Not) Keeping Up with Our Parents*. One person profiled in the 2008 book is Diana, thirty-six, a licensed psychologist with a doctorate in clinical psychology. Her husband, Byron, is a trained engineer who makes his living as a technical writer for a patent attorney. The couple has two young children. Besides bringing up her kids, Diana holds down two part-time jobs, one as an assessment director for a nonprofit organization that places school counselors, the other building her private practice as a psychologist. She makes $35,000 a year. Her husband, a contract worker paid on a per-project basis, makes $40,000. When interviewed by Mooney, their credit cards were loaded with debts totaling $17,000. Their mortgage cost them $1,150 a month. Diana was paying $450 a month on her school loans, but that figure was about to get bumped to $550 a month. Rent on her office, plus condo fees, added another $750 a month. The couple had little equity in their property and had wiped out their savings.

"I feel like we've cut every corner we can cut," Diana told Mooney. "We don't take vacations. We never go out. Right now, I just keep my fingers crossed that nothing breaks. We need a new roof and new tires for the car. And we're going to get hit hard by taxes this year." At that point, Diana's voice began to crack. "I'm scared. I'm scared we'll never be able to retire. I'm scared we won't be covered for health care. I'm scared we won't be able to send our kids to college. We've never had much, but before I always felt like we were doing our time. We were working our way toward a more comfortable future. That doesn't seem true anymore. At this point, I see no way out at all."

Diana and Byron's tale is an increasingly common one. Their high-priced college education—the kind many see as a safeguard against economic hard times—is no longer enough at a time when the jobless rate is almost 10 percent and twenty-six million people are out of work or underemployed.

Troy Renault is one of them. In August 2009, Troy, his wife, Tammy, and their five children were living in a three-bedroom home in Lebanon, Tennessee. Two years earlier, Troy had lost his construction job. Ultimately, as the Huffington Post's Laura Bassett reported, they lost their home and had to move into a donated trailer on a local campground. They downgraded from a 1,900-square-foot house to a 215-square-foot trailer.

Says Troy, "You wind up starting to think to yourself, 'Okay. Do we go ahead and make the house payment and keep a roof over our head but have no lights and no water, or do we go ahead and keep those utilities on and forgo the house payment, and hope that you can get caught up?'"

Rebecca Admire is another of the more than eight million people who have lost their jobs since December 2007. A single mom with two kids, Admire was laid off from her job at the Family Guidance Center for Behavioral Healthcare in St. Joseph, Missouri. After several months of struggling to pay her rent, she invited her cousin and two children to move in with them and share costs. There are now eight people living in Admire's two-bedroom house. The four children sleep in one bunk bed, two to a mattress. But with so many in the house, the utility bills have gone through the roof. "I cry every time a bill comes in the mail," Admire says.

In some cases, entire towns are falling into permanent decline when their central industries disappear. Mount Airy, North Carolina, for example, which has a population of just 9,500, historically relied largely on the textile industry for jobs. But, as Paul Wiseman reported in a March 2010 piece in

USA Today, one after the other, the city's textile and apparel factories shuttered, shedding more than three thousand jobs between 1999 and 2010. It's a trend bound to continue: According to the Bureau of Labor Statistics, openings in textile and apparel manufacturing will nearly halve by 2018, as work is increasingly outsourced overseas and replaced by technological advances.

And in Mount Airy—the city where Andy Griffith grew up, and the inspiration for Mayberry, the epitome of small-town America for TV viewers for half a century—the transition has rattled an entire generation that had banked on the security of manufacturing jobs. "When you started work, you thought you'd be there until you retired," Jane Knudsen, who began working in a textile mill in 1973, told *USA Today.* But Knudsen's mill closed down, and now she works as a part-time cook at the local jail for two dollars less per hour. Another local, Steve Jenkins, opted to skip college and go straight into apparel manufacturing. He worked at Perry Manufacturing for more than thirty years, advancing through the ranks to earn a salary of $103,000 as director of purchasing. But Perry shut down in 2008. For Jenkins, who received no severance and had few other skills, life was suddenly upended.

"We were not prepared," Mount Airy City Council member Teresa Lewis conceded. "We've had a huge loss of jobs in the textile industry. A lot of those people had devoted 30, 35 years to one particular company, and they found themselves in their early to mid-50s without a job or without the skills to go into something else."

The aggregate effect of these stories—and tens of thousands more like them—is deeply troubling for our country. Through an enviable mix of jobs created by innovative American businesses and a national culture based on self-reliance, America has always had unemployment rates far lower than other developed nations. But this historic advantage is coming to an end. By the end of 2009, the unemployment rate among sixteen-to-twenty-four-year-olds was 19.1 percent. And 19.7 percent of American men aged twenty-five to fifty-four (prime working years) were unemployed—the highest figure since the Bureau of Labor Statistics began tracking this data in 1948.

"Every downturn pushes some people out of the middle class before the economy resumes expanding," wrote Peter Goodman in the *New York Times* in February 2010. "Most recover. Many prosper. But some economists worry that this time could be different. An unusual constellation of forces—some embedded in the modern-day economy, others unique to this wrenching recession—might make it especially difficult for those out of work to find their way back to their middle-class lives. . . . Call them the new poor: people long accustomed to the comforts of middle-class life who are now relying on public assistance for the first time in their lives—potentially for years to come."

OPEN SEASON: SETTING A TRAP FOR THE MIDDLE CLASS

There are those in our country who look at the struggles of the middle class—mortgages underwater, foreclosure notices on the door, mounting credit card bills in the mailbox, bankruptcy on the horizon—and think, "They got into this mess of their own free will; they're just getting what they deserve." Who told them to buy that house they couldn't afford, sign that mortgage without reading the balloon payment fine print, and run up those balances on a credit card that came with a teaser interest rate that is now 30 percent? Why should the rest of us, who were more prudent, be expected to carry the burden of the irresponsible?

This response ignores the ugly truth of what brought about this crisis. It wasn't a sudden spike in irresponsibility on the part of middle-class Americans. It was the inevitable by-product of tricks and traps deliberately put in place to maximize profits for a few while creating conditions that would soon maximize misery for millions. The devastation was predictable—and, in fact, had been predicted by any number of Jeremiahs who saw the writing on the wall. Indeed, looking at the foreclosure crisis and the credit crisis—and the resulting bankruptcy crisis—it's hard to avoid the conclusion that, in many ways, things are working out exactly as planned.

In hindsight, it's as if a giant bear trap had been set for the middle class—a bear trap that was sprung by the economic crash.

Let's start with the bursting of the housing bubble and the foreclosure crisis that followed. For a century, from the mid-1890s to the mid-1990s, home prices rose at the same pace as the overall rate of inflation. The bubble started to inflate in 1996 and within a decade home prices had jumped 70 percent—an $8 trillion bubble.

That bubble was no accident. We've just seen the way middle-class incomes had fallen behind expenses over the past three decades. How is it that more and more Americans were able to buy more and more houses—even as incomes stagnated? By taking on more debt, of course, provided by an underregulated army of lenders pitching seductive new mortgage vehicles. By 2005, subprime mortgages had skyrocketed to 20 percent of the market.

Fueling the boom was the development of securitized mortgages—including collateralized debt obligations (CDOs)—in which mortgages of varying degrees of risk were bundled together in "tranches" and sold to investors. Since lenders were selling off the risk to someone else, they felt much freer to make loans to borrowers who never would have been able to qualify for a prime mortgage.

The Fed did its part, too, contributing extremely low interest rates and lax oversight to the increasingly toxic housing mix. In the words of economist Dean Baker, "The Federal Reserve Board completely failed to do its job."

And both sides of the political aisle aided and abetted the bubble. Even after a spate of accounting scandals, many Democrats continued to support Fannie Mae and Freddie Mac, seeing them as valuable facilitators of affordable housing. Between 2004 and 2007, Fannie and Freddie became the top buyers of subprime mortgages—exceeding $1 trillion in loans. George W. Bush and the GOP also helped inflate the bubble by pushing to dismantle some of the barriers to homeownership—part of Bush's vision of "an ownership society" that sought to, as he put it in his second inaugural address, "give every American a stake in the promise and future of our country." The road to hell continues to be paved with good intentions.

Refinancing homes and offering home equity lines of credit—the better to be able to buy all those things you see on

TV but really can't afford—became a fee-generating bonanza for financial institutions. Protected and encouraged by their political cronies in Washington, banks were given free rein to push ticking time bomb mortgages on the middle class—mortgages they could then slice and dice and sell as swaps, derivatives, and all sorts of complex financial products to investors around the world.

So banks, confident in the securitization of their loans, began selling mortgages to anyone who had a pulse, and they often neglected to confirm that borrowers could afford the mortgages they were selling them. By 2006, 62 percent of all new mortgages were so-called liars' loans—loans that required little or no documentation.

We got a glimpse into the back rooms of the mortgage industry in April 2010 when a Senate panel investigated the collapse of mortgage giant Washington Mutual. Among the findings, as reported by Sewell Chan of the *New York Times,* was that the bank offered its loan officers pay incentives to originate riskier loans. Loan officers and salespeople "were paid even more if they overcharged borrowers through points or higher interest rates, or included stiff prepayment penalties in the loans they issued."

The behavior of the WaMu bankers, and the many others just like them, was no different than the behavior of corner drug dealers—and while they weren't peddling crack or meth, they were selling something every bit as addictive: a no-money-down, no-proof-of-income-needed, interest-only, teaser-rate ticket to the good life. The bankers, with a green light from Congress, were determined to turn everyone into irresponsible consumers.

THE MORALLY BANKRUPT BANKRUPTCY BILL

Of course, the bankers knew that the housing bubble, like all bubbles before it, had to eventually burst. And when it did, massive foreclosures and bankruptcies would result. So they needed to set up their self-protecting bear traps.

Enter the bankruptcy bill that banking lobbyists pushed through Congress and President Bush signed into law in 2005. It was a bill so hostile to American families that it could have come about only in a place as corrupt, cynical, and unmoored from reality as Washington.

Instead of cracking down on predatory lending practices, closing loopholes that favor the wealthy, and strengthening the safety net for working people, single mothers, and elderly Americans struggling to recover from a financial setback, the Senate put together a nasty little bill that:

- made it harder for average people to file for bankruptcy protection;

- made it easier for landlords to evict a bankrupt tenant;

- made it more difficult for small businesses to reorganize, while opening new loopholes for the Enrons of the world;

- allowed creditors to provide misleading information; and

- did nothing to rein in lending abuses that all too frequently turned manageable debt into unmanageable crises.

Even in failure, ordinary Americans could not get a level playing field.

And make no mistake, the inequitable nature of the bill—bending over backward to help the credit industry while sticking it to working people who fall on hard times—was not the result of chance. Time and again, the Senate shot down amendments that would have made the bill less mean-spirited. Senators denied proposals that would have made it easier for military veterans, the sick, and the elderly to qualify for bankruptcy protection. They even rejected an amendment that would have put a 30 percent ceiling on the interest rates credit card companies can charge. Thirty percent—that's more than your neighborhood loan shark charges.

According to the Institute for Financial Literacy, in 2009, 9.1 percent of the people who filed for bankruptcy earned $60,000 a year or more, up from 4.7 percent in 2005. And among those who declared bankruptcy in 2009, 57.7 percent had attended college, an increase of 3.9 percent.

The institute's executive director, Leslie Linfield, also points out that there is an alarming bell curve for bankruptcy filings in the thirty-five to fifty-four age group. "Fifty-six percent of bankruptcy filers," she says, "are in this age group. This is concerning because you are looking at a group of people who are middle-aged and very unprepared for retirement. As a society we can't help but ask the question what will happen in twenty years when this group does in fact retire?"

Our elected leaders utterly ignored the fact that the vast majority of people who file for bankruptcy are middle-class folks who can't pay their bills because they've lost their jobs or been hit with high medical bills. In fact, a 2009 study by researchers at Harvard and Ohio University showed that health-care problems were the root cause of 62 percent of all personal bankruptcies in America in 2007. Using that rate, roughly 900,000 of 2009's 1.4 million bankruptcy filings were medical bankruptcies. Or, to put it another way: Just over every thirty seconds someone in this country files for bankruptcy in the wake of a serious illness. How's that for a shocking stat? Here's another: 78 percent of the so-called medically bankrupt had health insurance at the time of their illness. It just wasn't enough to cover the dramatic rise in health-care costs.

Barry Bosworth and Rosanna Smart of the Brookings Institution found that the catastrophic collapse of the 2008 subprime mortgage market resulted in the disappearance of $13 trillion in American household wealth between mid-2007 and March 2009. Bosworth and Smart also found that "on average, U.S. households lost one quarter of their wealth in that period."

The abrupt meltdown of the subprime mortgage and financial markets dramatically changed the lives of millions. Once-attainable goals like owning a home, achieving financial security, and being able to retire were suddenly out of reach. And, as we have not yet hit bottom, millions more may soon find their standard of living lowered—and their dreams of a brighter future dashed.

We are facing nothing less than a national emergency: 2.8 million homes faced foreclosure in 2009, and an estimated 3 million more are expected to be foreclosed on in 2010. If there was ever a middle-class Katrina, this is it. Yet even modest attempts to loosen the trap that snapped shut on so many have had a hard time getting traction in special interest–dominated D.C.

Take Senator Dick Durbin's attempt to allow homeowners

in bankruptcy a so-called cramdown, a means to renegotiate their mortgage with the bank under the guidance of a bankruptcy judge. Currently, mortgages are exempt from bankruptcy proceedings. Until 1978, allowing cramdowns was standard practice. Subsequent court battles eventually eliminated their use. The mortgage industry, not surprisingly, has been vehemently opposed to bringing the cramdown back. The banks scored a lopsided victory in late April 2009 when the Senate rejected Durbin's measure, which would have helped 1.7 million homeowners keep their homes and preserved an additional $300 billion in home equity.

Given the tidal wave of foreclosures that so destabilized our economy, this seemed like a no-brainer. There had already been more than eight hundred thousand foreclosures in the first three months of 2009. But even after major concessions that diluted the bill, the Mortgage Bankers Association (whose members' subprime schemes helped bring our economy to the brink), the Financial Services Roundtable, and the American Bankers Association fought tooth and nail against it. And won.

Making matters worse is the fact that America's banks and mortgage lenders are often so disorganized that people are being erroneously foreclosed on.

As ProPublica's Paul Kiel reported: "Sometimes the communication breakdown within the banks is so complete that it leads to premature or mistaken foreclosures. Some homeowners, with the help of an attorney or housing counselor, have eventually been able to reverse a foreclosure. Others have lost their homes." Kevin Stein, associate director of the California Reinvestment Coalition, told Kiel, "We believe in many cases people are losing their homes when they should not have."

You want an economic nightmare? How about a foreclosure bear trap that snaps shut on your leg even when you haven't stepped in it?

YOU HAVE THE RIGHT TO AN ATTORNEY . . . UNLESS YOU'RE ABOUT TO LOSE YOUR HOUSE

America's foreclosure crisis is being made even worse by the shortage of legal assistance available to beleaguered homeowners. According to a study by the Brennan Center for Justice, "the nation's massive foreclosure crisis is also, at its heart, a legal crisis." The vast majority of homeowners face foreclosure without legal counsel.

In New York's Nassau County, in foreclosures involving subprime or nontraditional mortgages (which are disproportionately targeted at minorities), 92 percent of homeowners did not have a lawyer. Having legal help can be the difference between families keeping their homes and being evicted. A lawyer can stop foreclosure proceedings or put enough pressure on lenders to convince them to rework the terms of the loan. A lawyer can also intervene in other ways, such as enforcing consumer protection laws or spotting legal violations by banks and lenders.

The barriers keeping homeowners from obtaining proper legal representation are twofold. The first is funding. In 1996, the budget for the Legal Services Corporation, the primary agency that provides help for low-income Americans in civil cases, was cut by a third. At this point, to match the funding level the Legal Services Corporation received in 1981 would require an increase of $753 million. If Goldman Sachs or Bank of America needed that kind of cash (or even ten times that kind of cash), Washington wouldn't think twice. But low-income homeowners have no clout in D.C.

The second barrier is that restrictions to adequate legal help have been deliberately built into the system. Remember the 1994 "Contract with America"? It turns out that one of its provisions severely limited the ability of homeowners to get legal protection from predatory lenders. Homeowners represented by the Legal Services Corporation are barred from bringing class-action suits. Nor are they able to make the other side pay attorneys' fees, even when the law would normally allow it. The chance to recoup attorneys' fees when a defendant wins his case is critical in discouraging lending companies from dragging out proceedings merely to exhaust a defendant's financial resources. The Obama administration has asked Congress to remove many of these limitations, to no avail. The $789 billion stimulus plan didn't contain a single dollar for foreclosure-related legal help.

Although Americans losing their homes are being treated like an afterthought, foreclosures are actually a gateway calamity. Every foreclosure is a crisis that begets a whole other set of crises. When families lose their homes, they are forced to move in with relatives, or into a motel, or live out of a car, or on the street. Meanwhile, the home sits vacant. Surrounding home values drop. Others in the neighborhood move out. In many communities, squatters move in. Crime goes up. Tax revenues plummet, taking school budgets down with them.

Almost forty-one million homes in the United States are located next door to a foreclosed property. The value of these homes drops an average of $8,880 following a foreclosure. This translates into a total property value loss of $356 billion. And vacant properties take a heavy toll on already strapped local governments. A 1 percent increase in foreclosures translates into a 2.3 percent rise in violent crimes.

But the collateral damage of the foreclosure crisis is even more grave and far-reaching. It has a huge impact on future generations and on our children. A September 2009 *New York Times* story by Erik Eckholm on the surge of homeless schoolchildren caused by the foreclosure crisis haunts me to this day. A photograph that accompanied the article showed nine-year-old Charity Crowell of Asheville, North Carolina, modeling the green and purple outfit she intended to wear on the first day of school. The previous spring, when her parents lost their jobs and their car, she received Cs on her report card. She vowed to bring her grades back up. "I couldn't go to sleep," nine-year-old Charity said of her last semester. "I was worried about all the stuff." As a result, she often fell asleep in class.

· The family had been evicted and forced to move into a series of friends' houses, then a motel, and then a trailer.

The National Center on Family Homelessness estimates that 1.5 million children in the United States are homeless—that is one in fifty children. San Antonio, for example, enrolled one thousand homeless students in the first two weeks of the 2009–10 school year—double the number during the same period the previous year. The National Center on Family Homelessness also found that homeless children are four times as likely to get sick and twice as likely to have learning and developmental problems as non-homeless children.

"We see eight-year-olds telling Mom not to worry, don't cry," said Bill Murdock, who works with homeless schoolchildren.

It's hard to hear stories like these and not feel outraged that we have given hundreds of billions of dollars to save Bank of America, Citigroup, JPMorgan Chase, and Wells Fargo, and yet those same banks are turning around and refusing to modify mortgages so that families can stay in their homes.

Moreover, despite common perception, most of the people losing their homes today are not recent buyers with crazy subprime mortgages, or families who took out massive loans they couldn't afford. They are middle-class Americans who have lost their jobs and are struggling to make ends meet.

The foreclosure crisis hasn't gotten the attention it deserves because the public's interest—people being able to keep their homes—is not aligned with corporate and financial interests. Banks don't want to adjust nonperforming mortgages down to their actual values because that would lead to marking down the value of the massive asset pools they have rolled the mortgages into. The four largest banks (Bank of America, Wells Fargo, Chase, and Citibank) service two-thirds of all distressed mortgages. These banks collectively hold about $477 billion in second liens.

When it came to the foreclosure crisis, Obama's audacity to win morphed into a timidity to govern. Bolder action earlier by the administration and our paralyzed, polarized Congress would have kept millions of families in their homes and cleared the decks more quickly for an economic revival on Main Street. But that, of course, would have meant giving the public the same sort of breaks the gluttonous bankers got.

"The banks are too big to fail" has been the mantra we've been hearing since September 2008. But apparently it's okay when American homeowners are thrown out of their homes and out of the middle class—perhaps forever.

A HOUSE OF CARDS

Mortgages, of course, are far from the only kind of debt Americans are saddled with. Indeed, we have become a nation fueled by plastic and financed by revolving credit.

The numbers are stunning:

- As of January 2010, U.S. consumers were carrying $2.46 trillion in consumer debt; $864 billion of that was made up of revolving credit (98 percent of which is credit card debt).

- There are more than 576 million credit cards in circulation in America, and another 507 million debit cards. We used those cards to make more than 56 billion transactions last year.

- The average credit cardholder has 3.5 cards, and of the households with credit card debt, the average debt is $16,000. During 2009, 56 percent of consumers carried an unpaid balance.

Americans no longer use their credit cards just to buy the things they want; they use them to make ends meet. "For much of America," says Elizabeth Warren, "the credit card is now the health insurance policy, the unemployment insurance, the way to deal with a child who's off in college and you haven't got enough to cover expenses." For more and more Americans, credit cards have become a plastic lifeline. In fact, in 2007, even before the economic crisis began, 14.7 percent of American households had debt totaling more than 40 percent of their annual income.

In 1958, American Express pioneered the use of widely accepted credit cards. BankAmericard (later to become Visa) followed in 1959 with the first general-use card that allowed balances to be paid over time. MasterCard (originally known as Master Charge) launched in the late 1960s.

But the modern credit card industry really kicked into high gear after a 1978 Supreme Court ruling allowed banks to charge the top interest rate permitted by the state where a bank is incorporated as opposed to the borrower's home state. Hoping to lure banks' business, states such as South Dakota and Delaware repealed their usury laws—which had kept interest rates in check—and we were off to the customer-gouging races.

The arrival of nationwide banking, combined with bank deregulation and the tech revolution, sealed the deal. It also opened the floodgates on banks soliciting our credit card business, and the creation of all manner of tricks and traps designed to separate consumers from their hard-earned money. "In 1980, the typical credit card contract was a page and a half long," Elizabeth Warren says. "Today, the typical credit card contract is about thirty-one pages long. The other twenty-nine and a half pages are the tricks and traps. I teach contract law at Harvard Law School," she continues, "and I can't understand my credit card contract. It's just not designed to be read."

As a result, for years the credit card companies have been fattening their bottom lines with an ever-widening array of fees: late fees, cash-advance fees, balance-transfer fees, over-the-limit fees. Fees now account for 39 percent of card issuers' revenue. In fact, last year, lenders collected more than $20 billion in penalties and fees. And even with the passage of the new credit card regulations that took effect in early 2010, banks are coming up with sneaky new ways to soak customers, including (if you can believe it) an "inactivity fee" for *not* using their card!

One of the best things the new credit card regulations do is make it harder for credit card companies to go after customers under the age of twenty-one. For years, the companies have aggressively, recklessly, and successfully targeted young consumers. As a result, according to CreditCards.com, 76 percent of all undergraduates now have credit cards: "Undergraduates are carrying record-high credit card balances. The average (mean) balance grew to $3,173, the highest in the years the study has been conducted. . . . Twenty-one percent of undergraduates had balances of between $3,000 and $7,000, also up from the last study." Half of all college undergraduates have more than *four* credit cards, and more than a third of them are unable to pay their balance in full. And, of course, this credit card debt is piled on top of their student loans. According to FinAid, 66 percent of college graduates ended their four-year bachelor's degree in debt—owing an average of $23,186 in student loans. These middle-class students—young, educated, and maxed out—will have a difficult time getting out from under the crushing debt as they start their careers. Priceless.

Our country now stands on the verge of a major credit card crisis. Every day, Americans, faced with layoffs and tough economic times, are forced to use their credit cards to pay for essentials such as food, housing, and medical care—the costs of which continue to escalate. But, as their debt rises, they find it harder to keep up with their payments. When they don't, banks, trying to offset losses in other areas, turn around, hike interest rates, and impose all manner of fees and penalties— all of which makes it even less likely consumers will be able to pay off their mounting debts. It's a vicious cycle, as Janet H. recounted:

"Back in 2008," she told me, "we had just a few minor credit card balances less than $1,000, which we would pay off within a couple of months. It was what we used for vacations or maybe for an extra Christmas splurge.

"When I lost my job as an office manager, however, we came to live off of credit cards—we had no other choice. Gas and groceries were a large portion of that, as gas was almost $4 per gallon and my husband commuted 50 minutes each way to work.

"Now our interest rates, which a couple of years ago ranged from 2.9 percent to 12 percent, have risen as high as 29.9 percent, even though we continued to make credit card payments.

"At the same time, each credit card decided to lower our credit limit and that, in turn, gave us a higher debt-to-available-credit ratio. A couple of months later, another credit card company would see the higher percentage and then they, too, would lower our credit limit. This is a cycle and we are now at the point where our credit card with a $16,000 credit limit has a $3,000 credit limit, thus giving us the dubious distinction of looking like we've maxed out all of our cards. These days we do not use credit cards often because, since all of them are maxed out, we cannot make a purchase without going over the limit.

"We have more debt than we can handle now, no savings, a house going back to the bank. All I hear is people saying that people in my situation 'are just bad with money' or 'overspend' or 'should never have bought a house if they could not afford it.' I do not want a handout; I do not want to file for bankruptcy. I make less money now, my husband makes less money now.

I am getting pretty fed up with people who judge us like we are of a lower class due to circumstances that really were beyond our control. Meanwhile, the banks get bailouts and pay large bonuses."

Credit card experiences like Janet's contribute to the growing anger, as well as to our economy's downward spiral. Many experts feel that as more and more Americans default on their credit card debt, banks will find themselves faced with a stomach-turning replay of the toxic securities meltdown from the mortgage crisis. In another example of Wall Street "creativity," credit card debt is routinely bundled together into "credit card receivables" and sold to investors—often pension funds and hedge funds. In 2008, securities backed by credit card debt added up to a $365 billion market. It motivated credit card companies to offer cards to risky borrowers and to allow greater and greater amounts of debt.

As these borrowers continue to default, banks and the investors who bought their packaged debt will take a serious hit. So how are the credit card companies trying to offset the rise in bad debts? By raising rates and fees for the rest of their customers, causing more of them to fall into arrears. And round and round and round we go.

Americans are encouraged to spend in order to help get the sputtering economy humming again. But the problem is, many Americans are broke, or barely scraping by, so the only way they can spend is to charge it, running up balances on credit cards that are structured in a way that makes it harder and harder to pay them off. Getting dizzy yet?

Elizabeth Warren worries that the credit card crisis "could be the knockout blow to the middle class."

FEAR, ANXIETY, DEPRESSION, ANGER . . . OTHER THAN THAT, AMERICA, HOW ARE WE DOING?!

Americans everywhere are anxious.

In March 2010, a FOX News poll found that 79 percent of voters—including the vast majority of Democrats, Republicans, and independents—think it's possible the economy could collapse. An April 2010 Gallup Poll revealed that only 41 percent of Americans think their financial situation is "good" or "excellent"—the lowest percentage in the past ten years. And 21 percent of workers think it's likely they will be fired during the next year.

This pessimistic outlook can have a profound impact on the American psyche, shaking our celebrated self-confidence. As reported by Don Peck in the March 2010 issue of the *Atlantic,* University of Warwick economist Andrew Oswald believes that "involuntary unemployment lasting six months or more is the worst thing for a person's mental health—just as bad . . . as the death of a spouse. . . . And the psychological effect is lasting—lingering even after a new job has been found."

Researchers at Rutgers University interviewed one thousand unemployed people in the summer of 2009. By the spring of 2010, 80 percent of them were still out of work. Of the people who did find work, only 13 percent had landed full-time jobs. To deal with the extended unemployment, "70 percent of the people dipped into retirement funds, 56 percent borrowed money from family or friends, and 45 percent turned to credit cards. Forty-two percent skimped on medical care, 20 percent moved in with family or friends, and 18 percent visited a soup kitchen."

"The cushion's completely gone," says Cliff Zukin, one of

the authors of the study. "It's a much deeper economic gash this time." And no occupation, at the middle-class level, has been spared.

Henry Chalian was a vice president and relationship manager at JPMorgan when he was laid off in May 2009. "It was a shock to everyone, in every way possible," he explains. "That said, the year before had been an unsettling one where every morning we came in, we said to each other: 'We are still here!'" Chalian, who has a master's degree from the London School of Economics, worked for Bear Stearns before he was hired by JPMorgan. "I managed relationships with some of the top independent research firms in the country," he says. "A lot of changes occurred in the last year, but we thought our jobs were secure. I was laid off on the last day Bear Stearns' severance was in place."

Chalian considers himself luckier than most: His former company has an in-house career center for displaced workers for up to one year. He has access to career counselors on a weekly basis, and the center offers classes on networking, speaking, and interviewing skills. He even participated in a six-week seminar on using social media for job searches. "I have joined a number of LinkedIn groups associated with finance, prior employers, and school alumni," he says, "I follow discussions, ask questions, and make comments." Chalian has also been using Twitter, which he discovered can be a powerful job-searching tool. "There are a lot of smart and helpful career advisers, bloggers, and recruiters that I have discovered and now follow."

He has participated in a variety of programs offered by his city and state to assist newly unemployed individuals, such as JumpStart NYC, which is a combined effort by Mayor Michael

Bloomberg and the New York City Economic Development Corporation for displaced financial service employees; he attended a one-week boot camp with educators from Harvard Business School; he spent six months at a digital media and e-commerce start-up incubator as part of an unpaid fellowship and consulting program; and he used a National Emergency Grant to participate in a two-week "Columbia Essentials of Management" program at Columbia Business School. He also contributes to a blog on WSJ.com called Laid Off and Looking, and he appeared in a CNN Money segment entitled "Castaway Bankers."

It has now been a year since Chalian was laid off, and, despite all these efforts, he is still looking for a job. His severance package exhausted, he is now relying on unemployment and has cut into his retirement savings. "I have been very frugal," he says, "but that goes only so far. I'm in a constant state of worry about money and the future. As busy as I have been, it has not been easy."

One of the offshoots of this undercurrent of fear and anxiety is the anger building up across America.

In April 2010, hot on the heels of an outbreak of threats against members of Congress, came word that an Oklahoma Tea Party group was planning to form an armed militia to help defend the state against the perceived encroachment of the federal government—this in a state where, fifteen years earlier, Timothy McVeigh's rage had turned deadly.

The FBI was investigating an antigovernment extremist group that was sending letters to America's governors demanding they resign or be "removed." This followed the arrests of members of the Hutaree group, a radical Christian militia organization in Michigan that was plotting to kill police officers.

When Tea Party members gathered for tax-day protests across the country, we were treated to a fresh wave of debate about whether these groups are fueled by anger, fear, racism, or class divisions. There was also talk about how much responsibility media outlets and certain political figures bear for inciting Tea Party crowds with violent rhetoric. (Sarah Palin urged her supporters to "reload," and U.S. representative Michele Bachmann said she wants her constituents "armed and dangerous.")

The rising tide of anger is part of a disturbing trend. According to *Rage on the Right,* a report released by the Southern Poverty Law Center, the number of so-called Patriot groups has skyrocketed in the past few years. In 2008, there were 149 active Patriot groups; in 2009, there were 512. The number of like-minded militia groups, meanwhile, rose from 42 in 2008 to 127 in 2009. And "nativist extremist groups," which advocate vigilante action against undocumented workers, went from 173 in 2008 to 309 in 2009.

While it's important that we take the threats and the rage seriously, it's just as important that we don't ignore the legitimate anger being directed at Washington and the political establishment of both parties. Thanks to the botched bank bailout, anti-government rhetoric has pervaded the public conversation. "Discontent with the present and apprehension about the future have become the background noise of our politics," wrote Tim Rutten in the *Los Angeles Times,* "yet both sides of the congressional aisle seem deaf to the din."

"There are times—they mark the danger point for a political system—when politicians can no longer communicate, when they stop understanding the language of the people they are supposed to be representing," wrote historian Ian Kersaw. Maybe that explains the lackadaisical, going-through-the-motions response of the political establishment to the rising chorus of middle-class anger.

In times of economic upheaval, when people are losing their jobs, losing their homes, and feeling powerless to do anything about it, people have always looked for scapegoats. We've seen this over and over again throughout American history.

For example, in the 1880s, as the post–Civil War Gilded Age came to an end, a severe economic crisis began that culminated in the depression of 1893. But the search for scapegoats among the American people began early. The Chinese Exclusion Act of 1882 suspended immigration from China, after Chinese immigrants had just helped build the transcontinental railroad. Attacks on the Chinese by white mobs took place all over the country.

One newspaperman captured the mood of the times:"Why permit an army of leprous, prosperity-sucking, progress-blasting Asiatics befoul our thoroughfares, degrade the city, repel immigration, drive out our people, break up our homes, take employment from our countrymen, corrupt the morals of our youth, establish opium joints, buy or steal the babe of poverty or slave, and taint with their brothels the lives of our young men?"

An ancestor of Glenn Beck's, perhaps?

Then, as now, the agitation resulted in the formation of a loose political party—the Populists. Here is how historian Richard Hofstadter described their agenda: "The utopia of the Populists was in the past, not the future," he wrote. "The Populists looked backward with longing to the lost agrarian Eden." Sound familiar? The myth of a golden age in America that existed before all our current problems existed has fueled many a political campaign.

Hofstadter also pointed to the Populists' rigid us-versus-them view of the world. It was the masses against the elites. Or, as Sarah Palin would put it, real Americans versus everybody else.

Conspiracy theories were rampant in the nineteenth century as well. In the wake of the depression of 1893, the Populists saw postwar American history as a "sustained conspiracy of the international money power," an obsession that also played into a virulent anti-Semitism.

History shows that such unconscionable credulity becomes much more ominous in times of economic hardship. It becomes even more heightened when our politicians, leaders, and members of the media pander to it, rather than addressing the underlying causes. While the shameful internment of Japanese citizens during World War II is well known, many Americans remain unaware that during the Great Depression, the United States, under President Hoover, actually deported large numbers of American citizens of Mexican ancestry.

As for anti-Semitism during the Great Depression, it wasn't just angry rhetoric—it was acted upon. In 1935, for example, many shops owned by Jews in Harlem were destroyed by a mob of African Americans, for whom the shopkeepers were simply the most available scapegoats. And, of course, the flames of bigotry were fanned by the wildly popular, xenophobic, and openly anti-Semitic Father Charles Coughlin, whose radio show was, at one time, listened to by one in three Americans.

In 1969, Pete Hamill published "The Revolt of the White Lower Middle Class" in *New York* magazine. It reads like it could have been published yesterday. "The working-class white man sees injustice and politicking everywhere in this town now," Hamill wrote, "with himself in the role of victim." He noted "an increasing lack of personal control over what happens to them." The result was a "growing talk of revolt." Hamill concluded, "If the stereotyped black man is becoming the working-class white man's enemy, the eventual enemy might be the democratic process itself."

By April 2010, over half the nation—and 92 percent of Tea Partiers—believed that President Obama was moving the country toward socialism. Combine our anxiety over the meltdown with today's downward economic mobility, and you get scapegoating run amok. A Harris Poll in March 2010 showed that, among Republicans, 57 percent believe Obama is a Muslim, 38 percent believe he "is doing many of the things that Hitler did," and 24 percent believe that the president "may be the Anti-Christ."

Even if the poll's methodology was flawed and the numbers are a fraction of these, this is crazy. But then again, according to psychologist Michael Bader, paranoia is a natural response to the suffering brought on by economic hard times. "Paranoid people are trying their best to make sense of and mitigate feelings of helplessness and worthlessness," Bader writes. "People can't tolerate feeling helpless and self-hating for very long. It's too painful . . . too demoralizing, too frightening. They have to find an antidote. They have to make sense of it all in a way that restores their sense of meaning . . . their self-esteem, and their belief in the possibility of redemption." To do so, they often create "a narrative—a set of beliefs about the way the world is and is supposed to be—[that] helps make sense of chaos." This often involves projecting blame onto others and creating an enemy to go after.

As we head into the 2010 midterm elections, and get more and more reports of extremist behavior and more news bites of the rhetoric of rage, let's keep in mind that the explanations people give to pollsters and reporters are often a reflection of our growing economic anxiety. While we need the media to stop pouring gasoline on the bonfires of discontent burning across America, we also need to recognize the underlying reasons for this anger and discontent. Americans are afraid that we, as a nation, are losing our way, and to many of us, the nightmare of a Third World America is becoming frighteningly real.

JOHNNY PARKER

It's funny how life throws you for a loop. One day, my wife and I—who have a beautiful three-year-old daughter—have a nice home, drive two newish cars, and don't have to choose between paying the bills and buying food. We were financially stable.

I worked full-time in a mental rehabilitation center. It wasn't the best pay, but it was more than enough for us. We lived simple lives—no extravagant vacations, no splurging at holidays or birthdays. We never had the money to build up savings, but we always had enough.

In April 2007 all that changed. I worked hard at my job, I'd never gotten in trouble, never been late. I got praise from my supervisors. I was working double and triple shifts and taking on new responsibilities, so I asked for a pay raise.

A month later I got called into a meeting with the program director and the director of nursing. I was told I'd done nothing wrong, but they would have to let me go. They would not tell me why, but just said I should file for unemployment.

So I did. The checks were enough to cover the rent, but not utilities and food. We rented out our office and our daughter's playroom. But one day the renters both suddenly left without notice. We applied for food stamps and welfare. My unemployment was too much for us to get welfare but we did get food stamps: eighty-two dollars a month. My car got repossessed but we were able keep my wife's car. June came and we didn't have enough for rent. We were served eviction papers. At the end of July we put all our stuff in storage but had nowhere to go.

Our county worker was able to get us a voucher to stay in a motel for a week while we looked for a place to live. That weekend, I went to a gas station to get something to drink. I asked the lady there for a job. She told me to come back tomorrow. I started working the cash register—two graveyard shifts a week and the other five days the swing shift. Thursday we found a one-bedroom in downtown Modesto. It was very small in a pretty bad area—the stove and heater didn't work—but it was a roof over our heads.

In February our car broke down. I called the gas station owner to tell them that I would not be able to make it in time for my shift. When I got home, there was a message—he had hired his brother-in-law to take my place. I went back on unemployment.

Money is still tight. Our food stamps aren't quite enough to buy food for the month. So in order to make sure there's enough for our daughter, my wife and I usually don't eat during the day. I've lost almost forty pounds.

I recently found out that I will receive my very last unemployment check at the end of this month. I applied for welfare when my unemployment was temporarily stopped, and it was not enough to cover the rent on even our small apartment.

I spend around thirty hours a week looking for work. But there just is not work available. I have offered to work off the clock and overtime. But no offers.

I used to consider myself middle class. I have some education and I have a wide variety of skills and experience, but almost every company I talk to says the same thing: Until the economy gets better, they are not hiring.

3

AMERICA THE ~~BEAUTIFUL~~ DILAPIDATED

* ★ ★

E ven before there was a Constitution, our founding fathers were already thinking about building America's infrastructure.

George Washington knew that without a national system of transportation, especially canals that would connect the East Coast to the Ohio and Mississippi river systems, we could never truly come together as a "more perfect union."

Thomas Jefferson put Washington's vision into effect, creating a concrete national plan for roads and canals—a farsighted plan that served as the touchstone for the next hundred years of development and led to America's transcontinental railroad, championed by Abraham Lincoln.

Franklin Delano Roosevelt spent massive federal dollars, even in the midst of the Great Depression, to bring electricity to rural America. Dwight Eisenhower pushed through the interstate highway system.

Building things—amazing things, grand things, forward-looking things, useful things—has always been an integral part of who we are as a country. We created highways, waterways, railroads, and bridges to link us together and forge a strong nation.

We created an infrastructure—including electrical grids, dams, sewers, water pipes, schools, waste-treatment facilities, airports—second to none. It was the skeleton that held our country up, the veins and arteries that kept our economy pumping, our prosperity flowing, and our quality of life high. But those once-glorious systems are falling apart at an alarming rate—a casualty of lack of funding, old age, and neglect.

In 2009, the American Society of Civil Engineers (ASCE) released its comprehensive infrastructure report card. It's not a pretty read. The nation's overall infrastructure grade was an appalling D. The report noted a downward trend since 2005: transit and aviation fell from a D+ to a D, while roads dropped from a D to a nearly failing D−. Dams, hazardous waste, and schools maintained their lowly D grade, while drinking water and wastewater remained mired at D−.

"It's the kind of report card you would have expected on the eve of the collapse of the Roman Empire," Stephen Flynn, a senior fellow at the Council on Foreign Relations, told a reporter from *Scientific American.*

Or from a Third World nation.

But despite the desperate state of affairs, America remains in denial. According to the ASCE, we would need to invest $2.2 trillion over the next five years just to bring our existing infrastructure up to a passable level (let alone a level appropriate for the twenty-first century). But we've only budgeted $975 billion for that period.

America is like a middle-aged man, still clinging to a perception of himself at age twenty-three, refusing to take in the wrinkles and the bald spot showing up in the mirror. And the bad knee. And the clogged arteries that could make his heart stop beating at any moment. We still see ourselves as a youthful nation, when it simply isn't true anymore. But unless we snap out of it and grow up enough to look reality in its sagging face, we are in for a world of trouble.

The fact is, America's antiquated infrastructure is desperately in need of an extreme makeover.

THE FLINTSTONES VERSUS *THE JETSONS*

Our infrastructure problems are so extensive, you don't have to look far to encounter them. Flip on a light switch, and you are tapping into a seriously overtaxed electrical grid. Go to the sink, and your tap water may be coming to you through pipes built during the Civil War. Take a drive, and pass over pothole-filled roads and cross-if-you-dare bridges. The evidence of decay is all around us.

But while the present state of disrepair is disturbing, looking down the crumbling, congested, traffic-clogged road at what lies ahead for us is chilling. America's population is expected to reach 438 million by 2050—a 48 percent increase since 2005. But instead of preparing for this growth and the attendant demands it will make on our run-down systems, America is nickel-and-diming its way into the future.

We invest just 2.4 percent of gross domestic product in infrastructure, compared with 5 percent in Europe and 9 percent in China—a surefire way to ensure that we will not be leading the twenty-first century. While we try to hold the American jalopy together with duct tape, chewing gum, some wire, and a prayer, China is busy building the most up-to-date, bells-and-whistles infrastructure money can buy, dramatically increasing that country's mobility.

For example, from 2006 through 2009, China spent $186 billion on its railways alone—which World Bank officials have described as "the biggest expansion of railway capacity undertaken by any country since the nineteenth century." And by 2020 China plans to construct 26,000 additional miles of track. It's making a similar commitment to other modes of transportation. In 2009 China built over 230,000 miles of roads and announced plans to build ninety-seven airports by 2020.

In a column headlined "Time to Reboot America," *New York Times* columnist and author Tom Friedman recounted flying from Hong Kong's "ultramodern airport" (following a ride on a high-speed train with top-of-the-line wireless connectivity) to New York's JFK airport and compared it to "going from the Jetsons to the Flintstones." The experience left him wondering: "If we're so smart, why are other people living so much better than us?"

And it's not just Asia. Armando Carbonell, chairman of the Department of Planning and Urban Form at the Lincoln Institute of Land Policy, says that while "the European Union is working across national boundaries to integrate the continent," in America "there's been at least a fifty-year gap in national planning for comprehensive infrastructure across water systems, energy systems and transportation."

This is about a lot more than just fixing potholes or getting from place to place faster. It's about keeping America competitive and keeping its people healthy and productive.

Felix Rohatyn, author of *Bold Endeavors: How Our Government Built America, and Why It Must Rebuild Now,* serves up the bracing bottom line: "The aging of our nation's infrastructure has lessened our productivity, undermined our ability to compete in the global economy, shaken our perceptions about our own safety and health, and damaged the quality of American life."

Then there is Pennsylvania governor Ed Rendell, who in 2008 teamed up with California governor Arnold Schwarzenegger and New York City mayor Michael Bloomberg to form Building America's Future (BAF), a bipartisan coalition looking, in Rendell's words, to "deliver a message to Washington that if America is going to have a future, an economically viable future, a quality-of-life future, a future that involves public safety, we have to begin the business of repairing infrastructure." In a February 2010 speech at an economic conference, Rendell warned, "If we don't do something quickly, by the time 2030 rolls around, America will be a second-rate economic power." Telling the businessmen in the room that "nothing significant will change until the businessmen step up," he urged: "We need entrepreneurs to step up and say, 'Guys, we're having the living daylights beaten out of us. If we don't do something quickly, we're sunk—we're a cooked goose.'"

The Flintstones, a cooked goose, a collapsing empire, a Third World nation. Pick your metaphor. They all translate into the same takeaway: The stakes for America couldn't be higher.

MISSED OPPORTUNITY: THE STIMULUS BECOMES A FISCAL PIÑATA

By the beginning of 2009, in the wake of the economic meltdown and the election of Barack Obama, it looked like investing money in a massive infrastructure-spending plan would be that rarest of things these days in American politics: a win-win initiative with bipartisan support.

With the economy in desperate need of a boost, building roads, updating our electrical grid, and repairing bridges, dams, and levees could create millions of high-paying jobs—jobs that would have to be located in America and couldn't be outsourced. According to Department of Transportation estimates, 47,500 jobs would be created for every $1 billion the government spends on highway improvements alone.

In addition, it could also produce what Rendell described as "a whole boatload of orders for American steel and concrete and timber companies. . . . it would be a huge shot in the arm for the economy, probably the best economic stimulus you could do."

As the debate over the stimulus began, Tom Friedman, knowing the need and seeing the opportunity, declared: "The next few months are among the most important in U.S. history."

But our leaders certainly didn't act like that was the case. Instead of focusing on infrastructure and job creation—and the gravity of the crisis at hand—we got a load of business-as-usual partisan bickering, special interest lobbying, and pork barrel spending.

The result was a bill Jeffrey Sachs, the Columbia University economist who was instrumental in transitioning the economic system of the former Soviet Union, called "a fiscal piñata," an "astounding mish-mash of tax cuts, public investments, transfer payments and special treats for insiders," and "a grab bag of hasty short-run spending."

In the end, the $787 billion American Recovery and Reinvestment Act allotted only $72 billion to infrastructure projects. "I fear that we may soon look back and say that we missed a huge chance to go bigger and bolder," Van Jones, author of *The Green*

Collar Economy, told me at the time the bill was being debated. "After all, there were three flaws with the old economy that has crashed: It favored consumption over production; debt over smart savings; and environmental damage over environmental renewal. Some parts of the stimulus package seem to be more of the same—trying to prop up the old, failed economy. That strategy simply won't work—but we could waste a lot of money and time trying. Instead, we need a new direction for our economy."

Faced with an even more devastating economic crisis, FDR responded with a large-scale public works program, including the Tennessee Valley Authority, the Works Progress Administration, and the Civilian Conservation Corps—programs that gave us much of the infrastructure that needs to be updated today. But instead of doing something similar—and instead of constructing a new economic vessel capable of navigating the stormy seas of the twenty-first century—we chose to grab a bucket and try to bail out the old sinking ship.

Moving forward, the price we'll pay for getting it wrong is extremely high. Think of a patient suffering from a grave viral infection who is treated with antibiotics, effective only against bacterial infections. Not only will the treatment be unsuccessful, it will also dangerously delay the proper care.

POWER BLACKOUTS, RUSTY WATER, COLLAPSED BRIDGES, RAW SEWAGE LEAKS: A GUIDED TOUR OF THIRD WORLD AMERICA

Extending the medical metaphor just a tad longer: Having failed to treat our ailment properly, we must continue to deal with the symptoms that rage all around us. What follows are the results of our nation's latest infrastructure checkup. The prognosis is definitely not good.

Let's start this examination of what's ailing America with that most elemental of elements: water. No society can survive without clean water. It's essential for life and civilization (imagine the Roman Empire without its aqueducts). Clean, fresh water is so essential that many believe that, in the coming decades, wars will be fought over it. Among them is Steven Solomon, author of *Water: The Epic Struggle for Wealth, Power, and Civilization,* who believes the world can be divided into water haves and water have-nots (Egypt, China, and Pakistan are among the have-nots).

"Consider what will happen," he writes, "in water-distressed, nuclear-armed, terrorist-besieged, overpopulated, heavily irrigation-dependent and already politically unstable Pakistan when its single water lifeline, the Indus River, loses a third of its flow from the disappearance of its glacial water source."

Despite the indispensable nature of water, America's drinking-water system is riddled with aging equipment that has been in the ground for one hundred years—or longer. Indeed, some of the nation's tap water continues to run through cast-iron pipes built during the Civil War. As a result of leaking pipes, we lose an estimated seven billion gallons of clean water every day.

According to a *New York Times* analysis of data from the Environmental Protection Agency, "a significant water line bursts on average every two minutes somewhere in the country." Washington, D.C., averages a water line break every day. "We have about two million miles of pipe in this nation," says

Steve Allbee of the EPA. "If you look at what we're spending now and the investment requirements over the next twenty years, there's a $540 billion difference."

Even now, our tap water is becoming less and less safe to drink—in some places our citizens are already forced to fetch fresh water from tanks stored on the back of trucks, our version of the Third World communal pump.

Meanwhile, America's wastewater treatment facilities are also fast deteriorating. According to the American Society of Civil Engineers, "Older systems are plagued by chronic overflows during major rainstorms and heavy snowmelt and are bringing about the discharge of raw sewage into U.S. surface waters. The EPA estimated in August 2004 that the volume of combined sewer overflows discharged nationwide is 850 billion gallons per year. Sanitary sewer overflows, caused by blocked or broken pipes, result in the release of as much as 10 billion gallons of raw sewage yearly."

The wall between fresh water and tainted water has become increasingly porous.

PULLING THE PLUG ON OUR ELECTRIC GRID

Next up, electricity. America is an increasingly wired society. Advances in technology mean more electronic devices—and more demand for energy. Yet the delivery of electricity today doesn't differ much from the way it was done more than a hundred years ago when Thomas Edison brought the first commercial power grid online in New York.

While demand for electricity has risen 25 percent since 1990, the construction of transmission plants has dropped 30 percent.

Since we need all the power we can get, companies are finding it nearly impossible to take facilities offline for proper maintenance—leading to breakdowns and unplanned outages. These ongoing brownouts and blackouts—some lasting seconds, some lasting days—result in more than $80 billion in commercial losses a year. The ASCE estimates that it could take as much as $1.5 trillion to $2 trillion over the next twenty years to fully update and expand the grid.

On August 14, 2003, we got a glimpse of what we can expect a lot more of if we don't make that investment. That muggy Thursday, an estimated fifty-five million Americans and Canadians living in a nearly four-thousand-mile stretch from Michigan to Connecticut and Canada lost power in the largest blackout in North American history. In New York, traffic ground to a halt when 11,600 stoplights cut out, and stalled subways and trains stranded four hundred thousand commuters throughout the evening and into the night. The city was plunged into darkness. The impact was felt across the northern corridor of our country, from high-rise elevators to airports and communication networks. What happened? Power lines, heavy from increased demand, dipped into overgrown trees in Ohio, which triggered a series of malfunctions that led to the shutdown of at least 265 power plants throughout the Northeast.

ON THE ROADS TO RUIN

America's roads are also in miserable shape, with a third of the country's roadways rated "poor" or "mediocre." Again, our demand has far outstripped our capacity to meet it. From 1980 to

2005, the miles traveled by cars increased 94 percent (for trucks, mileage increased 105 percent). Yet there was only a 3.5 percent increase in highway lane miles.

But you don't need those numbers to know that our roads are badly congested. You see it—and experience it—every day. According to the American Society of Civil Engineers' Infrastructure Report Card, "Americans spend 4.2 billion hours a year stuck in traffic at a cost of $78 billion a year—$710 a year for each motorist." City drivers have it particularly bad: They are stuck in traffic over 40 percent of their time on the road.

In studying car crashes across the country, the Transportation Construction Coalition (TCC) determined that badly maintained or managed roads are responsible for $217 billion in car crashes annually—far more than headline-grabbing alcohol-related accidents ($130 billion) or speed-related pile-ups ($97 billion).

But Americans are paying an even higher price for our deteriorating roads: According to the TCC, 53 percent of the forty-two thousand road fatalities each year are at least partially the result of poor road conditions. We are currently spending $70 billion annually on improving our highways—nowhere near the $186 billion a year that is needed. It's a collision of need versus resources; for far too many of us, it can be fatal.

THE LONG AND GRINDING COMMUTE

There's an additional twist on the traffic story. Over the past decade, high housing prices have forced many middle-class families to move farther and farther away from the overpriced cities they work in. Doing so has meant ever-longer commutes.

By the year 2000, each day, 3.5 million Americans headed out on "extreme commutes," defined by the U.S. Census Bureau as travel times to and from work of three hours or more each day. That is twice the number of extreme commuters there were in 1990. One in eight workers—17.5 million Americans—are now out their front doors every morning and on their way to work by 6 A.M. For more and more of the middle class, life now consists of sleep, an arduous commute, work, another arduous commute, then back to sleep.

These stressed-out Americans turbo-charge their long journeys to work with PowerBars, vats of Dunkin' Donuts coffee . . . and loneliness. Robert Putnam, a Harvard political scientist, found that there is a direct connection between the duration of a person's commute and their sense of social isolation. By his calculations, every ten minutes of commuting results in 10 percent fewer social connections. "Commuting," Putnam says, "is connected to social isolation, which causes unhappiness." A study by Swiss economists at the University of Zurich discovered that commuters with a one-hour commute each way need to earn 40 percent more than noncommuters just to pull even with the noncommuters' level of satisfaction with their lives. It puts a whole new spin on the phrase "driven to succeed."

AMERICA'S TRAINS GO OFF THE RAILS

America's railway system is speeding down the tracks . . . in reverse. It's one of the few technologies that has actually regressed over the past eighty years.

Tom Vanderbilt of Slate.com came across some pre–World War II train timetables and made a startling discovery: Many train rides in the 1930s, '40s, and '50s took less time than those journeys would today. For instance, in 1934, the Burlington Zephyr would get you from Chicago to Denver in around thirteen hours. The same trip takes eighteen hours today. "The trip from Chicago to Minneapolis via the Olympian Hiawatha in the 1950s," Vanderbilt writes, "took about four and a half hours; today, via Amtrak's Empire Builder, the journey is more than eight hours."

At the moment, the only high-speed train in the United States is Amtrak's Acela, which travels the Washington–New York–Boston line. And I use the term "high-speed" very loosely. While in theory the trains have a peak speed of 150 miles per hour, the average speed on the Northeast Acela route is just 71 miles per hour, with its trains frequently stuck behind slower-moving ones on the heavily traveled tracks. Meanwhile, countries such as Japan, France, and Italy all have reliable train services that surpass 200 miles per hour. Same with China. For example, the six-hundred-mile ride between Wuhan and Guangzhou is completed in three hours by bullet trains reaching 217 miles per hour; the airport rail link in Shanghai reaches a top speed of 268 miles per hour.

The stimulus bill included $8 billion for high-speed rail projects in thirty states, linking cities such as Minneapolis, Milwaukee, and Chicago—$1.25 billion going to a high-speed rail corridor between Orlando and Tampa. Of course, high-speed rail systems everywhere would be great, but there are obvious political considerations behind sprinkling the money all over the country. The fact is, the highest trafficked section of the nation's rail system, the limping northeast corridor from

Boston to Washington, D.C., is in dire need of renovation but received only $112 million.

So while this new investment is a start, it's only a drop in the bucket. And while trains going over 200 miles per hour would be great, as Vanderbilt puts it, "We would also do well to simply get trains back up to the speeds they traveled at during the Harding administration."

TROUBLED BRIDGES OVER WATER

Out-of-date, overpriced, slow-moving, rickety, and routinely late trains can be frustrating and inconvenient. Out-of-date bridges can be downright deadly—as we've seen in the past decade with high-profile bridge collapses in Minnesota and Oklahoma.

According to the Department of Transportation, one in four of America's bridges is either "structurally deficient" or "functionally obsolete." The numbers are even worse when it comes to bridges in urban areas, where one in three bridges is deficient (no small matter given the higher levels of passenger and freight traffic in our nation's cities).

The problem is pretty basic: The average bridge in our country has a lifespan of fifty years and is now forty-three years old. We'd need to invest $850 billion over the next fifty years to get all of America's bridges into good shape. That's $17 billion a year. At the moment, we're spending only $10.5 billion a year.

As a result, we all too often find our attention drawn to places such as Webbers Falls, Oklahoma.

It was May 2002, and Webbers Falls, 140 miles east of Oklahoma City, had been pounded by heavy rains. But that didn't deter people from driving across Interstate 40 to get together with family and friends on a busy Memorial Day weekend. Some 35 miles west of the Arkansas state line, a long line of cars and trucks was crossing the 1967-built bridge, 1,988 feet of concrete and steel spanning the swollen Arkansas River.

Down in the river, towboat captain William Joe Dedmon was pushing two barges when he suffered an attack of cardiac arrhythmia, and the barges ended up hitting the bridge's support. Up above, a six-hundred-foot section of the bridge suddenly gave way—and a dozen cars, two tractor-trailer rigs, and a horse trailer plunged seventy-five feet into the water below.

In an instant, the Arkansas River turned into a graveyard—one littered with concrete slabs, diapers, dead horses, and broken car seats. Fourteen people died that day, including a three-year-old girl, and scores more were injured. "Officials set up a morgue inside city hall," the *Bowling Green Daily News* reported. "Victims' families were told to go to the community center in Gore, on the other side of the river." Because of the high and murky water, divers had a hard time retrieving the dead from the cars that were submerged and stacked on top of one another in the river's fast currents.

Six years later, one quarter of Oklahoma's bridges still needed overhaul or replacement. Indeed, the state had the dubious distinction of leading the nation in the percentage of structurally deficient bridges. And Oklahoma is far from alone. In August 2007, the Interstate 35W steel truss bridge over the Mississippi in downtown Minneapolis collapsed during evening rush hour, killing 13 and injuring 145. The bridge had been inspected each year by the state's Department of Transportation, but clearly the patchwork repairs were not sufficient.

All across the country, patch and pray remains the order of

the day . . . until the next bridge comes falling down. How many more will it take—and how many more people have to die—before a more serious effort is made?

AMERICA'S DAMS: DAMNED IF WE DON'T FIX THEM

We've seen similar tragedies with America's dams.

On March 16, 2006, the Ka Loko Dam in Kilauea, Hawaii, collapsed. "Seven people died when the Ka Loko Dam breached after weeks of heavy rain, sending 1.6 million tons of water downstream," the *Honolulu Star Bulletin* reported. Among the dead were a child and a woman eight months pregnant. The breach created an ecological disaster of torn-up streams, reefs, and coastal waterways. The Ka Loko Dam was not considered a "high-hazard dam." It was, however, like all dams, supposed to be regularly inspected. According to Hawaii congresswoman Mazie Hirono, it was not.

Dams are a vital part of America's infrastructure. They help provide water for drinking, irrigation, and agriculture, generate much-needed power, and offer protection from floods.

Yet our dams are growing old. There are more than 85,000 dams in America—and the average age is fifty-one years old. At the same time, more and more people are moving into developments located below dams that require significantly greater safety standards—but we've had a hard time keeping up with the increase in these so-called high-hazard dams. Indeed, we are falling further and further behind. According to the American Society of Civil Engineers, "Over the past six years, for every deficient, high hazard potential dam repaired, nearly two more were declared deficient."

It would take $12.5 billion over the next five years to properly upgrade our nation's dams. The estimated spending on dams over that time is $5.05 billion—a projected shortfall of $7.45 billion. Plus, of our 85,000 dams, the federal government regulates fewer than 10,000. The rest are the responsibility of the states—most of which are facing large budget deficits. For example, the ASCE reports that in 2007 Texas had "only seven engineers with an annual budget of only $435,000 to regulate more than 7,500 dams. Worse still, Alabama does not have a dam safety program despite the fact that there are more than 2,000 dams in the state."

In 2007, during congressional testimony on levee and dam safety programs, New York congressman John Hall gave an account of what some New York dams looked like after a period of heavy rains. "Yesterday," he said, "I visited three dams, all of which are over one hundred years old, in my district. The Whaley Lake Dam has boils on its surface. It's a dam that's largely earth and rock with some concrete structure. It has a frozen relief valve for the emergency release forty-eight-inch pipe, and that valve is in the middle of the dam, where it would not be accessible were the dam being overtopped by high water."

Similar stories could be told across the country.

AMERICA'S LEVEES: WHY HAVEN'T THE LESSONS OF KATRINA BEEN LEARNED?

In 2005, even those most determined to deny our deteriorating condition came face-to-face with Third World America as the levees around New Orleans burst during Hurricane Katrina. More than 1,800 people died. For weeks our government seemed incapable of even retrieving the bodies from the city's flooded streets, much less finding housing and food for those who were evacuated from their homes.

This great American tragedy was not created by the perfect storm of killer winds and driving rain, as President Bush told us. It was a catastrophe that was entirely man-made—produced by our compromised political process.

Like any number of agencies charged with protecting the public, the U.S. Army Corps of Engineers, which author and satirist Harry Shearer has called "the true poster child for federal incompetence," has lost its way. "The Corps," Shearer writes, "tasked by a 1960s Congress to protect New Orleans from severe hurricanes, failed, by its own standards, and according to its own post-mortem. More independent observers, like the UC Berkeley Independent Levee Investigation Team, had an even harsher verdict. Yet who's blithely going about fixing that which they screwed up so royally? The Corps. Who's reviewing their work? If anybody, engineers approved and paid by . . . the Corps." Instead of fulfilling its responsibility to build and efficiently maintain the country's waterways infrastructure, the Corps became yet another tool of a cabal of highly politicized officials using government for their own ends. After trying to deflect blame and cover up its shoddy work, the U.S. Army Corps of Engineers was forced to publicly own up to its systemic failures that led to the disaster that befell New Orleans.

The politicians who prioritize the Corps's workload and projects and grant it funding are also to blame, swayed as they are by the lobbyists and engineering firms whose contributions earn them the right to "recommend" what projects the U.S.

Army Corps of Engineers should be pursuing. You won't be surprised to learn that these projects often coincide with the very same services offered by clients of the lobbyists.

The American Society of Civil Engineers estimates it would cost $100 billion to refurbish the nation's levees. But even harder to come by are the political reforms needed to ensure that the $100 billion would be spent in a way that actually did what it was supposed to.

WIRED FOR FAILURE

Fortifying America's infrastructure is not just about patching up our antiquated systems. It's also about laying the groundwork for an efficient and equitable society that can compete with the fast-rising economies of the twenty-first century. This means that, along with repairing our decaying roads, bridges, dams, and electric grid, we have to invest in building the kind of high-tech infrastructure that can keep us in the game in the future.

For starters, we need to kick our high-speed Internet plans into high gear. A robust, broadband-charged, country-wide information superhighway is going to be key to staying ahead of the innovation curve. Over the next ten years, there will be a five-hundredfold increase in the amount of information traveling on the nation's information superhighway. New products coming onto the market—including video conferencing, video on demand, and geographic information systems mapping—will increasingly need to work on broadband's higher transmission speeds.

Federal Communications Commission chair Julius Genachowski explains that broadband isn't just important for faster email and video games—it's the central nervous system for democracies and economies of the future: "Broadband is indispensable infrastructure for the twenty-first century. It is already becoming the foundation for our economy and democracy in the twenty-first century . . . [and] will be our central platform for innovation in the twenty-first century."

How indispensable is it? In a study of 120 countries, researchers found that every 10 percent increase in broadband adoption increased a country's GDP by 1.3 percent. Even a farmer these days needs high-speed Internet to stay in touch with world commodity prices and access the latest information on weather and planting and seed technologies.

Unfortunately, when it comes to broadband, America is also falling behind.

In 2001, the United States ranked fourth among industrialized countries in broadband access. By 2009, we had dropped to fifteenth. As for average broadband download speed, we rank nineteenth. Over one hundred million Americans still don't have broadband in their homes. And while 83 percent of college graduates in the United States have access to broadband, only 52 percent of high school graduates do.

Breaking the numbers down by race and income reveals depressing discrepancies. For instance, around 65 percent of Asian Americans, Caucasians, and Hispanics use broadband at home; that usage rate falls to 46 percent for African Americans. Among households earning more than $100,000 a year, 88 percent have access to broadband versus 54 percent among households making between $30,000 and $40,000. And the split between rural and city folk? Broadband has penetrated just 46 percent of the farming community, compared to 67 percent for the rest of the country.

To help close the widening gap between us and the rest of the digitally connected world, the Obama administration has proposed a national broadband plan, with the goal of increasing broadband access from around 63 percent currently to 90 percent by 2020. The plan would also ensure that every high school graduate is digitally literate. This sounds great. But 2020? That hardly has the sense of urgency you'd expect from a country that is quickly falling behind. If it's truly a priority and important to national security and the relative position of the United States in the world, why put it off for a decade?

AMERICA'S SCHOOLS DON'T PASS THE TEST

As bad as America's sewers, roads, bridges, dams, and water and power systems are, they pale in comparison to the crisis we are facing in our schools.

I'm not talking about the physical state of our dilapidated public school buildings—although the National Education Association estimates it would take $322 billion to bring America's school buildings into good repair. The real devastation is going on inside our nation's classrooms. If America's public education system were a product, it would have been recalled. If it were a politician, it would have been impeached. If it were a horse, it would have been taken behind the barn and shot.

Nothing is quickening our descent into Third World status faster than our resounding failure to properly educate our children. This failure has profound consequences for our future, both at home and as we look to compete with the rest of the world in the global economy.

Historically education has been the great equalizer. The path to success. The springboard to the middle class—and beyond. It was a promise we made to our people. A birthright we bestowed on each succeeding generation: the chance to learn, to improve their minds, and, as a result, their lives. But something has gone terribly wrong—and we've slipped further and further behind.

Among thirty developed countries ranked by the Organisation for Economic Co-operation and Development, the United States ranked twenty-fifth in math and twenty-first in science. Even the top 10 percent of American students, our best and brightest, ranked only twenty-fourth in the world in math literacy.

A National Assessment of Educational Progress report found that just 33 percent of U.S. fourth graders and 32 percent of eighth graders were "proficient" in reading—while 33 percent of fourth graders and 25 percent of eighth graders performed below a "basic" level of reading.

In 2001, amid much fanfare, the D.C. establishment passed No Child Left Behind, shook hands, patted one another on the backs, and checked education reform off their to-do lists. But it turned out to be reform in name only. Despite a goal of 100 percent proficiency in reading and math, eight years later we are not even close. In Alabama, only 20 percent of eighth graders are proficient in math. In California, it's just 23 percent. In New York, it's 34 percent.

"Education," said President Obama during his May 2010

commencement address at Hampton University, "is what has always allowed us to meet the challenges of a changing world." But he made it clear that the bar for meeting those challenges has been raised, and that a high school diploma—formerly, in the president's words, "a ticket into a solid middle-class life"—is no longer enough to compete in what he called the "knowledge economy."

"Jobs today often require at least a bachelor's degree," he said, "and that degree is even more important in tough times like these. In fact, the unemployment rate for folks who've never gone to college is over twice as high as for folks with a college degree or more."

But rather than rising "to meet the challenges of a changing world," we're taking a tumble. Our high schools have become dropout factories. We have one of the lowest graduation rates in the industrialized world: Over 30 percent of American high school students fail to leave with a diploma. And even those who do graduate are often unprepared for college. The American College Testing Program, which develops the ACT college admissions test, says that fewer than one in four of those taking the test met its college readiness benchmark in all four subjects: English, reading, math, and science. And among those who are qualified, many are having trouble making the payments necessitated by large tuition increases.

University of California–Davis honors student Rajiv Narayan was raised in a two-income, solidly middle-class family. But shortly after he started college, his family's financial security was upended when both of his parents lost their jobs, driving their family income down from $90,000 to $30,000 per year. "Initially, I did not worry too much over my financial situation," he says. "I work hard, my grades are high, and from my understanding, FAFSA [the Free Application for Federal Student Aid] and the California grant system are designed to support good students from low-income backgrounds."

But the university's aid programs, it turned out, weren't flexible enough to accommodate his family's abrupt and radical change in financial circumstances. "For me to receive more aid, my parents would have to be unemployed for two years," he explained. Instead, the amount his family was expected to contribute toward his tuition jumped from $17,000 to $27,000. Set on finishing his degree, Rajiv applied for more loans and trimmed his expenses, budgeting just $18 per week for groceries, while his brother—who graduated from the University of California–Berkeley with about $80,000 in loans—took on a third job to help him cover the increased costs. "It appears I'm being punished for my new financial hardship," he says.

To save money and avoid going into debt, UC Berkeley student Ramon Quintero moved into a motor home. "They increased tuition, they increased the rent," he says. "But instead of giving you more grants, they give you more loans."

Patsy Ramirez says she was able to go to the University of California–Riverside with the help of a $10,000 grant, paying for the rest of her tuition, her books, and her living expenses with a part-time job. But the grant program was cut, and without it, she couldn't afford to continue college.

Amy Brisendine was a student at the University of California–Santa Barbara, studying to become a nurse. A 32 percent tuition increase in November 2009 forced her to drop out of college, and she now works five to six days a week waitressing and bartending at two restaurants. "I will try to finish my education if and when the economy gets better," she says, "but until then, I am continuing to work."

So as education becomes more and more important, why are we allowing our future workforce to become less and less educated?

Academy Award–winning filmmaker Davis Guggenheim set out to find the answer. The result is his film *Waiting for Superman* (the phrase comes from one young student's dream of being rescued by Superman). In it, he shows us the stories behind the statistics and exposes the bloody battlefield America's education system has become. The many opposing forces are deeply entrenched behind decades-old Maginot Lines—and our children are getting caught in the crossfire.

Guggenheim isn't afraid to point fingers. From politicians who pay lip service to education reform but never manage to change a thing to school boards and bureaucrats more concerned with protecting their turf than educating our kids, there is plenty of blame to go around. He turns a particularly withering spotlight on America's teachers' unions—which have gone from improving pay and working conditions for teachers to thwarting real reform and innovation and protecting incompetent teachers from being fired.

Guggenheim is not anti-teacher. Indeed, he sees good teachers as true heroes. In 2001, he made *The First Year,* a powerful look at a group of inspiring teachers battling to overcome soul-sapping obstacles to teach our children—particularly those in inner-city classrooms. But his new film shows how it's become next to impossible to get rid of bad or indifferent teachers.

By way of example, he cites the state of Illinois, which has 876 school districts. Of those, only 38 have ever successfully fired an incompetent teacher with tenure. "Compare that to other professions," says Guggenheim in the film's narration. "For doctors, one in fifty-seven lose their medical licenses. One in ninety-seven attorneys lose their law licenses. But for teachers, only one in twenty-five hundred has ever lost their teaching credentials."

In New York, tenured teachers awaiting disciplinary hearings on offenses ranging from excessive lateness to sexual abuse—along with those accused of incompetence—are allowed to bide their time, sitting around reading or playing cards for seven hours a day, in places dubbed "Rubber Rooms," while still collecting their full paycheck. On average, they remain in this well-paid limbo for over a year and a half—and some for three years or longer—costing the state $65 million a year. And, as Guggenheim points out, "None of this deals with the larger pool of teachers who just aren't good at their jobs."

This takes an enormous toll on the quality of the education America's children receive. In the film, Stanford's Eric Hanushek says if "we could just eliminate the bottom six to ten percent of our teachers and replace them with an average teacher, we could bring the average U.S. student up to the level of Finland, which is at the top of the world today."

The film charts the connection between the unions' clout and their generous political giving. Between them, the National Education Association and the American Federation of Teachers have made nearly $58 million in federal political contributions since 1989. Andrew Coulson of the Cato Institute points out that this is "roughly as much as Chevron, Exxon Mobil, the NRA, and Lockheed Martin combined."

According to Guggenheim, "Since 1971, educational spending in the U.S. has grown from $4,300 to more than $9,000 per student—and that's adjusted for inflation." But while spending is way up, results are not.

Unlike repairing America's roads, bridges, and dams, it will take more than just a massive infusion of dollars to fix our schools. Part of the problem is the system itself. Based on the Prussian educational model, which was designed to produce obedient soldiers and compliant citizens, the American version was a product of the Industrial Revolution—designed to ensure a pool of pliant, homogenized worker bees. Our schools were factories to produce factory workers, an assembly line to produce assembly-line drones. But this one-size-fits-all model is grotesquely out of step with the creativity and problem solving our modern age requires.

Plus, as President Obama pointed out, society's demands are different than they used to be. In the 1950s, only 20 percent of high school graduates were expected to go to college. Another 20 percent were meant to go straight into skilled jobs, such as accounting or middle management. The remaining 60 percent would become factory workers or go back to work on their farms. "The problem is," says Guggenheim, "our schools haven't changed—but the world around them has."

Once again, it's a question of priorities. Just look at the explosion of spending on America's jails over the past twenty years. During that time, new prisons have been popping up at a rate even McDonald's would envy—and the number of people living behind bars has tripled, to more than two million. In fact, America has more people living behind bars than any other country.

Sadly, in that prison population are close to 150,000 children. With their high dropout rates, too many of America's schools have become preparatory facilities not for college but for jail. Time after time, when the choice has come down to books versus bars, our political leaders have chosen to build bigger prisons rather than figure out how to send fewer kids to them. How is it that we are willing to spend so much more on kids *after* they are found guilty of crimes than we are when they could really use the help?

In the end, the blame for the chronic inability to fix our educational system has to be laid at the feet of our leaders in Washington. As predictably as a school bell, every election season our candidates promise to transform our schools—and, just as predictably, they fail to do so.

George W. Bush signed No Child Left Behind into law—but despite its passage, millions and millions of schoolkids have been left behind.

Bill Clinton started his second term vowing, "My number one priority for the next four years is to ensure that all Americans have the best education in the world." But as of 1999, America's eighth graders ranked nineteenth in the world in math and eighteenth in science.

We saw a similar pattern with George W's father, who promised to "revolutionize America's schools." "By the year 2000," Bush 41 vowed in his 1990 State of the Union address, "U.S. students must be the first in the world in math and science achievement. Every American adult must be a skilled, literate worker and citizen. . . . The nation will not accept anything less than excellence in education." But 2000 arrived, and out of twenty-seven nations, the United States ranked eighteenth in mathematics, fourteenth in science, and fifteenth in reading literacy.

Far from accepting nothing less than excellence, we've grown accustomed to our educational system's persistent failure, content to point out the occasional jewel spotted amid the dung: a marvelous charter school here, a high-performing inner-city academy there. We've allowed that old Washington motto to carry the day: "If it's broke, don't fix it."

But if we are to survive—and avoid turning into Third World America—it's essential that we make it easier for creativity and fresh thinking to flourish in our classrooms. We need to start looking at things in bold and different ways.

What Abraham Lincoln said in his second annual address to Congress in 1862 applies powerfully to today's educational crisis: "The dogmas of the quiet past are inadequate to the stormy present. . . . As our case is new, so we must think anew and act anew."

And when it comes to saving our children—and our future—there is not a moment to waste.

MATT STAGLIANO

I never thought I'd say this, but last week I lost my home. Despite my best efforts, on January 5, 2010, my house was sold at the Bexar County Courthouse (for less than I paid for it).

In retrospect, 2008 wasn't exactly the best time to start a new career as a Realtor. I was a guitarist in a touring band. It paid well, or at least allowed me to squeak by when it didn't.

But I had a plan for my life and wanted to follow it, instead of spending time regretting it. I wanted to focus on something tangible (like real estate), something I could be passionate about again.

It wasn't easy building a business in 2008. Many of the seasoned agents were struggling. As a new agent, I was told time and time again to be prepared to have some very lean months. And I certainly didn't make a fortune that year. Instead, I slowly ate through my savings, trying to hang on to what I had as tight as I could. As the bank accounts dwindled, my royalties from the band also dried up. With little coming in other than my wife's salary, we conserved everywhere we could.

And we did fine—until 2009. That's when we began to get behind. We'd get a month behind, then pay two, get two months behind and catch up. It was a constant cycle of getting behind and getting back. And each time, our credit went down. With less credit, we couldn't refinance. . . . One missed payment on a credit card leads to a higher interest rate, which results in more delinquency, which leads to even higher interest rates, and on and on it goes.

Late that year, I lost two commissions. We got a bit more

behind. So the mortgage company began the foreclosure process in November. I tried to work with the lender. We should have been a dream case for loan modification. There was no wild spending, no million-dollar home, no boats. We just hit an unfortunate set of circumstances and were making ground on them—but not fast enough.

In fact, I was having a great year (I was named "Mr. Zero-to-Sixty in Thirty Days" because of the complete turnaround in my business). My wife got a new job with a nice raise. All we needed was a little help from the lender. But lenders are flooded with people just like us. They never even looked at our package.

As a real estate agent, I took foreclosure extra hard. It wasn't easy talking to people about homes when I knew I'd just lost mine. The thought "I couldn't keep my own house" was always in the back of my head. Foreclosure is a deeply psychological event. When word got out, I heard from other Realtors who were in the same boat I was. Knowing that really helped me.

What will we miss? Things like the deck on which we had some fabulous BBQs with great friends. Knowing I won't have my neighbors anymore.

We're trying to get back on track. We've tightened our belts and given up extras. We talk a lot more about our finances—about what we're spending, and why.

And I have learned a lesson that will help me better understand my clients—have compassion. People all have their own hopes and dreams. So try to be compassionate. The emotions, the anger, the depression—if ever there was a time in a person's life when they need someone to lean on, this is it.

4

CSI USA: WHO KILLED THE AMERICAN DREAM?

★ ★ ★

So how did we get here?

How did we get to a place where our infrastructure is well past its sell-by date, our schools are failing, our middle class is on life support, and the American Dream is turning into a mirage?

Who took control of our national GPS and set as our ultimate destination the coordinates of a Third World future? Casting about for answers, the knee-jerk response is to point a finger and hurl an enraged *j'accuse!* at Washington. And, in this case, the knee-jerk response is right. But for all the wrong reasons.

Listen to the punditocracy and they'll tell you—loudly and often—that our politics is "broken" and "paralyzed." That government no longer works because of bipartisan bickering and polarization. That the parties have moved so far to their respective extremes on the left and the right that collaboration and consensus are no longer possible.

And while the GOP's decision to respond to the election of President Obama by transforming itself into the Party of No certainly gives that slice of conventional wisdom the surface patina of insight, dig a little deeper and you'll discover the much uglier truth: Over the past thirty years, the two parties have actually become much more alike—both deeply in the pocket of the big-business masters who fill their campaign coffers.

American politics is indeed "broken"—but not because our leaders are at one another's throats. It's broken because the founding democratic principle of "one man, one vote" has been replaced by the arithmetic of special interest politics: Thousands of lobbyists plus billions of dollars equal access and influence out of the reach of ordinary Americans.

The consequences of this corporate takeover of our democracy couldn't be more profound and far-reaching, affecting every aspect of our lives—from the cleanliness of the air we breathe and the water we drink to the safety of the food we eat, the medications we take, and the products we buy, to the stability of the economy that allows us to keep our jobs, afford our houses, and pursue our dreams.

All of these and more are being dictated by a system of government that determines its priorities in a bazaar of influence peddling.

There's an old joke about a cop who comes upon a drunk crawling around under a streetlight. "What are you doing?" he asks.

"Looking for my keys," the drunk answers.

"Where did you lose them?"

"Over there."

"Well, why are you looking for them here?"

"Because the lighting is better."

Do you ever find yourself wondering why laws that make no sense get passed while laws that would seem like no-brainers never make it out of committee? Why some issues get pushed to the front of the line, while others die from lack of attention? The answer is simple. Like the drunk following the light, politicians follow the money and the clamor of noisy special interest groups—leaving the interests of middle-class Americans, like so many car keys, forgotten and left behind.

Some people look at laws and ask, "Why?" or "Why not?" I look at laws and ask, "Who paid for them?"

THERE ARE NO LOBBYISTS FOR THE
AMERICAN DREAM

Since 1964, the American National Election Studies at the University of Michigan has regularly asked voters whether they think the U.S. government is run "for the benefit of all" or "by a few big interests." In the mid-1960s, only 29 percent thought "big interests" ran the nation. By the mid-1990s, that number had climbed to 76 percent. And in 2008, 80 percent of Americans surveyed told the Program on International Policy Attitudes that they believed government was controlled by "a few big interests looking out for themselves."

That shouldn't be a surprise. Over the years there has been an explosion in the number of lobbyists in Washington and the money they spend. In 2009, more than 13,700 registered lobbyists spent a record $3.5 billion swaying government policy the special interests' way, double the amount lobbyists spent as recently as 2002.

With 535 members of the Senate and the House, that means lobbyists in the halls of power outnumber our elected representatives almost 26 to 1. If we divide $3.5 billion evenly among the 535, it means each member of the legislative branch was at the receiving end of $6.5 million worth of special interest arm-twisting over the course of the year.

And that's just the money corporate America is spending on lobbying. Millions more are given directly to politicians and the political parties. From 1974 to 2008 the average amount it took to run for reelection to the House went from $56,000 to more than $1.3 million.

For an example of how special interests took advantage of this inflated price tag, let's look at the financial sector, which was front and center in the fund-raising explosion. Over the past two decades, it was the top contributor to political campaigns. According to Simon Johnson and James Kwak in their book, *13 Bankers,* from 1998 to 2008 "the financial sector spent $1.7 billion on campaign contributions and $3.4 billion on lobbying expenses." And the money was, of course, targeted to where it would have the most effect: the campaign coffers of such Senate Banking Committee powerhouses as Phil Gramm, Alfonse D'Amato, Chris Dodd, and Chuck Schumer. Notice that the bankers' money rained down on both sides of the aisle. To paraphrase Matthew, the rain falleth on the left and on the right.

The investment paid off in spades with the rollback of the financial regulations that had kept the worst excesses of corporate greed in check since the Great Depression, leaving in their place a shaky edifice of self-policing and cowed regulators powerless to rein in the galloping bulls of Wall Street. The results for corporate America: record profits, record pay packages, and record bonuses. The results for the rest of us: the savings and loan crisis, the corporate scandals of the Enron era, and the economic collapse we are still struggling to dig our way out of.

That collapse, by the way, has only caused the banking lobbyists to redouble their efforts in an all-hands-on-deck effort to thwart financial reform. Over the course of the debate about reforming Wall Street, the finance industry—which has been bailed out with trillions of taxpayer dollars and cheap loans from the Fed—has spent an estimated $1.4 million a day to convince our lawmakers to kill real reform.

For instance, when the Senate was crafting its financial reform bill, it included absolutely no reform of Fannie Mae and Freddie Mac. This despite the fact that in just the first quarter of 2010 Freddie—one-half of what the *New York Times*'s Gretchen Morgenson calls "the elephant in the bailout"—reported a loss of $6.7 billion.

As of May 2010, according to Morgenson, "serious delinquencies in Freddie's single-family conventional loan portfolio—those more than 90 days late—came in at 4.13 percent, up from 2.41 percent for the period a year earlier." And the number of foreclosed units Freddie controlled stood at nearly 54,000, up from 29,145 at the end of March 2009.

"I don't understand why people are not talking about it," says Dean Baker of the Center for Economic and Policy Research. "It seems to me the most fundamental question is, have they on an ongoing basis been paying too much for loans even since they went into conservatorship?"

And why would they do that? It's part of what Baker calls a "backdoor bailout" of the banks. In other words, an under-the-radar way to continue shoveling money from struggling taxpayers over to the richest Americans.

This unseemly link between money and political influence is the dark side of capitalism. And like a swarm of termites reducing a house to sawdust, moneyed interests and their lobbyists are making a meal out of the foundations of our democracy.

In 2008, the American people voted for change. But there's been a change in the plans for change. The detour was created by D.C. lobbyists who, since President Obama took office, have watered down, gutted, or out-and-out killed ambitious plans for reforming Wall Street, energy, and health care.

The media like to pretend that something's at stake when a big bill is being debated on the House or Senate floor, but the truth is that by then the game is typically already over. The real fight happens long before. And the lobbyists usually win.

This disconnect between perception and reality reminds me of the time a friend took a family trip on a cruise ship. Her ten-year-old son kept pestering the crew, begging for a chance to drive the massive ocean liner. The captain finally invited the family up to the bridge, whereupon the boy grabbed hold of the wheel and began vigorously turning it. My friend panicked—until the captain leaned over and told her not to worry, that the ship was on autopilot, and that her son's maneuvers would have no effect.

And that's the way it is with our leaders. They stand on the bridge making theatrical gestures they claim will steer us in a new direction while, down in the control room, the autopilot, programmed by politicians in the pocket of special interests, continues to guide the ship of state along its predetermined course. America won't be able to change the disastrous direction it's heading in until the people elected to represent us go down into the boiler room and disengage the autopilot—which means taking on the hordes of lobbyists who continue to dictate policy in D.C.

Unfortunately, the middle class doesn't have a gaggle of lobbyists patrolling the corridors of power, offering cash incentives to Congress and the White House to protect the American people from the corporate crooks fattening their bottom lines (and filling their personal coffers) while our jobs, our houses, and our pensions disappear.

There are no lobbyists for the American Dream.

DEMOCRACY GOES ON THE AUCTION BLOCK

The epic struggle between financial powerhouses and the American democratic experiment—between the wealthy few and the struggling many—is as old as the country itself.

From the trust busting of Theodore Roosevelt to the major banking reforms put in place by FDR in the wake of the Great Depression, from the monopoly that was Standard Oil to today's Goldman Sachs, there have always been powerful special interests pitted against the interests of the public.

Indeed, as far back as 1910, Roosevelt warned about the danger of corporations exerting influence on the body politic: "There can be no effective control of corporations while their political activity remains. To put an end to it will be neither a short nor an easy task . . ." Of course, far from being put to an end, corporate political activity has only gotten more pervasive, more aggressive, more ruthless, and more effective. Not only have we failed to control corporations, corporations have flipped the equation and taken control of us.

Teddy Roosevelt must have been spinning in his grave in January 2010 when the Supreme Court, in *Citizens United v. Federal Election Commission*, voted 5–4 to extend the right of free speech to corporations and unions, lifting any limits on so-called independent expenditures on political campaigns. President Obama called the decision "a major victory for Big

Oil, Wall Street banks, health insurance companies, and the other powerful interests that marshal their power every day in Washington to drown out the voices of everyday Americans."

This decision will allow the giant pharmaceutical companies that knowingly permit unsafe drugs to remain on the shelves, the people running chemical plants releasing deadly toxins into the water and air, and the factory farm conglomerates filling our food with steroids to spend unlimited amounts of money to get their water carriers into office and defeat the all-too-rare candidates who actually stand up for the public good.

It has now become even easier to auction off our democracy to the highest bidder.

A VERY RISKY BUSINESS

Corporate America is a lot like Tom Cruise's teenage character in *Risky Business,* who convinces his parents he can look after himself while they are away. Then, as soon as they are gone, he orders up a hooker, trashes his father's Porsche, has his family's furniture stolen by a killer pimp, and throws an out-of-control party—turning his parents' house into a makeshift suburban brothel.

Corporate America bribed and browbeat our political leaders, convincing them that private industries could regulate themselves. So out went effective oversight . . . and in came an orgy of unrestrained capitalism and risky business that made the Cruise blowout look like a get-together at Mother Teresa's house.

The destructive—and often deadly—consequences of this capitalism without a conscience have been on full display for years now. Just take a look at the immoral behavior of giant drug companies that have routinely sacrificed the health of the public on the altar of higher and higher profits, time and again leaving deadly drugs on the market despite the loss of innocent lives. Or the chemical industry's long-term cover-up of the poisonous effects on unsuspecting workers and consumers of many of the eighty thousand synthetic chemicals created in the past sixty years. Or the way Big Tobacco has fought tooth and nail to keep marketing a product that still kills more than 440,000 Americans a year. Or the outrageous ripping off of the American taxpayer by Halliburton and other contractors throughout the Iraq war.

In 2010 there were three headline-grabbing examples of what happens when corporations get their way in Washington and our public watchdogs become little more than obedient lapdogs, unwilling to bite the corporate hand that feeds them: the explosion at the Upper Big Branch coal mine in West Virginia; the BP oil blowout in the Gulf of Mexico; and the ongoing aftershocks of the financial collapse, including the fraud charges against Goldman Sachs.

All these disparate events are linked by the same root cause: a badly broken regulatory system.

The loss of life in the Upper Big Branch mine and on the Deepwater Horizon oil rig happened in one horrific instant. The economic collapse has not killed people, but it has gradually destroyed the lives of millions of Americans. All three calamities occurred because elected officials who should have been enforcing a regulatory system that protects working families instead allowed the system to protect the corporations it was meant to watch over.

Most of the systemic breakdowns that led to the regulatory failure at Upper Big Branch and on the BP rig were the same ones that led to the housing bubble, credit-default swaps, toxic derivatives—and, by extension, the bank bailout, long-term unemployment, and the rapid decline of America's middle class.

Days after the Upper Big Branch disaster, the *New York Times* described the Mine Safety and Health Administration (MSHA), the regulatory agency that so atrociously failed the Upper Big Branch miners, this way: it is "fundamentally weak in several areas"; "the fines it levies are relatively small, and many go uncollected for years"; "it lacks subpoena power, a basic investigatory tool"; "its investigators are not technically law enforcement officers"; "its criminal sanctions are weak"; "fines remain so low that they are mere rounding errors on the bottom lines" of the companies being regulated; and it shows a "reluctance to flex all of its powers."

In an eerie echo, in the wake of the Deepwater Horizon disaster, the *Wall Street Journal* described the Minerals Management Service (MMS), the government agency that oversees offshore drilling, this way: it "doesn't write or implement most safety regulations, having gradually shifted such responsibilities to the oil industry itself"; it "seldom referred safety or environmental violations to the Justice Department for criminal prosecution, even when it should have done so"; and it "got out of the business of telling companies what training was necessary for workers involved in keeping wells from gushing out of control." Florida senator Bill Nelson summed it up: "If MMS wasn't asleep at the wheel, it sure was letting Big Oil do most of the driving." Chris Oynes, the Interior Department's top official overseeing offshore oil and gas drilling, announced his retirement shortly after the disastrous explosion, and Elizabeth Birnbaum, the head of MMS, was forced out thirty-seven days after the spill began—just another pair of resignations that came too late to make a difference.

The problem isn't a shortage of regulators. It's the way we've allowed the regulated to game the system. The federal government has entire agencies dedicated to overseeing offshore drilling and the mining industry. Indeed, a federal inspector was at the Upper Big Branch mine hours before it blew up.

Similarly, there are plenty of financial regulatory agencies. In fact, before the economic meltdown there were dozens of federal regulators dedicated to keeping an eye on each of the big banks—in many cases, with offices inside the premises of the banks themselves. Fannie Mae and Freddie Mac had the Office of Federal Housing Enterprise Oversight dedicated to them, and the SEC, which monitored their securities filings, provided an additional layer of oversight. And, after Bear Stearns crashed, the New York Fed had a team of examiners at Lehman Brothers every day. And yet they still missed the impending economic collapse.

Regulations are "very difficult to comply with," and "so many of the laws" are "nonsensical," in the words of Don Blankenship, the chief executive officer of Massey Energy, the company that owns the Upper Big Branch mine, which just happens to have a shocking history of safety violations.

The *Wall Street Journal* cites the arguments of oil industry executives and regulators who claim "that offshore operations have become so complicated that regulators ultimately must rely on the oil companies and drilling contractors to proceed safely." "There has been a very good record in deep water [drilling]," said Lars Herbst, head of the MMS's Gulf of Mexico region, "up until the point of [the Deepwater Horizon] accident." Other than that, Mrs. Lincoln, how did you enjoy the play?

Similarly, the reason the financial industry can't be regulated adequately is because, as Alan Greenspan put it during his 2010 testimony before the Financial Crisis Inquiry Commission, "the complexity is awesome," and regulators "are reaching far beyond [their] capacities."

That is, of course, exactly the way Wall Street designed it. To the financial world, "awesome complexity" is a feature, not a bug.

The mining and oil-drilling stories are remarkably similar to what happened in the financial industry over the past decade. A disaster occurs. Politicians are "outraged" and demand reform. Laws are passed. And then, when the next disaster occurs that the new laws were supposed to protect against, we find out about the loopholes in the last set of "reforms."

Massey offers a textbook—and tragic—example of how this works. After the 2006 Sago mine disaster killed twelve miners in West Virginia, mining regulations were enacted that called for a company with a "pattern of violations" to be subject to a much greater level of scrutiny.

If you're looking for the poster child for the phrase "pattern of violations," it's Massey Energy. In 2009, its Upper Big Branch mine was ordered to be temporarily closed more than sixty times. That same year, the mine was cited for 515 violations. In 2010, by the time of the explosion, it had already received another 124 violations. What's more, in the ten years before the Upper Big Branch explosion, twenty people had been killed at mines run by Massey.

So how did Massey escape greater oversight following its

pattern of violations? It turns out that a loophole written into the law says that if a company contests a violation, it can't count toward the establishment of a pattern while the matter is being contested. At the time of the explosion, Massey was contesting 352 violations at the Upper Big Branch mine alone.

According to another loophole in the law, a company can delay paying a fine while it contests the violation. The result? Only $8 million of $113 million in penalties levied against mining companies since April 2007 had been paid by April 2010—around 7 percent. To people like Don Blankenship—or any big bank CEO, for that matter—that kind of money is seen simply as the cost of doing business; it's factored into the bottom line, like bribes are in the Third World.

The BP disaster has a similar story line. Between 2001 and 2007, U.S. offshore drilling accidents resulted in 41 deaths and 302 injuries. Over the last decade, the Minerals Management Service expressed concerns about the safety of off-shore oil rigs and warned oil companies about the need to have backup safety equipment of the kind that could have prevented the Gulf spill. But, in the face of aggressive lobbying from the oil industry, the agency backed away from its concerns, crossed its fingers, and hoped that the industry would voluntarily police itself.

The piece of equipment that the industry resisted because it was too costly, known as an acoustic trigger, runs about $500,000. The replacement value of the Deepwater Horizon platform, which that $500,000 trigger might have saved, is about $560 million—to say nothing of the untold billions the disaster will cost the company and the entire Gulf region, and the irreplace-able human lives lost when the oil rig exploded.

As for fines for safety violations levied by the Minerals

Management Service, between 1998 and 2007, BP racked up a dozen safety violations but paid less than $580,000 in penalties—an infinitesimal figure for a company that made $5.6 billion in profits in just the first quarter of 2010.

Even after the Gulf catastrophe, oil companies were handled with a velvet glove. According to the *New York Times*, in the five weeks after the Deepwater Horizon blew up and millions of gallons of oil came gushing out, "federal regulators . . . granted at least 19 environmental waivers for gulf drilling projects and at least 17 drilling permits." And, wouldn't you know—one of the exempted projects was run by BP.

I have no doubt that new regulations will be written in response to these latest oil and mining disasters, just as we have new financial regulations in response to the financial disaster. But by the time these regulations make their way through Congress, the lobbyists will make sure that loopholes are part of the deal—and that the American people are on the losing side of the trade once again.

Disasters—mining, environmental, and financial—are going to keep happening until we reevaluate our priorities and force our elected officials, and the regulators they pick, to put the public interest above the special interests, and until the lives of hardworking Americans take precedence over the corporate bottom line.

FOXES GUARDING THE HENHOUSE

Not content with controlling politicians and kneecapping effective government oversight and regulations, corporate America has taken things one step further. As Janine Wedel, author of

Shadow Elite, and Linda Keenan put it, "businesses aren't just *sidestepping* or fighting regulators. Their M.O. is to try to make *themselves* the de facto regulators of their own self-interested conduct . . ."

That's something else that the mining, oil, and financial industries share: the revolving door between regulators and those they're supposed to be regulating. The names of the Wall Streeters who have moved into positions of power in Washington are familiar: Hank Paulson, Robert Rubin, Josh Bolten, Neel Kashkari, Mark Patterson—and that's just from Goldman Sachs.

But the revolving door between Wall Street and Washington goes far beyond these marquee names. The finance industry has 70 former members of Congress and over 900 former federal employees on its lobbying payroll. This includes 33 chiefs of staff, 54 staffers of the House Financial Services Committee and Senate Banking Committee (or a current member of those committees), and 28 legislative directors. Five of Senate Banking Committee chair Chris Dodd's former staffers are now working as banking lobbyists, as are eight former staffers for Senate Banking Committee heavyweights Richard Shelby and Chuck Schumer. Of course, the revolving door spins both ways: 18 percent of current House Financial Services committee staffers used to work on K Street.

On the mining front, former Massey chief operating officer Stanley Suboleski was appointed to be a commissioner of the Federal Mine Safety and Health Review Commission in 2003, and four years later was nominated to run the U.S. Department of Energy's Office of Fossil Energy. At the time of the Upper Big Branch accident he was back on Massey's board. And President Bush named Massey executive Richard Stickler to head the Mine Safety and Health Administration in 2006. Stickler had such a lousy safety record at the companies he'd run, his nomination was twice rejected by senators from both parties, forcing Bush to sneak him in the back door with a recess appointment. In other words, the guy Bush tapped to protect miners was precisely the kind of executive the head of the MSHA is supposed to protect miners from.

Picking foxes to guard the henhouse was standard operating procedure during the Bush years, when appointments to federal regulatory agencies were often used as a payback mechanism for rewarding major political donors, with industry hacks getting key government positions not because they were the best people to protect the public interest but because they were willing to protect the very industries they were meant to supervise.

That's what happened when Bush put Edwin Foulke, a lawyer with a long history of open hostility to health and safety regulations, in charge of the Occupational Safety and Health Administration (OSHA), the agency meant to oversee workplace safety. Earlier in his career, while serving as chairman of the federal agency that hears appeals from companies cited by OSHA, Foulke led a successful effort to weaken OSHA's enforcement power. With Foulke in charge of his former target, OSHA, not surprisingly, issued fewer significant standards than at any time in its history.

Then there was Bush's choice of Mary Sheila Gall to head the Consumer Product Safety Commission, despite her tendency to blame consumers rather than manufacturers when defective products injured or killed. In her ten years on the commission, Gall voted against regulating baby walkers, infant bath seats, flammable pajamas, and children's bunk beds. She even adopted a "Let them eat marbles" stance on the need for toy labeling, voting against choke-hazard warnings on marbles, small balls, and balloons. Consumers, she argued, are aware of "the well-known hazard of very young children putting marbles in their mouths."

In other words, if a kid chokes on a small toy, it's because the parent is defective, not the product. And while I'm all for slapping warnings on defective parents, Gall's attitude dishonors the lives of the twenty thousand people, many of them children, who are killed every year by defective products—to say nothing of the close to thirty million people a year who are injured by them. Thankfully, the Senate refused to confirm Gall. Undeterred, Bush filled the slot with Harold Stratton, a vocal opponent of states pursuing consumer protection cases.

The Food and Drug Administration is another agency that has long had an overly cozy relationship with the very companies it is supposed to oversee—in this case, the pharmaceutical industry. This dysfunctional dynamic has proved especially deadly over the years, with numerous drugs pulled off the market after causing deaths and serious injuries to patients.

Following the money once again, we see that Big Pharma contributed more than $124 million to federal candidates between 2000 and 2008. In return, the Bush administration served up FDA commissioners such as Lester Crawford, who was forced to resign after failing to disclose that he owned stock in companies regulated by his agency.

And, if you want to see "overly cozy" run amok, look no further than the Minerals Management Service, which, according to government watchdog reports, featured "a culture of substance abuse and promiscuity" wherein government employees did drugs and had sexual relationships with oil and gas industry officials. So not only is the fox guarding the henhouse, it's doing blow and sleeping with the hens. But it's middle-class Americans who are getting screwed.

We have a regulatory system in which corporate greed, political timidity, and a culture of cronyism have rendered the public good a quaint afterthought.

THEY'VE GOT LOW FRIENDS IN HIGH PLACES

The third leg in the Access Triple Crown is the way corporate America has used its economic clout to cultivate—okay, "buy"—friends in high places. It's so much easier to get a politician to take your call when you have donated millions to him or used to work in the office next to him. Facebook is great, but the crony capitalism of Washington takes social networking to a whole different level.

We saw how all those former Senate and House staffers are making a buck by lobbying their former bosses and colleagues on behalf of the big banks looking to gut reform. It's the same thing we saw during the health-care battle when those fighting against reform hired 350 former members of Congress and congressional staffers to influence the debate, including half a dozen former staffers of Senator Max Baucus, the influential chairman of the Senate Finance Committee. Among those lobbying Baucus were two of his former chiefs of staff. And among those on his staff being lobbied was Baucus's chief health adviser, Elizabeth Fowler, who before joining Baucus's team had been the vice president of public policy for WellPoint, the giant health insurance company.

We got an unsettling glimpse of what this kind of cozy setup leads to in the spring of 2009, when the big stimulus bill was being finalized in Congress. At the time, there was much public outrage directed at bailed-out companies that continued to pay their executives big bonuses. In response, Senator Chris Dodd inserted a clause in the bill that would have barred bailed-out companies from awarding bonuses. But, somewhere along the way, behind closed doors and without public debate, the Treasury Department insisted that a loophole be added to the bill that would allow AIG to pay out bonuses. Think about that: Even after having been bailed out to the tune of $182 billion, AIG still had the inside juice to get a special favor served up.

It's the same kind of inside juice that allowed Goldman Sachs chairman Lloyd Blankfein to have a prime seat at the table during the emergency weekend meetings in September 2008 when Treasury Secretary—and Goldman Sachs alumnus—Hank Paulson was deciding the fate of AIG—a fate that would have a multibillion dollar impact on Goldman's bottom line.

It's the same kind of juice that allowed Enron to become a major Washington player during the Bush years—before it became synonymous with corporate mendacity and greed. The crooked firm's chairman, Kenneth Lay, and his senior management doled out $2.4 million to federal candidates in the 2000 elections and were among George W.'s biggest donors. Enron also spent $3.45 million lobbying Congress in 1999 and 2000, all of which helped the outfit push its "deregulation" agenda—which really meant creating enough "wiggle room" to get away with wholesale fraud.

"Kenny Boy" Lay was known to boast about his "friends at the White House"—friends who helped him engineer the replacement of the head of the Federal Energy Regulatory

Commission, the agency charged with regulating Enron's core business. He also had a lot of input on energy policy at the Bush White House: Vice President Dick Cheney and his staff had six meetings with Enron representatives—including two with Lay—as part of their energy task force. The last of those meetings took place six days before Enron was forced to reveal it had vastly overstated its earnings, starting the energy giant's slide into bankruptcy.

Another energy company, Upper Big Branch mine operator Massey Energy, has also realized the investment value of buying friends in high places. Back in 2000, Massey was responsible for a coal slurry spill in Kentucky that was three times larger than the *Exxon Valdez* oil spill. The company very successfully limited the damage—not to the environment, but to its bottom line. According to Jack Spadaro, a Mine Safety and Health Administration engineer investigating the spill, once Kentucky senator Mitch McConnell's wife, Elaine Chao, became secretary of labor—the labor department oversees the MSHA—she put on the brakes. Two years after the spill, Massey was assessed a slap-on-the-wrist $5,600 fine. The same year, Massey's political action committee donated $100,000 to the National Republican Senatorial Committee, which McConnell chaired from 1997 to 2000. Cozy.

And you can't get any cozier than Linda Daschle, who, while her husband, Tom, was Senate minority leader, was one of the airline industry's top lobbyists—although I'm sure pillow talk had nothing to do with her clients Northwest and American Airlines raking in one billion dollars from the government's post-9/11 bailout of the airline industry.

But there is no need to worry about familial conflicts of interest anymore because, since leaving the Senate, Tom

Daschle has moved over to the influence-peddling side of the street and made a bundle working as a "special policy adviser" at Alston & Bird, a lobbying firm that makes almost 50 percent of its income from health-care clients. Daschle, you'll recall, came within a few unreported chauffeur-driven rides of being Obama's health-care reform czar. *Very* cozy.

Daschle has also bolstered his personal bottom line doing lucrative side gigs, such as serving on the advisory board of BP. Hopefully he wasn't the one who advised BP CEO Tony Hayward to try to calm fears about the ecological catastrophe facing the Gulf of Mexico by saying that the spill was "relatively tiny" compared to the "very big ocean," or who advised BP Chairman Carl-Henric Svanberg to refer to those affected by the spill as "the small people."

DÉJÀ *WHO?*

Have you noticed how the same names keep popping up again and again? It makes it seem as if establishment Washington is the political equivalent of a small theatrical repertory company: production after production, you always see the same actors— they just keep switching parts.

Tom Daschle is a senator, then a near–cabinet member overseeing health-care reform, then a "special adviser" to companies looking to undermine health-care reform.

Robert Rubin is co-chairman of Goldman Sachs, then secretary of the Treasury, then a senior counselor of Citigroup— pocketing more than $126 million in cash and stock during his almost ten years there.

Dick Cheney is a congressman, then secretary of defense,

then CEO of Halliburton, then the most powerful vice president in history—helping lead America into a war with Iraq that ends up netting his former company billions in sweetheart contracts. During the Bush-Cheney years, Halliburton became the poster child for crony capitalism, which is why it was both surprising and utterly predictable when the company came roaring back into the headlines during the BP oil spill fiasco.

It's like one of those horror movie killers who keeps popping back up from the grave. You thought Halliburton had been eradicated when government audits showed the company had bilked taxpayers out of a billion dollars during the war in Iraq? You thought it was over when the Justice Department brought a civil fraud suit against a Halliburton subsidiary in 2010 for charging the government for tens of millions in unauthorized security services in Iraq? You thought reports that Halliburton had allowed U.S. troops to bathe in contaminated water had left them dead and buried? Well, they're baaa-aaack! And their work sealing the bottom of the BP oil well will very likely be found to be at least a contributing factor in the catastrophic Deepwater Horizon blowout.

Doing a segment on Halliburton's involvement with the BP disaster—including the fact that, after taking office, Cheney restaffed the Minerals Management Service with what Robert F. Kennedy, Jr., called "oil industry toadies including a cabal of his Wyoming carbon cronies"—MSNBC's Chris Matthews couldn't contain his indignation. "How do we stop this?" he sputtered. "It seems like a Third World banana republic would do things this way!"

Third World America . . . it's closer than you think.

POWERBROKERS 2.0

These are the new breed of movers and shakers. Powerbrokers 2.0. Public shape-shifters, they effortlessly glide in and out and around government. They can be found on both sides of the ideological aisle—serving their own agendas more than either party's. Janine Wedel calls them "flexians": "top players who move in and out of government, corporate, and think tank roles, gathering exclusive information at each stop, and using that privileged asset to benefit themselves and their allies." The members of this shadow elite keep morphing into their next incarnation no matter how often their conflicts of interest and their undermining of the public good are revealed.

With this merging of state and private power, we're getting to the point where the only difference between senior congressional staffers and the lobbyists and influence launderers whose ranks they'll soon join is the size of their paychecks. They just have to put in a few years in Congress, and then they can join, or rejoin, the lobbyist herd. It's like putting in a few semesters getting your master's degree in influence peddling. And you don't have to pay off those irritating school loans.

The state-of-the-art modern powerbroker is the aforementioned Robert Rubin.

His résumé is the personification of the flexian in action, as he moved seamlessly between political positions (director of the National Economic Council, Treasury secretary), private positions (a board member and senior counselor at Citigroup), advisory positions (including serving on the President's Advisory Committee for Trade Negotiations and the SEC's Market

Oversight and Financial Services Advisory Committee), stints on a World Bank task force on growth and development, work as an unofficial economic adviser to President Obama, and his current position as co-chairman of the Council on Foreign Relations and founder of the Hamilton Project on challenges facing the U.S. economy.

Early in 2010, he penned a lengthy essay in *Newsweek* called "Getting the Economy Back on Track," in which he completely failed to explain or acknowledge—let alone apologize for—the key role he played in getting the economy off track in the first place.

What grabbed my attention was not the 2,500-word piece, but the 28-word bio at the end of it: "Rubin is a former secretary of the Treasury (1995–99). He now serves as co-chairman of the Council on Foreign Relations and is a fellow of the Harvard Corporation." Given that the piece is about the economic meltdown, it's telling that the bio doesn't include his nearly ten years at Citigroup—during the very time that ended with the bank having to be saved by the American taxpayers.

But that's how our system "works" these days: Someone like Rubin is able to wreak destruction, collect an ungodly profit, then go along his merry way, pontificating about how "markets have an inherent and inevitable tendency—probably rooted in human nature—to go to excess, both on the upside and the downside." This from the man who, as Bill Clinton's Treasury secretary, was vociferous in opposing the regulation of derivatives—a key factor in the current economic crisis—and who lobbied the Treasury during the Bush years to prevent the downgrading of the credit rating of Enron—a debtor of Citigroup.

The hidden costs of such crony capitalism are monumental for the middle class. Why would people strive to build businesses—risking their money and their sweat equity—when they know there will always be someone on the other side of the table playing with a stacked deck?

THE VULCAN MIND MELD BETWEEN WASHINGTON AND WALL STREET

So the deck is stacked. The fix is in. The cards are marked. And our economy is as rigged as a carnival ring-toss game.

But it's even worse than that. Corporate America's takeover of our democracy runs deeper than the simple quid pro quo of a donor swaying a politician. It has captured our leaders' hearts and minds. It's one thing for moneyed interests to be able to buy influence. It's another for that industry's agenda to become conventional wisdom across party lines.

"Politics is like sales," write Simon Johnson and James Kwak in *13 Bankers*. "If you are trying to close a large deal with a major corporation, it helps to have friends on the inside, it helps to have buyers who see their fortunes aligned with yours, and it can even help to dangle the prospect of a high-paying job before the key decision-maker. But it is even better if the buyers really, independently want what you are selling. It is best of all if they believe that buying what you are selling is a symbol of their own judgment and sophistication—that buying your product marks them as part of the informed elite."

That is what happened with the Vulcan mind meld between Wall Street and Washington, and it's what laid the groundwork for the financial crisis—and the bailout with no strings attached that followed. Our leaders have completely bought what corporate America has been selling. It's become part of their DNA. This includes the key members of President Obama's economic team. They are operating on the basis of an outdated cosmology that places banks at the center of the economic universe.

Talking about our financial crisis with them is like beaming back to the second century and discussing astronomy with Ptolemy. Just as Ptolemy was convinced we live in a geocentric universe—and made the math work to "prove" his flawed theories—Obama's senior economic advisers are convinced we live in a Wall Street–centric universe and keep offering their versions of "epicycles" and "eccentric circles" to rationalize their approach to dealing with Wall Street. And because, like Ptolemy, they are really smart, they are really good at rationalizing.

If you believe the universe is revolving around the earth—when, in fact, it isn't—all the good intentions in the world will be for naught. It's no surprise that people such as Tim Geithner and Larry Summers believe in bank centrism—they're both creatures of it. And in a bank-centric universe, funneling no-strings-attached money to too-big-to-fail banks is the logical thing to do.

The longer this remains the dominant cosmology in the Obama administration—and the longer it takes to switch to a plan that reflects a cosmology in which the American people are the center of the universe and are deemed "too big to fail"—the greater the risk that the economic crisis will be more prolonged than necessary. And the greater the suffering. There is an enormous human cost to this dogma.

Writing about the "grand book" that is the universe, Galileo declared that it "cannot be understood unless one first learns to comprehend the language and interpret the characters in which it is written . . . without these, one is wandering about' in a dark labyrinth."

That's where we find ourselves today, wandering about in a dark financial labyrinth—being led by good men blinded by an obsolete view of the world.

DO THE CRIME, DO THE TIME . . . UNLESS YOU'RE WORKING ON WALL STREET

"The struggle of man against power is the struggle of memory against forgetting." So wrote Milan Kundera in *The Book of Laughter and Forgetting*. It is one of my favorite quotes and it popped into my head as I was thinking about how short our collective memory is when it comes to holding the powerful accountable.

Until the Securities and Exchange Commission sued Goldman Sachs for fraud in April of 2010, it was easy to forget that we have a regulatory agency designed to protect the public from the pillaging of corporate America. Six months earlier, the SEC had arranged a settlement with JPMorgan that showed how rigged the system is. The banking giant agreed to pay a $25 million penalty and cancel $647 million in fees owed by Alabama's Jefferson County as the result of a complicated derivatives deal that blew up in the county's face.

As part of the settlement, JPMorgan neither admitted nor denied wrongdoing—despite overwhelming evidence that it had engaged in plenty of wrongdoing. This is what passes for justice these days. If you commit a petty crime and hammer out a plea bargain, you'll have to admit wrongdoing as part of the agreement. But put on a suit and commit a billion-dollar crime and you won't even have to admit you did anything wrong—which makes it much more likely that you'll do it again.

We saw the same dynamic played out in the saga surrounding the $3.6 billion in bonuses that was awarded to Merrill Lynch executives just before the failing firm was acquired by Bank of America (with a lot of help from American taxpayers, who handed BofA $45 billion).

Bank of America executives failed to inform their shareholders that, as part of the acquisition, they were going to give billions to the executives who had been at the helm while Merrill lost $27 billion in 2008. Had the shareholders been told, the news would have put a major crimp in the shotgun marriage of the two firms.

Bank of America agreed to pay a $33 million fine to the SEC but—you guessed it—admit no wrongdoing. A heroic U.S. district judge, Jed Rakoff, refused to rubber-stamp the deal, which he called a breach of "justice and morality" that "suggests a rather cynical relationship between the parties." The SEC and Bank of America came back with a $150 million settlement. The judge said he was forced by judicial restraint to accept the new deal, but did so reluctantly. "While better than nothing, this is half-baked justice at best," Judge Rakoff said.

The total amount of fines levied by the SEC in 2008 was the lowest since the corporate scandals of 2002 led to stricter enforcement regulations. So while the financial system was on a fast track to collapse, the SEC was taking its hand off the brake. And even now the perpetrators of that near-collapse are avoiding accountability. When crimes are uncovered and the culprit is allowed to simply move on without even acknowledging that a crime was committed, that's a recipe for anarchy—not for a healthy democracy.

It's really not that complicated: If you do the crime, you do the time. But the people who run the show like to make it seem like it is very complicated—all the better to obscure the simple moral principle of right and wrong. Why should it matter whether you commit your crimes in a boardroom or on the street? You should have to admit wrongdoing when you're caught and pay a commensurate penalty. If that means jail for the street crime, it should mean jail for the boardroom crime.

Of course, it's not just our too-big-to-fail banks that have been allowed to do wrong without having to admit any wrongdoing. The pharmaceutical, mining, oil, and health-care industries have been doing the "pay the fine but admit nothing" dance for years—chalking up the millions (and sometimes billions) in penalties as the cost of doing business.

But with corporate America earning major profits and middle class America struggling to stay afloat, now is a very good time to revoke the "Get Out of Jail Free" card those at the helm of these companies have been given for far too long.

"WHO COULD HAVE KNOWN?"

Three weeks after the Deepwater Horizon rig exploded in the Gulf of Mexico, BP finally released underwater video showing a massive column of oil gushing out of a broken pipe a mile below the surface.

Watching the unrelenting geyser-like spew, it struck me as an inverse visual metaphor for the plight of America's middle class: While the thick black oil was being pushed inexorably upward, hour after hour and week after week, the quality of life for tens of millions of hardworking Americans is being pushed inexorably downward—month after month after month. And our leaders watch them both, either wringing their hands or waving them in anger and frustration.

When the oil spill first happened, it seemed troubling but nothing to be too concerned about. Within a week, Obama administration officials were describing it as "a very grave scenario" and "potentially . . . very catastrophic." In other words, it was much worse than we thought it would be. Has there been a crisis in the last decade that turned out to be better than we thought it was going to be?

- We are still fighting two wars that were going to be cakewalks but have now lasted nine years and seven years—much worse than we thought it would be.

- Katrina looked like it could be bad but—even though there were plenty of people warning about a Category 5 storm breaching the levees—the devastation ultimately was much worse than we thought it would be.

- Warnings were issued about the housing bubble that was fueled by the Wall Street casino. Even though we now know that people in the Fed were forecasting big trouble ahead as early as 2004, the warnings were ignored—and when the bubble burst in 2008, it was much worse than we thought it would be.

- The foreclosure crisis hit hard in 2009. But the government promised to protect homeowners . . . so when the first quarter of 2010 brought the highest number of fore-closures since they began keeping records, it was clear the scope of the calamity was much worse than we thought it would be.

- In October 2009, the unemployment rate hit 10.2 per-cent, a twenty-six-year high. But the $787 billion stimu-lus package was going to bring that down. It has, but not by much. Turns out, the unemployment crisis is also much worse than we thought it would be.

- When BP first applied to operate the Deepwater Hori-zon rig, it submitted plans to the Minerals Management Service stating that "no significant adverse [environ-mental] impacts are expected" and predicting that a spill was an "unlikely event." Of course, as we've seen, the historic disaster is much worse than they thought it would be.

Perhaps we should start calling this the age of "Much Worse Than We Thought It Would Be." Or, in honor of the standard excuse we hear in these situations, the "Who Could Have Known?" era.

See if this sounds familiar: An ambitious and risky under-taking is carried out with hubris and features the weeding-out of anyone who raises alarm bells, little to no transparency, an oversight system in which no central authority is accountable, and the deliberate manufacturing of ambiguity and complexity so that if—*when*—it all falls to pieces, the "Who Could Have Known?" defense can be trotted out.

Am I describing Iraq? The subprime mortgage market? The Enron-led financial scandals of the early 2000s? The BP oil spill? The Upper Big Branch mine disaster? The Lehman Brothers and AIG–led financial meltdown of 2008?

The correct answer: All of the above.

When you look at the elements that were crucial to the creation of each of these debacles of the past decade, it's amazing how much they all have in common. And not just in how they began but in how they ended: with those responsible being amazed at what happened, because . . . who could have known?

Well, I'm amazed at the amazement, because each of these disasters was entirely predictable. And, indeed, every one of them *was* predicted. But those who rang the alarm bells were aggressively ignored, and we let those responsible get away with the "Who Could Have Known?" excuse ("the struggle of memory against forgetting" continues).

Let's start with Iraq, an unnecessary war that has cost America's parents the lives of more than 4,300 sons and daughters, and American taxpayers three-quarters of a trillion dollars and counting (not to mention the future cost of $422 billion to $717 billion to care for American veterans through health-care and disability coverage)—money desperately needed for some long-overdue nation rebuilding here at home. And for what? As the Center for American Progress's "Iraq War Ledger" puts it: "there is simply no conceivable calculus by which Operation Iraqi Freedom can be judged to have been a successful or worthwhile policy. The war was intended to show the extent of America's power. It succeeded only in showing its limits."

In the run-up to the war, General Eric Shinseki, a heroic combat officer who had risen to become the army's chief of staff, told Congress that a successful occupation of Iraq would require "several hundred thousand" troops on the ground. U.S. deputy secretary of defense Paul Wolfowitz told Congress he found that "hard to imagine." But when defense secretary Donald Rumsfeld's attempt to win the war on the cheap failed, everyone acted shocked. Who could have known?

The Bush administration also told the public that the rebuilding of Iraq would cost taxpayers no more than $1.7 billion. To say the administration massively underestimated would be a massive understatement. The *New York Times* described our reconstruction efforts there as "an effort crippled before the invasion by Pentagon planners who were hostile to the idea of rebuilding a foreign country, and then molded into a $100 billion failure by bureaucratic turf wars, spiraling violence and ignorance of the basic elements of Iraqi society and infrastructure." Who could have known?

At the same time the warning signals about Iraq were being ignored in Washington, many on Wall Street were ignoring the signs of their own impending disaster.

In late 2002, Charles Prince was put in charge of Citigroup's corporate and investment bank. The banking giant was already knee-deep in toxic paper and aggressively looking the other way. Prince was so successful at averting his eyes that, five years later, when he was told that his bank owned $43 billion in mortgage-related assets, he claimed it was the first he'd heard of it. Isn't that something he should have known? Or did he prefer not knowing?

Prince had plenty of help ignoring the obvious, particularly from Robert Rubin. According to a former Citigroup executive, despite ascending to the top of the Citi food chain, Prince "didn't know a CDO from a grocery list, so he looked for someone for advice and support. That person was Rubin."

But when it all came tumbling down, both Rubin and Prince portrayed themselves as helpless victims of circumstance, because, well . . . who could have known?

"I've thought a lot about that," Rubin said when asked if he made mistakes at Citigroup. "I honestly don't know. In hindsight, there are a lot of things we'd do differently. But in the context of the facts as I knew them and my role, I'm inclined to think probably not." What he means, of course, is the facts as he chose to know them at the time.

Former Fannie Mae CEO Franklin Raines suffered from the same affliction. According to Raines, he can't be blamed for what happened at Fannie Mae because mortgage stuff is so, well, complicated. In fact, he can't even understand his own home mortgage: "I know I can't and I've tried," Raines told a House committee. "To this day, I don't know what it said. . . . It's impossible for the average person to understand." In other words, who could have known?

But isn't it interesting that the complexity and opacity of these things somehow always redounds to the benefit of those in charge?

We saw a familiar insistence on ignoring all warnings in the Bernie Madoff scandal. "We have worked with Madoff for nearly twenty years," said Jeffrey Tucker, a former federal regulator and the head of an investment firm that lost billions to Madoff. "We had no indication that we . . . were the victims of such a highly sophisticated, massive fraudulent scheme." Who could have known?

Well, financial fraud investigator Harry Markopolos, for

one. Not only did he know, he did everything he could to make sure everybody else knew as well. In 1999, after researching Madoff's methods, Markopolos wrote a letter to the SEC saying, "Madoff Securities is the world's largest Ponzi Scheme." He pursued his claims with the feds for the next nine years, with little result.

One would think the "Who Could Have Known?" excuse has been exposed as a sham enough times to render it obsolete, but there are always new incentives to not know.

In the wake of 9/11, Condoleezza Rice assured us nobody "could have predicted" that someone "would try to use an airplane as a missile." Except, of course, the 1999 government report that said "Suicide bomber(s) belonging to al-Qaeda's Martyrdom Battalion could crash-land an aircraft packed with high explosives (C-4 and semtex) into the Pentagon, the headquarters of the Central Intelligence Agency (CIA), or the White House."

After Katrina, the Bush White House read from the "Who Could Have Known?" hymnal: No one could have predicted that the storm would be a Category 5, and that this could result in the levees being breached. We now know, of course, that plenty of people knew that the levees could be breached and said so before the storm hit.

Then there is the high priest of "Who Could Have Known?", Alan Greenspan, who, looking back in October 2008 on the makings of the financial crisis he helped create, delivered this "Who Could Have Known?" classic: "If all those extraordinarily capable people were unable to foresee the development of this critical problem . . . we have to ask ourselves: Why is that? And the answer is that we're not smart enough as people. We just cannot see events that far in advance."

In other words, it's simple biology: We humans are only smart enough to create situations in which the rich are benefi ciaries of huge wealth transfers from the middle class—but we have not yet evolved to the point where we can foresee that this is what we're doing.

In truth, the problem is not that we are "not smart enough as people." As we've seen time after time, smart enough people are all too willing to ignore facts they don't like or that don't happen to benefit them in the short term. And to lessen personal culpability, they institutionalize not knowing—constructing oversight systems deliberately designed to be ineffective and accordingly unable to provide those in power with information they don't really want to know.

We had our warning signals for the financial crisis: They were called Enron and WorldCom and Global Crossing. Those outrages set the stage for the much larger, more sophisticated, and much more dangerous excesses that drove the housing and banking meltdown.

But the broken system that allowed the scandals at Enron and the rest was never really reformed. Yes, there were window-dressing changes and Band-Aid legislation. But the guiding philosophy—that the free market would regulate itself, and that corporate America always knew best—remained in place. Indeed, it was given much freer rein.

So it's been déjà vu all over again, with one big difference that makes this latest crisis so painful: the scale of it all. The impact on average Americans has been so much more devastating and long lasting. And here's the bottom line: If we don't reform the system—really reform it—the next financial collapse will surely be more than we can withstand.

It's the thing that will send us over the edge, making the

idea of Third World America more than just a scary harbinger of things to come. It will be our reality. So it's time to say goodbye to the "Who Could Have Known?" era. It's time to know things again—and to acknowledge that we know them. And to make things right before it is too late.

LINDA D. WILSON

Perhaps my story is no different from that of millions of other middle-class workers who are experiencing an enormous test of their faith. I have an MBA and more than twenty-five years of human resources experience. I worked for the same company in Louisiana for twenty-two years. Despite countless layoffs and downsizings, I was either promoted or changed positions every two to three years, expanding my HR skills and knowledge. I can honestly say I never concerned myself with getting a pink slip. I served on local boards and committees, volunteered for good causes, donated to charities, and served at my church. My near-perfect credit score and disposable income allowed me to live with little debt and pay down my mortgage from thirty to seven years.

I overcame a birth defect—a cleft palate. After surgery, I had to learn to talk again. I attended college on a track scholarship, and in my senior year I competed in the U.S. Olympic Track & Field trials. From there, I earned my bachelor's degree and started my career. While working full-time and successfully climbing the corporate ladder, I had an idea for an event planning system. I filed for and received a U.S. patent. However, working full-time in a competitive environment left me with little time to launch a business and new product, so I put it on the back burner. Instead, I focused on a seemingly safer and more stable corporate career path—guaranteed paychecks, benefits, pension, and a 401(k). Like most other members of the middle class I believed that with enough hard work and determination I would be successful. It was what my parents taught me by example and what they expected me to demonstrate in everything I did.

In 2005, I adopted two girls—sisters. My ten-year-old was diagnosed with HIV and works *extra* hard to learn and be successful in school. I set them up with a financial plan and invested in real estate, which I planned to leave them for their inheritance.

Then, Hurricane Katrina destroyed my home and rental properties in New Orleans. My family and friends were displaced and scattered across the country. So after working for the same company for twenty-two years, I resigned and relocated to Texas, along with my parents and five sisters. I put my career on hold to rebuild our lives. Two years later, I'm still unable to land a suitable full-time position (at any level)—despite more than twenty-five years of expertise.

The world has obviously changed for the middle class. Now the only guarantee that today's worker can expect is that you put in a day's work, you get a day's pay—that's it.

So, like millions of other middle-class workers, I'm being forced to reexamine my career, lifestyle, priorities, interests, goals, and future. Although I've exhausted my savings and face insurmountable debt, I've decided to step out in faith—or better yet, take a leap. I'm managing my own business full-time, designing products to help people plan and organize their everyday lives. I'm determined to establish a business as an inheritance for my children.

5

SAVING OURSELVES FROM A THIRD WORLD FUTURE

★ ★ ★

A nd now for something completely different . . . some good news: *Third World America is not a done deal.*

Despite the overwhelming evidence that the wheels are coming off our national wagon, I believe deeply that America can still accomplish great things: that our greatness is not necessarily a thing of the past—indeed, that our best days can still lie ahead of us.

I realize that coming after the litany of all the ways America is falling apart, this might sound overly optimistic. Or delusional. Or the result of hitting the ouzo in despair. I understand that the initial response to the first four parts of this book might be to walk onto one of our crumbling bridges and contemplate jumping off.

But that's not how the American psyche works. We've always been a positive, forward-looking people. A can-do attitude is part of our cultural DNA. And that mind-set is a prerequisite for turning things around. Without it, the seeds of change and innovation will wither in a soil that is an arid mix of negativism and defeatism. With it, we can shake off our cynicism and avoid the slow slide to Third World status.

As a country, we have an unparalleled track record for marshalling our forces and rising to meet great challenges. It is one of our greatest strengths.

After Pearl Harbor, America's naval force was decimated. But just three years later, as John Kao points out in his book *Innovation Nation*, "America had a hundred aircraft carriers fully armed with new planes, pilots, tactics, and escort ships, backed by new approaches to logistics, training methods, aircraft plants, shipyards, and women workers" along with "such game changing innovations as the B-29 . . . and nuclear fission."

We had a similar reaction to the Soviets' launch of Sputnik. "We responded with massive funding for education," writes Kao, "revamped school curricula in science and math, and launched a flurry of federal initiatives that eventually put Neil Armstrong in position to make his 'giant leap for mankind.'"

President Obama captured this essential part of the American character when he announced the kickoff of his Educate to Innovate campaign—a nationwide effort to move American students back to the top in science and math education. "This nation wasn't built on greed," he said. "It wasn't built on reckless risk. It wasn't built on short-term gains and shortsighted policies. It was forged on stronger stuff, by bold men and women who dared to invent something new or improve something old—who took big chances on big ideas, who believed that in America all things are possible."

Many economists and historians are warning that our current economic downturn has created a new normal—that the country will never be the same. Things are, of course, going to be different. But that doesn't mean that they are predestined to be worse. However, if we don't get serious about the crises we face, they will be.

America is rich with resources—both natural and human. "America—with its open, free, no-limits, immigration-friendly society—is still the world's greatest dream machine," says Tom Friedman. "The Apple iPod may be made in China, but it was dreamed up in America."

We must stop squandering these resources. If the middle class is to thrive and continue to be the backbone of America, we need to create the conditions that will allow these dreams to flourish—and our country to move forward in wiser ways.

"You can't cross a chasm in two small jumps," said World War I–era British prime minister David Lloyd George. And you can't cross it in a series of little steps either. Instead, we have to reconnect with our bold national identity and once again take "big chances on big ideas."

Stopping our descent into Third World status won't be easy. It will take daring initiatives from both the private and public sectors—supercharged with an infusion of personal responsibility.

On the one hand, this moment in our history demands that we stop waiting on others—especially others living in Washington, D.C.—to solve the problems and right the wrongs of our times. Now, more than ever, we must mine the most under-utilized leadership resource available to us: ourselves.

On the other hand, the problems our society and, indeed, much of the world are facing are too monumental to be solved solely by individuals. We still need the raw power that only big government initiatives—and big government appropriations—can deliver.

But, as we've seen, in today's Washington, the fix is in. So that's the first thing we need to fix.

I.
ON A NATIONAL LEVEL

THE MOTHER OF ALL REFORMS

It's a classic catch-22: The most effective way of fixing the multitude of problems facing America is through the democratic process, but the democratic process itself is badly broken. That is why the first step toward stopping our relentless transformation into Third World America has to be breaking the choke hold that special interest money has on our politics.

This has to start with a complete reboot of the way we finance our elections. The most effective means of restoring the integrity of our government is through the full public financing of political campaigns.

It's the mother of all reforms—the one reform that makes all other reforms possible. After all, he who pays the piper calls the tune. If someone's going to own the politicians, it might as well be the American people. Think of it: No hard money, no PAC money, no endless dialing for dollars, no *quid pro dough* deals. No more lobbyists sitting in House and Senate offices literally writing tailor-made loopholes into laws. No more corporate welfare giveaways buried in huge spending bills. No more dangerous relaxation of safety regulations that can be traced to campaign donations. Just candidates and elected officials beholden to no one but the voters.

Among those working to make this happen are Harvard law professor Lawrence Lessig and Joe Trippi, who ran Howard Dean's Internet-fueled 2004 presidential campaign. Together they've founded Fix Congress First!—an attempt to build a grassroots movement to pressure Congress to pass public financing legislation. And to make sure the legislation can't be struck down by an activist Supreme Court, the group is also pushing for a Constitutional amendment. "We must," says Lessig, "establish clearly and without question the power in Congress to preserve its own institutional independence."

In May 2010, I was one of about 430,000 people to receive an email from the group with the eye-catching subject line "300 Million Lobbyists," promoting an effort to create "the biggest lobby in the history of American politics." And who is part of this all-powerful lobby? You, me, and the rest of the 300 million citizens of the United States.

As the Fix Congress First! founders put it: "This isn't a Democratic issue or a Republican issue—it's a fundamental question about what kind of democracy we want to have."

If you want to know what a democracy no longer beholden to special interests would mean for the political process, look no further than Senator Ted Kaufman of Delaware. When Kaufman, Joe Biden's longtime chief of staff, was appointed to serve out his old boss's term, he was originally thought of as a Senate placeholder.

But, far from biding his time, Kaufman soon emerged as one of the Senate's fiercest critics of Wall Street and a champion of the need to push for a serious overhaul of our financial system to protect the middle class. What transformed this behind-the-scenes staffer into a fire-breathing accidental leader? A healthy sense of outrage.

In March 2010, on his seventy-first birthday, he took to the Senate floor to lambast the loss of the rule of law on Wall Street. He reminded his colleagues that the American taxpayer has laid out more than $2.5 trillion to "save the system," and asked, "What exactly did we save?" His answer: "a system of overwhelming and concentrated financial power that has become dangerous . . . a system in which the rule of law has broken yet again. . . . At the end of the day, this is a test of whether we have one justice system in this country or two. If we don't treat a Wall Street firm that defrauded investors of millions of dollars the same way we treat someone who stole five hundred dollars from a cash register, then how can we expect our citizens to have faith in the rule of law? . . . Our markets can only flourish when Americans again trust that they are fair, transparent, and accountable."

Watching his determination to fix the financial system offers a window on how we can fix our political system. Aside from his personal character, which we cannot duplicate, there is a dynamic that helped turn Kaufman into a fearless crusader that we *can* duplicate: the absence of money as a factor in his political life.

Kaufman didn't need to raise money to become a senator—he was appointed. And he doesn't need to raise money for his reelection campaign—because he's not running. So he is completely unencumbered by the need to curry favor with the moneyed interests. Kaufman is a great test case—a shining example of what it looks like when our representatives are not beholden to special interests and are only serving the public good.

Another important means of fighting the disillusionment, cynicism, and doubt that have infected the body politic in recent years is a top-to-bottom commitment to transparency. "Sunlight," Justice Louis Brandeis famously said, "is said to be the best of disinfectants." But real transparency means more than just putting up a website for every government agency. Creating a system in which the people feel confident that they know what their representatives are doing involves more than just throwing data at the problem. It requires context—and ways of helping the public yank back the curtain on the back rooms of power so it can see who is really pulling the levers.

A great early iteration of this was provided by the Sunlight Foundation during the health-care summit in February 2010. As part of its live streaming of the discussion, the group's website offered a dose of transparency by showing, as each of our elected officials was speaking, a list of his or her major campaign contributors. It was simple, powerful, and spoke volumes about the extent to which many players in the summit were bought and paid for.

In the future, a souped-up version of this kind of technology will allow us to see who is funding whom, and who is carrying water for which special interest, in real time and across every imaginable platform. The Sunday political shows will be a whole different animal when we are able to effortlessly, instantly, and literally follow the money—and discover why a seemingly irrational policy becomes the law of the land.

American politics has become a rigged game. But, moving forward, innovative technology can give us the chance to level the playing field.

KILLER APPS FOR A TWENTY-FIRST-CENTURY DEMOCRACY

Among those looking to use technology to improve the way our government is run is Tim O'Reilly, the tech guru CEO of

O'Reilly Media. In 2004, O'Reilly popularized the term Web 2.0. He's now at the forefront of a movement to apply the concept to the way our democracy is run: Government 2.0.

He describes Government 2.0 as "a new compact between government and the public, in which government puts in place mechanisms for services that are delivered not by government, but by private citizens." It's about "government as a platform . . . If there's one thing we learn from the technology industry, it's that every big winner has been a platform company: someone whose success has enabled others, who's built on their work and multiplied its impact."

Using government as a platform is all about how the massive amount of information at the government's disposal is used, how widely it is shared, how low is the barrier for innovators to access it. After all, the Internet itself was a government project. The government built the platform and innovators ran with it. Same with GPS—a "killer app" that originated with the government.

Other examples of innovators building on government-provided information and services are popping up all over the country—and the Web. For instance, sites like Everyblock and StumbleSafely use crime statistics that are publicly available and remake them into public safety applications (kind of the opposite of a killer app!).

Many of the most interesting experiments in bringing technology and government together are going on at the local level. One leader who has enthusiastically embraced the new model is Newark mayor Cory Booker. "We are one part of a larger democracy that is learning how to master media to drive social change," says Booker. "Social media is a forum where people can come together to connect, talk, mobilize, and create a larger sense of community."

Booker has over one million followers on his very active Twitter page. Using Twitter, along with Facebook and YouTube, he maintains an open pipeline of communication with his constituents. He also uses these platforms to motivate them to take part in night patrols of troubled neighborhoods—patrols the mayor frequently joins. And he's formed an advisory working group called the Newark Tech Corps, made up of leading tech executives who advise him on the newest technologies and how he can best adapt them to serve Newark's residents.

We are reminded on a daily basis of the limits to what government can do. Going forward, it's clear that we are going to have to forge a new relationship with our government. "Citizens are connected like never before and have the skill sets and passion to solve problems affecting them locally as well as nationally," writes O'Reilly. "Citizens are empowered to spark the innovation that will result in an improved approach to governance."

We can't expect a government hobbled by centuries-old tools to deal with the challenges of the twenty-first century. That's why Government 2.0 needs to be taken out of beta and put into practice across the nation.

MAKING OUR SCHOOLHOUSES ROCK

Next up in our extreme makeover of America: education. Fixing our broken educational system is vital to rescuing America's middle class and preserving our standing as a First World nation.

Education is the most basic tool for changing one's life and circumstances. I think of it as a gateway opportunity: It makes everything else possible—which is why the failure of our leaders to truly address education reform is so troubling. Instead of fundamental reform, we get grandstanding and broken promises and reform in name only.

Real reform has to start with how we treat our nation's teachers.

Teacher effectiveness is the single most important factor driving student performance, with top teachers able to boost the test scores of students up to 50 percentage points above the scores of those under the tutelage of the least-effective instructors.

Yet, because of overly rigid union contracts, we cannot pay the best teachers more based on their performance—and we've seen how next to impossible it has become to fire even the worst teachers. Until we stop this insanity, our national education report card will continue to be littered with Fs.

We also have to put an end to our obsession with testing, which was supposed to be a way of assessing reform but is now treated as actual reform. It's as if the powers-that-be all decided that a checkup was as good as a cure. This focus on testing reduces teachers to drill sergeants and effectively eliminates from the school schedule anything not likely to appear on a standardized test—things such as art, music, and class discussions.

And cash-strapped states inevitably end up relying on multiple-choice questions instead of essays, which are up to one thousand times more expensive to score. So it's good-bye analytical thinking, hello rote memorization and educated guessing. Our all-out embrace of testing has given us the

standardization of education, the destruction of critical thinking, and the categorization of millions of our children as failures.

So what can we do to turn around this sorry state of
affairs?

For starters, we have to start looking at things in daring
and different ways. To paraphrase Einstein, you can't solve a
problem using the same type of thinking that created it. Unfortunately, in our current political climate, it's nearly impossible to get people to stop protecting their little parcels of
partisan turf and start thinking on a different level, allowing
them to connect the dots and see the possibilities that might
lie on the other side of the mountain.

And what I see on the other side of that mountain is a
single-payer system of education.

Single payer never made it out of the gate when it came to
health-care reform. But we should bring it into education
reform.

In a single-payer health-care plan, the federal government
provides coverage for all U.S. citizens and legal residents.
Patients don't go to a government doctor—they just have the
government pay the bill. And that's how it would work with
education. In a single-payer education plan, the federal government, in conjunction with the states, would provide an
education allotment for every parent of a K–12 child. Parents
would then be free to enroll their child in the school of their
choice.

In a single-payer health-care plan, all citizens would be
free to select the physician and hospital of their choice. And,
unlike in our education system, no one backing single-payer
health care ever suggested that patients can see only a doctor

in their own district or can be operated on only at the hospital down the street. If we don't hold our health hostage to the value of our property, why do we do this with our children's education? The annual educational cost per child—equalized for urban and suburban school districts across each state—would come from current education funding sources.

When it comes to quality control, in health care the guidelines incorporated by Medicare are used to manage the quality of health-care services. In education, the government would be responsible for accrediting the schools from which parents could choose.

It's simple, sensible, and, above all, just. And maybe instead of calling for an exorcist any time the words "competition," "choice," or "freedom" are used in connection with education, we can start singing hosannas for an idea that preserves what is truly public in public education—the government, that is, the public, paying for it—while allowing creativity, innovation, and parental empowerment to flourish.

IT'S THE JOBS, STUPID!

In January 2010, during his State of the Union speech, President Obama declared, "Jobs must be our number one focus in 2010." This was followed by a round of applause—but very little action. What else is new?

Everybody is in such total agreement we need "more jobs" that the words are in danger of becoming meaningless, of going from tangible policy to talking point. In Washington, saying you're for jobs has become just another obligatory, perfunctory throat-clearing preamble.

But we need to move beyond the lofty rhetoric and the desultory statistics and focus on the fact that every lost job is a social calamity. Child abuse and neglect, divorce, crime, poor health, and drug addiction are often the devastating side effects of job loss. No country can be considered healthy when twenty-six million of its people are out of work or underemployed.

The current job crisis is simply too large and too stubborn—and the suffering too great—to do anything less than be as bold as possible.

The first thing we should do is have the federal government offer direct aid to local and state governments. Since August 2008, more than 150,000 state and local jobs have been eliminated, and the states' combined budget gap for fiscal 2010 and 2011 is $380 billion. The Center on Budget and Policy Priorities estimates that state and local deficits could cost the country an entire point off the GDP, which would, in turn, lead to the loss of another 900,000 jobs next year. This is why the Economic Policy Institute (EPI) recommends the federal government spend $150 billion on aid to state and local governments over the next year and a half, an investment that would save up to 1.4 million jobs.

Congress and the president should also push through a muscular plan to create public-service jobs. "The federal government could provide jobs by . . . providing jobs," writes Paul Krugman. "It's time for at least a small-scale version of the New Deal's Works Progress Administration. . . . There would be accusations that the government was creating make-work jobs, but the W.P.A. left many solid achievements in its wake. And the key point is that direct public employment can create a lot of jobs at relatively low cost."

In fact, the EPI estimates that one million jobs designed to "put unemployed Americans back to work serving their communities" could be created with an investment of $40 billion a year for three years. This approach is also favored by Princeton's Alan Blinder. "Direct public-service employment is straightforward," he says. "As long as the new government jobs do not compete with the private sector, the net job creation should be one-for-one. So hire people to repair parks, not shopping malls."

We may have missed the chance to put rebuilding America's infrastructure front and center in the big stimulus package Congress passed in 2009, but we absolutely must redouble our efforts to do so, in the process creating millions of high-paying jobs that can't be outsourced.

One way to finance the massive rebuilding effort that is needed is through a national infrastructure bank. Modeled after the European Investment Bank, which has been successfully investing in European energy, telecommunications, and transportation infrastructure projects for more than fifty years, the U.S. version would use federal seed money to leverage private dollars for investment in high-priority rebuilding projects across the country.

An investment of $25 billion in government funds could leverage more than $600 billion worth of projects. That won't cover the $2.2 trillion needed to bring our infrastructure up to an adequate condition, but it's a significant start—and would be a powerful engine for job creation.

Washington needs to get its act together. The creation of a national infrastructure bank was first proposed in 2007. And even though President Obama threw his weight behind the legislation in early 2008, Congress was still holding hearings on the matter in mid-2010. It's time to up the intensity and move this idea from the drawing-board stage to the action stage, fixing roads, bridges, sewers, and electrical grids and laying high-speed rail tracks.

We also need to pass a comprehensive legislative package to plug the drain of jobs heading overseas. It must include tax credits for companies that keep and create jobs for American workers and close loopholes that encourage employers to ship jobs abroad.

It would also be smart to incentivize green jobs. Investing in renewables will both lessen the likelihood of another disaster, like the BP one in the Gulf, and tap into a multibillion-dollar world market, creating an explosion of well-paying high-tech jobs and nurturing the next generation of job-creating entrepreneurs.

To take just one example, as the rest of the economy was shedding jobs in 2009, the solar energy industry added nearly twenty thousand. The Solar Energy Industries Association estimates that the solar industry could add up to 200,000 jobs over the next two years if Congress renews various incentive programs that are expiring in 2010.

Another way of promoting the green economy would be the creation of a national green bank, which, in the words of John Podesta and Karen Kornbluh of the Center for American Progress, would "open credit markets and motivate businesses to invest again," and "enable clean-energy technologies—in such areas as wind, solar, geothermal, advanced biomass, and energy efficiency—to be deployed on a large scale and become commercially viable at current electricity costs."

Such a bank would help loosen the available credit for small businesses and establish a reliable source of funding for entrepreneurs who wish to devote themselves to green technologies and start-ups.

Reed Hundt, the Federal Communications Commission chair under President Clinton, is the head of a group called the Coalition for Green Capital, whose goal is "to establish a government-run non-profit bank that would fill the void that exists in clean-energy legislation in America today." According to Hundt, a green bank would create "about four million jobs." Hundt's proposal has been included in several House and Senate climate and energy bills. And he is in talks with state governments to help them set up their own green banks.

Small businesses have long been the biggest creators of American jobs. According to a May 2010 report by the Congressional Oversight Panel, "More than 99 percent of American businesses employ 500 or fewer employees . . . and create two out of every three new jobs." And there are many ways we can help support them: Expand the Small Business Administration's lending programs; enact a one-year payroll tax holiday (creating a moratorium on Social Security, Medicare, and FICA taxes that will encourage businesses to hire new workers); offer businesses a tax credit for every job created over the next twelve months; and use bailout funds left in the TARP program to bail out Main Street (via increased lending to small businesses and funding of public services being cut by states and cities).

Even more important than helping small businesses is helping new businesses. According to economist John Haltiwanger, a study of the past twenty-five years shows that roughly one out of every three new jobs is created by a start-up company. "These are the rocket ships of the economy," he says. As reported by *Time*, from 1980 to 2005, "the typical fifteen-year-old firm added jobs at a rate of 1 percent a year; the typical three-year-old firm at a rate of 5 percent."

One innovative way of promoting job-creating start-ups is by tweaking our immigration policy. Great ideas arise from all over the world, and if America doesn't welcome the people with those great ideas and make it easy for them to come here, they will go elsewhere. Indeed, they already are beginning to do so.

Right now, the United States has an immigration limit for skilled workers of sixty-five thousand, with an additional twenty thousand slots for those with advanced degrees from U.S. universities. This kind of rigid cap doesn't make sense in today's world. The "visa process has been plagued with backlogs resulting from this quota," says Jonathan Ortmans, a senior fellow at the Kauffman Foundation, a leading center for entrepreneurship. "As a result, high-skilled immigrants are looking for opportunities elsewhere in an increasingly competitive global labor market, taking their innovative ideas with them." If America is going to remain a First World country, it is going to have to step up the way it competes for first-class talent and ideas.

The people behind StartupVisa.com have a creative proposal for increasing America's share in the global idea marketplace. They want to make it easier for foreign entrepreneurs to come to America and start job-creating businesses. Our current law allows foreign investors to get a visa if they start a business in the United States with $1 million in capital and can create at least ten jobs right off the bat. The venture capitalists behind StartupVisa.com want to shift the emphasis from investors to entrepreneurs, providing visas to entrepreneurs who can get funding from American investors. The idea is to reward good *ideas* instead of just bringing in foreign money. The way the law stands now, by requiring those with good ideas to first get foreign funding, we make it more likely they'll decide to start their companies elsewhere.

The proposal, the StartUp Visa Act of 2010, is already in the legislative pipeline. It is being cosponsored by Senators John Kerry and Richard Lugar. According to the *Washington Post*, their bill "would create a two-year visa for immigrant entrepreneurs who are able to raise a minimum of $250,000, with $100,000 coming from a qualified U.S. angel or venture investor. After two years, if the immigrant entrepreneur is able to create five or more jobs (not including their children or spouse), attract an additional $1 million in investment, or produce $1 million in revenues, he or she will become a legal resident."

"At a time when many are wondering whether Democrats and Republicans can come together on anything, there is at least one area where we're in strong agreement," wrote Kerry and Lugar in an op-ed. "We believe that America is the best country in the world to do business. And now is the time to reach out to immigrant entrepreneurs—men and women who have come from overseas to study in our universities, and countless others coming up with great ideas abroad—to help drive innovation and job creation here at home."

The senators see the proposal as a jobs initiative, not an immigration reform initiative. As Kerry put it, "This bill is a small down payment on a cure to global competitiveness."

Clearly, when it comes to jobs, there is no lack of ideas. Just a lack of political will.

Yes, many of these job-creating proposals are expensive, but, in the long run, not nearly as expensive as long-term unemployment and the disappearance of America's middle class.

PERVERTED PRIORITIES: THE REMIX

Any time the idea of funding jobs programs or rebuilding America's moldering infrastructure is raised, our leaders immediately look at the price tag and go into sticker shock: We can't afford that! But they never seem to have the same reaction when the defense budget races past $700 billion or when it's time to sign the next check for funding the wars of choice in Iraq and Afghanistan (2010 price tag? $161 billion).

A perfect example of this came in May 2010 when, on the same day, the Senate approved a nearly $60 billion funding bill for the war in Afghanistan while the House took a hatchet to a spending bill, cutting out provisions that would have offered $24 billion in aid to cash-strapped states and helped laid-off workers pay for health insurance. The juxtaposition spoke volumes about what we've come to value in this country.

That's got to change. As a nation, we need to start redefining the meaning of "national security" by making sure our ports are protected, our railways are secure, and our nation's nuclear facilities, chemical plants, and storage facilities aren't vulnerable to attack. And we need to make sure that with all the budget cuts happening in states across the nation, we don't underfund our police and first responders. We've got to stop robbing our homeland security Peter to pay our foreign wars Paul.

For example, we are planning to spend $12.6 billion on ballistic missile defense in 2011. For the same amount, we could hire an additional 190,873 police officers for a year.

So let's end our disastrous—and Treasury-draining—nation-building forays in Afghanistan and Iraq. And let's stop making a debate about cutting defense spending an electrified third rail that must never be touched.

There is plenty of fat in the Defense Department. Representative Barney Frank suggests a good place to start cutting: doing away with one prong of America's hugely expensive nuclear triad—bombers, submarines, and intercontinental ballistic missiles—designed to deal with Cold War–era threats, but still siphoning off twenty-first-century dollars. "My radical proposal," said Frank, "is that we say to the Pentagon that they can pick two of the three, and let us abolish one."

Targeting Defense Department waste is not the exclusive province of progressives like Frank. Senator Tom Coburn, a social conservative and fiscal hawk—and a Republican member of President Obama's deficit commission—has called for a full audit of spending by the Pentagon. He sums up the need succinctly: "The Pentagon doesn't know how it spends its money." In a damning letter to the deficit commission's chairmen, calling for an audit, Coburn said, "An ethic continues to predominate in the Pentagon that consistently paints an inaccurate picture—one that is biased in the same unrealistic and ultimately unaffordable direction. The errors are not random: actual costs always turn out to be much higher than, sometimes even multiples of, early estimates." According to a Coburn aide, there hasn't been a Pentagon audit in fifteen to twenty years because the department's "books are so disorganized it would be impossible to do." Not exactly the description you want to hear about a place receiving more than $700 billion in taxpayer money this year.

Bottom line: We could trim the defense budget, change our national security priorities, and make the nation more secure. Even after cutting billions, defense spending would remain significantly higher, in real dollars, than it was at the height of the Reagan arms buildup.

As Defense Secretary Robert Gates put it in a speech at the Eisenhower Library (fitting given Ike's warnings about the military-industrial complex): America cannot survive as "a muscle-bound, garrison state—militarily strong, but economically stagnant and strategically insolvent."

SAVING OUR HOMES FROM FORECLOSURE

We cannot truly secure our homeland without also protecting America's besieged middle class. The best place to start is finding a way to reduce foreclosures, allowing people to keep their homes.

The single most valuable thing the government could do to help people facing foreclosure is to pass a cramdown bill allowing homeowners in bankruptcy to renegotiate their mortgages under the guidance of a bankruptcy judge.

Cramdown legislation, facing intense opposition from mortgage-industry lobbyists, has been repeatedly voted down in Congress. But those senators and members of the House representing the interests of average Americans—as opposed to the special interests—need to keep trying. The banks' resistance to the idea of judicial modification is showing signs of weakening. Some, including Bank of America and Citigroup, have already changed their tune and expressed support for it.

We should also make it mandatory that homeowners and lenders engage in mediation prior to any final foreclosure. A pilot program along these lines, the Residential Mortgage Foreclosure Diversion Program, started in Philadelphia in 2008, has proven very successful in preventing or delaying foreclosures in 75 to 80 percent of the cases that have made it to mediation. Currently, many homeowners don't even talk to their lenders until they have been foreclosed on—partly because the lenders often make it next to impossible to reach them. Or, if your mortgage has been sliced up and sold to speculators, to even find them.

"I've been to the City Hall courtroom where the mediation hearings take place," Senator Bob Casey of Pennsylvania told me, "and they are crammed with lenders and borrowers and counselors and lawyers, and they are remarkably effective."

Judge Annette Rizzo, who has been working hard to keep Philadelphians in their homes, told the *Philadelphia Daily News*: "There is hand-to-hand outreach to each client here. There is individual caretaking here. The lender lawyers get to know the homeowners as people here. We put a human face on this and they embrace it. So as I work the room, I feel a humanism here on both sides. If necessary, our volunteer lawyers pick up clients and bring them here. Housing counselors make house calls. Our mission is to save lives, one address at a time."

The foreclosure prevention program has worked so well in Philadelphia, it has spread to Boston, Pittsburgh, Cook County, Prince George's County, Louisville, and New Jersey. We should take this model and apply it on a national level.

Until we do, we'll need to rely on officials like Judge Rizzo and Judge Arthur Schack of the New York State Supreme Court in Brooklyn, described by the *New York Times* as "a judicial Don Quixote, tilting at the phalanxes of bankers, foreclosure facilitators and lawyers who file motions by the bale." Judge Schack regularly refuses banks' petitions for foreclosure if every "i" is not dotted and every "t" is not crossed. "If you are going to take away someone's house," he told the *Times*, "everything should be legal and correct. I'm a strange guy—I don't want to put a family on the street unless it's legitimate."

His humanity—and his rulings—should become a national model.

GIVING CREDIT WHERE CREDIT IS DUE

We also need to protect middle-class Americans from all the tricks and traps being set by credit card companies and banks. And make no mistake: While the new credit card reform law that took effect early in 2010 reined in some of the industry's most egregious practices, credit card companies are working overtime to come up with new ways to separate us from our money. So the game of "catch you because I can" continues.

Of course, our elected officials made sure to include some banking lobbyist–designed loopholes in the legislation. For example, the new law still allows promotional teaser interest rates that hook in new customers for a short period of time—before the far higher real rate kicks in.

As Elizabeth Warren sees it, "That's exactly the sweet spot for the credit card companies. It's the person who can just barely make it, who's lost a job, who's having trouble finding another job, diligently tries to pay, and struggles to pay. Boy, that's the one you want. And that's the one you want to hit with 29 percent interest. . . . Those are staggeringly profitable accounts. I mean, that's the big bucks. That's where it happens."

According to the new law, the credit card issuer needs to

give a forty-five-day notification before it raises interest rates. But you must stop using the card if you refuse to accept the new rate. And the banks, of course, know the havoc it would create in most peoples' lives to have to regularly close down their credit cards and seek new ones. However soul sapping it may be, you have to read all the stuff that comes from your credit card company—including the small print about service fees on top of late fees on top of "inactivity" fees. If you can, set up automatic bill pay so you don't miss a payment. Because fees account for 39 percent of credit card issuers' revenue, the banks will keep dreaming up new ways to trick us that are not covered, or even contemplated, by existing laws.

And the new law doesn't prevent banks from gouging their credit card customers with sky-high interest rates. Senator Bernie Sanders, whose attempts at capping credit card interest rates have been voted down by his colleagues, says, "When banks are charging thirty percent interest rates, they are not making credit available. They are engaged in loan sharking"—also known as usury.

Throughout history, usury has been decried by writers, philosophers, and religious leaders. Aristotle called usury the "sordid love of gain" and a "sordid trade." Thomas Aquinas said it was "contrary to justice." In *The Divine Comedy,* Dante assigned usurers to the seventh circle of hell. Deuteronomy 23:19 says, "Thou shalt not lend upon usury to thy brother." Ezekiel 18:8–13 compares a usurer to someone who "is a shedder of blood . . . defiled his neighbor's wife . . . oppressed the poor and needy . . . [and] committed abomination." The Koran is equally unequivocal: "God condemns usury."

We need to return to that approach to outrageous lending

practices. We need to once again become a country where it's not acceptable to financially trick millions of working families, binding them to the whims of bankers who have lost all sight of fairness.

CLOSING DOWN THE WALL STREET CASINO

Right after President Obama's election, Rahm Emanuel famously declared, "Rule one: Never allow a crisis to go to waste. They are opportunities for big things." But since the financial meltdown, it is actually the very people who created the crisis who have taken advantage of it and achieved "big things"— especially big profits and bonuses.

We obviously need to fix Wall Street. Desperately. And there is much to be fixed. But on a nuts-and-bolts level, the three things we absolutely must do are:

1. Regulate all derivatives and other exotic "financial instruments" that played such a big part in the meltdown and have turned Wall Street banks into much shadier versions of a Las Vegas casino (at least in Vegas, you know the odds going in).

2. Create a Glass-Steagall Act for the twenty-first century, restoring the Chinese wall between commercial and investment banking.

3. Follow the path of Teddy Roosevelt and break up the big banks. It's essential to end "too big to fail" in order to ensure that taxpayers are not on the hook next time.

Even Alan Greenspan, the oracle of free markets and a longtime cheerleader for banking deregulation, thinks the megabanks are too big. In October 2009, he said, "If they're too big to fail, they're too big. . . . So I mean, radical things— you know, break them up. In 1911, we broke up Standard Oil. So what happened? The individual parts became more valuable than the whole. Maybe that's what we need."

After the near-collapse of the economy, precipitated by Wall Street, you would have thought that reining in the big banks would have been a no-brainer. But the best Washington can muster are diluted reforms that won't prevent another meltdown.

Beyond new regulations, we need a new mind-set. We need to think bigger and begin eradicating the culture of greed and corruption that has come to dominate Wall Street. Discussing the economic crisis, Michael Lynton, chairman and CEO of Sony Pictures, told me, "I'm often asked if, given Hollywood's struggles, I were building a movie studio system from scratch, is the current model what I would build?"

The answer was no. Likewise, given the chance to rebuild America's economy, is the current system, even with a few hundred billion dollars' worth of patches, the one we would want to build? Of course not. Even Greenspan conceded there was a "flaw in the model." But there's not a flaw in the model—the model itself is flawed. It's not that capitalism isn't working. It's that what we have right now is not capitalism. What we have is corporatism. It's welfare for the rich. It's the government picking winners and losers. It's Wall Street having its taxpayer-funded cake and eating it, too. It's socialized losses and privatized gains.

A magnetic compass should always point north; a moral compass should always point out that cheating and fraud are dead wrong. But demanding that companies stop being bad is not enough. We have to demand that they start being good. That has to be the bottom line on financial and corporate reform.

We need to create an economy where productivity doesn't come at the cost of quality of life. In 1967, speaking at the University of Kansas, Robert F. Kennedy called on Americans to look at our economy in a radically different way. "Our gross national product is now over $800 billion a year," he said, "but that GNP—if we should judge America by that— counts air pollution and cigarette advertising, and ambulances to clear our highways of carnage. It counts special locks for our doors, and the jails for those who break them. It counts the destruction of our redwoods and the loss of our natural wonder in chaotic sprawl. It counts napalm and the cost of a nuclear warhead, and armored cars for police who fight riots in our streets."

America needs to engage in a similar soul-stirring questioning of many unquestioned assumptions. We need to move from a bottom-line-obsessed corporate culture to a "triple bottom line" approach that calls for corporations to pay attention to both their stockholders and their stakeholders—those who may not have invested money in the company but clearly have a de facto investment in the air they breathe, the food they eat, and the communities they live in.

We can't afford to just remodel the Wall Street casino. We need to collectively decide that we want to return to being a country where middle-class Americans are put first, and where trickle up—not trickle down—is the economic order of the day.

THIRD WORLD AMERICA WILL NOT BE TELEVISED . . . IT WILL BE BLOGGED, TWEETED, AND UPLOADED TO YOUTUBE

There is a reason our founding fathers made sure that freedom of the press was guaranteed in the very first amendment. As we've seen time and time again, governments—as well as giant corporations and Wall Street banks—are prone to corruption. And when that corruption has metastasized and actually overtaken the political and financial systems, a dogged and independent press becomes more essential than ever.

As Justice Potter Stewart wrote of the Pentagon Papers, "Without an informed and free press there cannot be an enlightened people." He might have specified a free press not in bed with the government it is supposed to keep an eye on. Far too often over the past twenty years, members of the media have traded their independence for an all-access pass to the halls of power.

Don't forget: With a few honorable exceptions, the media failed to serve the public interest by missing the two biggest stories of our time—the run-up to the war in Iraq and the financial meltdown. In both instances, there were plenty of people who got it right—who saw what was coming and warned about it—but they were drowned out by the thumping sound of journalists walking in lockstep. As a result, we've had far too many autopsies of what went wrong and not enough biopsies of what was about to go wrong.

The media is also addicted to covering what Bill Maher describes as the "bright, shiny objects" over here, distracting attention from the real story over there—trivial stories that draw our attention away from harder-to-understand stories, such as what caused the financial meltdown or why Congress isn't reforming Wall Street.

We saw this last year with the media's breathless, wall-to-wall coverage of the Balloon Boy nonstory—coverage that continued on for days even after we learned the balloon was empty, with TV anchor after TV anchor expressing deep concern for Attic Boy (a more fitting name since he never was in the balloon).

Who knew the media was so worried about the welfare of children? Well, as it turns out, their concern extends only to children in certain circumstances—such as when they are thought to be trapped in a runaway balloon. Why do we feel so much for Balloon Boy and so little for the hundreds of thousands of children affected by the financial meltdown and the downward spiral their families' lives are in?

What if we could repurpose some of that concern for the more than 1.5 million children who are homeless or the 51 percent of homeless children who are under the age of six? How about some attention to the 75 to 100 percent increase in the number of children who are newly homeless because of the foreclosure crisis? Or the 14 million American children living in poverty?

If we are going to halt our transformation into Third World America, we need the media to step up to its role as watchdog and storyteller, holding our leaders' feet to the fire and speaking truth to power. Stories that put flesh and blood on the data connect us with one another and put the spotlight on the effects that lobbyist-driven laws have on the day-to-day lives of middle-class families.

"People work for justice when their hearts are stirred by specific lives and situations that develop our capacity to feel empathy, to imagine ourselves as someone else," says Paul Loeb, author of *Soul of a Citizen*, who has been writing about citizen movements for forty years. "New information—the percentage of people out of work or children in poverty, the numbers behind America's record health-care costs, the annual planetary increases in greenhouse gases—can help us comprehend the magnitude of our shared problems and develop appropriate responses. But information alone can't provide the organic connection that binds one person to another, or that stirs our hearts to act. Powerful stories can break us beyond our isolated worlds."

Luckily, thanks to the expansion of online news sources, new media platforms such as Twitter and Facebook, and the ever-decreasing size and cost of camera phones and video cameras, the ability to commit acts of journalism is spreading to everyone. As a result, citizen journalism is rapidly emerging as an invaluable part of delivering the news.

Nothing demonstrated the power of citizen journalism better than the 2009 uprising in Iran. People tweeting from demonstrations and uploading video of brutal violence taken with their camera phones were able to tell a story, in real time, that a tightly controlled mainstream media was unable to cover with the same speed and depth.

Citizen journalism often works best when filling a void— attending an event that traditional journalists are kept from or have overlooked—or by finding the small but evocative story happening right next door. People are becoming increasingly creative in exploring ways to find these facts and tell these stories.

New media and citizen journalists are taking traditional journalism's ability to bear witness, and spreading it beyond the elite few—thereby making it harder for those elite few to get it as wrong as they've gotten it again and again.

Our slide into Third World America may not be televised . . .
but it will be blogged, tweeted, posted on Facebook, covered
with a camera phone, and uploaded to YouTube. And by shining
the spotlight on it, we may be able to prevent it.

II.
ON THE PERSONAL LEVEL:
LOOK IN THE MIRROR

There is no doubt: Times are hard. The "new normal" is a punch
in the gut, a slap across the face, and a pitcher of icy water
dumped on our heads. It's a chill running up our national
spine.

The question is, What are we going to do about it? Are we
going to shut off the lights, curl up in a ball, and slap a victim
sticker on our foreheads? Or are we going to shake off the blows,
take a deep breath, hitch up our pants, and head back into the
fray?

Are we going to wallow in despair or rage against the fading
of the American Dream?

The preamble to the Constitution starts with "We the
People." And we have never needed the active participation of
each one of us more urgently than now.

It's becoming clearer by the day that we're not going to be
able to rely solely on the government to fix things. Yes, we need
our leaders to tackle the things on our "How to Avoid Third
World America" checklist. But we can't save the middle class
and keep America a First World nation without each of us
making a personal commitment and taking action—without

each of us doing our part. We can't just sit on the sidelines and complain. It's up to us: We the People.

Leadership is, after all, about breaking old paradigms—about seeing where society is stuck and providing ways to get it unstuck. And right now, the point at which we're most stuck, the site of the primary bottleneck that prevents us from adequately addressing our problems, is in Washington itself. So the job of getting us unstuck is increasingly going to be the responsibility of those outside that center of power. Learning to mine the leadership resources of ordinary Americans means no longer relying only on elected officials to solve our problems. You don't have to lead vast nations or command huge armies to make a difference. In looking at the leader in the mirror we are just following that very American urge to take matters into our own hands and get things done.

Tip O'Neill said, "All politics is local." And, in the end, all problem solving is personal. So we have to ask ourselves: What are we going to do to help ourselves—and one another?

Moving your money is a good place to start.

BREAKING UP WITH YOUR BIG BANK

It was a lightbulb moment. A group of us, including economist Rob Johnson, political strategist Alexis McGill, filmmaker Eugene Jarecki, and Nick Penniman of the Huffington Post Investigative Fund, was having dinner, talking about the huge, growing chasm between the fortunes of Wall Street and Main Street, and the outrageous behavior of America's megabanks—how they'd taken our bailout money but cut back on lending, paid themselves record bonuses, and kept on with all the greedy, abusive, ruthless practices that have earned them billions a year—year after year. We were getting madder by the minute.

Then the lightbulb clicked on: Why don't we take our money out of these big banks and put it into community banks and credit unions? And why don't we see if we can encourage everyone in America to do the same thing?

The concept was simple: If enough people who had money in one of the Big Six investment banks (JPMorgan Chase, Citigroup, Bank of America, Wells Fargo, Goldman Sachs, and Morgan Stanley) moved their money into smaller, more local, more traditional community banks and credit unions, collectively we, as individuals, would have taken a big step toward transforming the financial system so it again becomes the productive, stable engine for growth it's meant to be. And since deposit insurance at small banks is the same as at big banks—up to $250,000— there is zero risk involved. While it may not be in our power to change the system single-handedly, we do have the power to take our money out of the banks that undermined our economy and move it to more responsible banks to help rebuild it. We don't have to wait for Washington to act. We can do a complete end run around the closed ecosystem of lobbyists and politicians.

We launched the Move Your Money campaign on the Huffington Post in late 2009, and it took off like wildfire. The video Eugene Jarecki made (playing off the classic film *It's a Wonderful Life,* where community banker George Bailey helps the people of Bedford Falls escape the grip of the rapacious and predatory banker Mr. Potter) went viral. Bill Maher compared moving your money to ending "a loveless, abusive relationship with your big bank." Media coverage was extensive. Top financial analysts Chris Whalen and Dennis Santiago created a tool that allowed people to plug in their zip codes and quickly get a list of small, safe banks and credit unions operating in their communities. About 2 million people, in every region of the country, ended up moving their money—more than $5 billion in the first quarter of 2010—as did a growing number of cities, states, and large pension funds.

The idea is neither liberal nor conservative—it's productive populism at its best—and has been embraced by those on both sides of the ideological spectrum who are sick and tired of the megabanks and are ready to do something about it.

The big banks may still be "too big to fail"—but they are not too big to feel the impact of hundreds of thousands of people taking action to change a broken financial and political system. The key thing is we don't have to wait on Washington to get its act together.

People from all walks of life have written in to say how empowering the small act of moving their money was. One of them, H. Lee Grove, wrote, "Thank you so much. I have been so depressed about the apathy I had fallen into, being able to do nothing as the bully on the playground beat everyone to hell right in front of my eyes, that I would just lie in bed for days at a time. I moved my money to a credit union and I feel fantastic."

EVERYBODY KNOWS THE DICE ARE LOADED . . . SO CHANGE THE GAME

Leonard Cohen wrote his classic song "Everybody Knows" in the late 1980s, but it couldn't feel timelier:

Everybody knows that the dice are loaded
Everybody rolls with their fingers crossed

Everybody knows that the war is over
Everybody knows the good guys lost
Everybody knows the fight was fixed
The poor stay poor, the rich get rich
That's how it goes
Everybody knows

Knowing that when it comes to getting ahead in America the dice are loaded—and that it's getting harder and harder to insulate yourself and your family from the consequences of America's misguided policies—is fostering anger, resentment, cynicism, and despair across the country. But if we're ever going to change the rigged game, we first have to break that cycle of despair at the personal level. And the greatest antidote to despair is action. Move Your Money is one example.

Another is arming yourself against the predatory behavior of unscrupulous businessmen—especially bankers, mortgage lenders, and credit card companies. This requires becoming smarter and more vigilant about what kinds of companies we give our business to. When it comes to credit cards, pick an issuer—such as a credit union—that's not busy figuring out ways to get you to pay a 30 percent interest rate or charging every manner of fee and penalty to fatten its bottom line.

Consumer credit unions are not owned by shareholders, who are looking for maximum quarterly profits, but by members, who are looking for stability and service. Since their goal is not to maximize short-term profit, credit unions by and large steered clear of risky subprime loans. Nearly ninety million Americans belong to credit unions, which usually offer lower fees and higher interest rates on savings.

Around 70 percent of credit union mortgages are held by

the credit unions themselves, as opposed to being sliced up into pieces and sold off on secondary markets for players in the Wall Street casino to bet on. (The exceptions are corporate credit unions that began behaving like investment banks and dove into the toxic securities market.)

"A credit union saved me from Bank of America," wrote Joe McKesson on the Huffington Post. "Every day BoA had a way to take some amount of money from me—every day a fee ranging from 25 cents to 35 dollars. Once I went credit union, transparency came back into my life. I woke up with the same amount of money I went to bed with. . . . The robbery was over. I will never trust a large bank again."

"All I can say is that nothing beats the personal attention a credit union offers," wrote Consuelo Flores. "It's the 'Cheers' bar where everybody knows your name."

Deborah Bohn's nineteen-year-old daughter, who had no credit history, was unable to get a car loan, even when she was offering to put 50 percent down. "Our credit union came through for her," wrote Bohn.

The truth is that millions of people today are unnecessarily losing money every year to banks and other lenders. That is due, in part, to the fact that only 20 percent of households can afford to get quality financial advice. But new technology now exists that can change that.

Witness HelloWallet.com, a start-up company that, for a very small fee, acts as an online personal money manager, identifying savings opportunities for its users and alerting them to threats to their financial health before they become economic catastrophes. Launched in 2009 with a grant from the Rockefeller Foundation and touted by Bill Clinton, Ernst & Young, and dozens of nonprofits across the country, HelloWallet is giving

America something that hasn't been available before: affordable financial guidance.

The site will automatically find you the best rates on financial products such as mortgages and credit cards and will alert you when your bank tries to increase your rates or charge fees. It also makes it easy to create, and keep, a budget: it keeps track of your accounts in a single place, categorizes your spending, and presents you with a breakdown of where you're spending your money.

Best of all, the site is independent from banks, which means it can help you avoid fees and can give you unbiased guidance about how to make the most out of your money. The result is that HelloWallet could, for the first time in a long time, put banks back to work for their customers, saving the public billions of dollars every year.

Another good online tool is Mint.com, a free service that allows you to securely link all of your credit card, loan, bank, and retirement accounts for a great overview of your finances. The site also helps you to budget your spending with tools that easily divide your expenditures into a variety of categories, helps you plan the optimal repayment of your debts, and can send you alerts when accounts get low or when certain bills need to be paid.

If you are getting a tax refund at the end of the year, you might want to consider having less money withheld from your paycheck and using the additional cash to pay off debts rather than let the government hold on to it without paying you interest. And it's important to keep track of your credit report and credit score, which can determine what type of interest rate you are eligible for. Also, start making saving a habit—even if you can only save a little each month.

In April 2010, President Obama issued a proclamation for National Financial Literacy Month. "While our government has a critical role to play in protecting consumers and promoting financial literacy," the proclamation read, "we are each responsible for understanding basic concepts: how to balance a checkbook, save for a child's education, steer clear of deceptive financial products and practices, plan for retirement, and avoid accumulating excessive debts."

On top of this practical caveat emptor advice, perhaps the proclamation should have added "And remember: The people you think of as 'service providers' are actually out to get you. They may appear friendly, but they're not your friends. They're hoping to hook you and your family into a vicious cycle of debt. This is financial combat. If you want you and your family to survive, you'd better learn how to spot the financial land mines buried in your mortgage and credit card contracts, and keep yourself out of harm's way."

I GET KNOCKED DOWN . . . BUT I GET UP AGAIN

Earlier this year, I was reading *Consumer Reports* and came across an article offering "10 New Rules for a New Economy." The first seven rules touched on the kind of personal finance tips you'd expect, things such as "assess risk" and "control spending." But the last three rules caught me by surprise. They were:

8. "Stay healthy. The best investment tip of all is to invest in your health."

9. "Don't stress. Forget about your 'relationship' with money. It's just a tool."

10. "Move on . . . consider only what you can make or lose going forward, not how much you have lost."

Or, as Suze Orman puts it, "No Blame, No Shame. . . . The first, and most difficult, step is to absolve yourself and your spouse or partner of any guilt. . . . Whatever mistakes you feel you have made with money, whatever moves you wish you had or hadn't made, are irrelevant." That's not the kind of counsel you'd normally get from a financial adviser—but it is spot-on. Focusing on the deeply personal aspects of "personal finance" is essential if we are going to effectively navigate these challenging times.

Karen Reivich and Andrew Shatté, authors of *The Resilience Factor*, have identified resilience as the key to how we deal with what life brings us: "Where you fall on the resilience curve—your natural reserves of resilience—affects your performance in school and at work, your physical health, your mental health, and the quality of your relationships. . . . We all know resilient people. They inspire us. They seem to soar in spite of the hardship and trauma they face. . . . Resilient people understand that failures are not an end point. They do not feel shame when they don't succeed. Instead, resilient people are able to derive meaning from failure, and they use this knowledge to climb higher than they otherwise would.

"Resilient people," they continue, "have found a system— and it is a system—for galvanizing themselves and tackling problems thoughtfully, thoroughly, and energetically. Resilient people, like all of us, feel anxious and have doubts, but they have learned how to stop their anxiety and doubts from overwhelming them. We watch them handle threat with integrity and grace and we wonder: Could I do that?"

Luckily, resilience, like fearlessness, is a muscle we can build up. The more we use it, the stronger it becomes, and ultimately, how we deal with adversity depends on how much we have developed this inner strength.

Dominique Browning, who lost her job as editor in chief of *House and Garden,* describes the long months after being knocked off her career path: "Privately, I was in a whiplashing tailspin. My nightmare had finally come true. For years, I had a profound dread of unemployment that went way beyond worrying about how to pay the bills. I would like to say that this was because of the insecure nature of magazine publishing, but my anxiety had more to do with my own neuroses—though I didn't think of it that way. Work had become the scaffolding of my life. It was what I counted on. It held up the floor of my moods, kept the facade intact. I always worried that if I didn't have work, I would sink into abject torpor."

Indeed, after being fired she went through "months of depressed sloth." But, slowly, she began to take daily walks, sometimes for miles every day, giving herself lectures: "Buck up. Just because something has failed doesn't mean I am a failure. Just because something has ended doesn't mean it was all a mistake. Just because I have been rejected doesn't mean I am worthless and unlovable. Sound familiar? It would if you or anyone you know has gone through a divorce. I had hauled myself through one of those many years earlier. This felt like the same thing. Worse. A divorce you choose. Unemployment chooses you."

Obviously, faith helps people develop the resilience they need in difficult times, but so do simple things such as learning to reduce stress by unplugging and recharging, getting enough sleep, and the walks and daily lectures like Browning gave herself.

Eventually, things turned around for her. "I hate to be the one to bring up silver linings, or worse, windows opening while doors are slamming," she says, but over time she came to feel as if she had grown a new taproot, "one that reaches deeper into nourishing soil. I am more resilient. If I had to pin it down, I would say I finally fell open to the miracle of this world."

Jim Laman of Holland, Michigan, is another great example of how resilience can get you through tough times. He spent twenty-one years working at furniture manufacturer Herman Miller before he was "downsized" in the economic tailspin that followed 9/11. He found his next job at a smaller company, but in 2006 he abruptly lost it in a mass layoff. "There was absolutely zero warning," he says. "My benefits ended that night at midnight, as did my pay. I was devastated. Never saw it coming. They even kept the bonus that I had earned for the past year. I was bitter for a long time about that and it still bothers me, as the company was supposedly so 'family oriented.' I guess that came with a caveat!"

Laman found another job, this time at a manufacturer of truck transmissions in southwest Michigan. It was sixty-five miles away, but he kept his gas bill down by riding his motorcycle, even through treacherous weather, which saved him about sixty dollars per week. Then, in November 2008, as the economy reeled from the financial crisis, his company issued a round of pink slips—and once again, with just twenty-four hours' notice and a month before Christmas, he was out of a job.

"It was not a merry Christmas," he remembers, "but we got a few gifts for the kids and a free tree to put them under. I started selling things on eBay to help make ends meet, and have continued to do so sporadically to this day. Classic Herman Miller furniture is quite valuable, so we sold a few pieces and I parted with a classic Saab and the parts I had collected for it for many years. I've sold about five thousand dollars' worth a year on eBay, and it has helped tremendously. In the meantime, my wife lost her contract job at Herman Miller, which was another blow to us. During this time we were very worried about losing our home, and my parents helped us a little. I was so stressed that there were days I wondered if I could go on much longer, frankly. Unemployment benefits and the remainder of our retirement savings got us through. I looked into selling blood, any sort of factory work, doing odd jobs, anything for some income . . . but no takers."

He filled out almost five hundred job applications. Frustrated, Laman broadened his search, first to Indiana, and then as far as Chicago, where he finally received an offer in mid-March 2009. In a complete upheaval of his life, he accepted the job.

"Soon after, I found a room to rent up in Evanston, about six miles north of where I work, and I still live there. I commute home to Michigan every Friday night, returning on Sunday evenings, so weekends are rather short, but we are making it work. People thought at first that my wife and I were separated or getting a divorce. But no, we are fine. We just live in different states! Kind of funny really, but I got a better cell phone plan and with that and email, we stay in fairly good communication. At times, I find out what is going on via Facebook, too! . . . I think it is about attitude and priorities: If you go in with a good attitude, good things will come your way. As a result I am involved in many things that I never would have done before, including company volunteer work, a soft-ball league, and exploring the city on my own on my motorcycle. All new stuff—and kind of fun. Things I never would have imagined doing back in 2006 when I lost my job."

For many left jobless by the recession, resilience has meant hitting the books, so as unemployment rose, college enrollment—particularly at community colleges—also increased. When Patty C., a director of service for a health-care company in Denver, Colorado, was laid off from her job in June 2009, for example, she kept herself busy for the six months she spent unemployed by earning new certifications and heading back to school for a degree in health-information management. For Patty, losing her job was a chance to sharpen her skills and upgrade her qualifications: "We have spent our lives dedicated to the companies we worked for," she said. "Now is the time to focus on ourselves and rethink our next career move." Unemployment also forced Patty to slash her family's expenses, which she did with the guidance of coupon blogs and websites dedicated to frugality. When she did land her next job, as an operations manager for a nonprofit organization, she said that despite a 25 percent pay cut, she felt "secure about the future," confident in her ability to get by with less and certain that her new education would "open doors . . . that were closed before."

Lesa Deason Crowe, a small business owner who lives in Oklahoma City, Oklahoma, saw the financial crisis nearly destroy her twelve-person advertising firm. "It started in the news," she recalled. "Every night, there would be another story about the recession, depression. This was in fall 2008. Clients started to get jittery and began to proactively get ready for 'disaster.' Part of that planning was to get rid of all the 'fat' in their budgets, which in my case meant cutting all advertising, marketing, and public relations work. My lowest point was when three clients quit in one day. I walked in, prepared for a typical monthly meeting, and the next thing I knew I was fired on the spot. Three in a row. Our two largest clients and our fifth largest. Gone."

She tried to keep her prized employees busy, but she couldn't shield herself from worry, which kept her up nights. "My husband was in Iraq, my son would be asleep, the house was clean and I would lie there awake, staring at the ceiling, unable to sleep. Something like this haunts you. I worried about the people I work with, as well as my clients, because I care for them, they're friends. I worried about the bills, about my business, about absolutely everything."

Things finally started to take a turn for the better when Lesa got involved with the Rural Enterprises' Women's Business Center in Oklahoma City. "One of the ladies in my peer advisory group leaned over and handed me a business card. 'Here's a heck of a client for you,' she said. It turned out to be the biggest client I have." Soon after, her former clients began to trickle back. "It took about a year but every client but one has returned." Lesa credits the Women's Business Center and the women she met there with helping her keep both her business and her sanity.

Lesa draws inspiration from her mother, who divorced in 1964 with four daughters under the age of seven. "Every day I saw this magnificent woman with a college degree do everything from taking in sewing to working at a canning factory. She used to say: 'How do you clean up the house? Well, you pick up one thing and put it away. You pick up another thing and put it away. You do that again and again and soon your house is clean.' The same thing is true in business. We get so scared and we sit there, bummed out. You have to look up and say, even if I do something very, very small, I'm going to keep plugging along and accomplish something today!"

FINDING THE SILVER LINING

"When you are helping others, you are helping yourself." It's amazing, when hearing stories of resilience, how often that sentiment pops up.

It's an unexpected twist: Taking the one thing you have an abundance of when you are out of work—time—and using it to help others turns out to be remarkably empowering and energizing. Moving beyond a sense of helplessness to make a difference in the lives of others—whether working at a food bank, delivering meals to seniors, or mentoring a child—can transform our experience of even the most stressful times. The consequences of being jobless are not just economic—they're also psychological. And the psychic toll is greatly lessened by taking a look outside ourselves and finding ways to serve others even less fortunate. It can bring both perspective and meaning to our lives. Plus, evidence shows that when we look outward, reach out, and connect—especially in times of trouble—good things follow.

Take the case of Annette Arca, a Las Vegas commercial real estate professional. After she lost her job, she began to spend some of her newfound free time volunteering in her community. Even though she couldn't afford to make the payments on her town house, she figured there were still people in worse situations who needed help, so she set aside a chunk of hours each week to help deliver lunches to medical centers and work with homeless families. "It's a great opportunity to get involved, to help other people," she told the *Las Vegas Review-Journal*. But volunteering also lent Arca a sense of purpose and positive outlook that complemented her job search. "If I'm negative, nothing's ever going to happen for me," she said.

Then there's Seth Reams, who lost his job as a concierge in December 2008. He took an energetic approach to his job hunt, circulating his résumé to more than three hundred potential employers. But when he got no bites, Reams told KOMO Newsradio in Seattle, he felt useless, "like I wasn't a member of society anymore, like I wasn't contributing to [my] household anymore." Frustrated, he and his girlfriend, Michelle King, who worked as an assistant administrator analyst at a health insurance company, brainstormed ways for him to stay productive during his job search. Together, they came up with We've Got Time to Help, an online platform for locals who have extra time—generally people who were laid off—and want to contribute to the community in Portland, Oregon, where Reams and King live. For the blog's first project, Reams helped a single pregnant woman, who also cared for her three siblings, move furniture into her home. More projects soon followed: painting a room in a battered-women's shelter, teaching refugees how to drive, helping a needy family repair the roof on their home. Within sixteen months of the site's launch in January 2009, We've Got Time to Help assembled more than a hundred volunteers, who've assisted hundreds of struggling locals.

"People call us with tales of hunger, home loss, job loss, personal loss, and myriad difficulties," Reams and King wrote on their blog in May 2010. "But, most still have hope. Hope that things will change. Hope that times will get better. Hope that their situation will get better. Hope that someone still cares. And if someone calls us that seems to have lost their hope, we do our best to give them a little. We tell them that we will do everything in our power to help them. We will not walk away from them. We will stand by them in their darkest hour."

"The ultimate measure of a man or woman," said Martin

Luther King, "is not where he stands in moments of comfort and convenience, but where he stands at times of challenge and controversy."

LESSONS FROM THE FINANCIAL FOXHOLE

After spending months embedded with a thirty-man platoon in Afghanistan's remote Korengal Valley, Sebastian Junger, who wrote *War* based on the experience, says that he was struck by how, after being put through "the worst experience possible," soldiers often miss it upon returning home. It's not because they are adrenaline junkies, he says. They are addicted to the brotherly love. "Every guy in that platoon was necessary to everyone else and that necessariness, I think, is actually way more addictive than adrenaline is," says Junger. "You have an unshakable meaning in a small group that you can't duplicate in a society."

We actually *can* duplicate "unshakable meaning" and "necessariness" outside the battlefield. Indeed, we have to. In times of mortal danger, soldiers unconsciously create a sense of purpose and community and kinship. Right now, the perils we are facing here at home are not as tangible and deadly as those faced by our soldiers in Afghanistan. Nobody is shooting at us—and I don't mean to draw an equivalency to the lethal threats our men and women in uniform are bravely facing every day. But twenty-six million people are unemployed or underemployed, and over 4 percent of U.S. workers have been unemployed for more than six months—nearly twice the percentage it was back in 1983. Forty-six percent of the unemployed have been out of work for over six months; 23 percent have been unemployed for a year or more.

And more and more people are entering the ranks of "the 99ers"—those who have been unemployed for ninety-nine weeks, after which all unemployment benefits end. Since Congress has been unwilling to extend benefits beyond that point, by the end of 2010 over a million people will likely have exhausted all available benefits. Of course, a third of America's unemployed never receive any financial support when they lose their jobs; they're ineligible to receive unemployment benefits.

Making matters worse, there is a growing—and disturbing—trend among some employers: job listings that explicitly ban unemployed workers from applying, with lines like "No unemployed candidates will be considered at all," "Must be currently employed," and "Client will not consider/interview anyone NOT currently employed regardless of reason."

"In the current economy, where millions of people have lost their jobs through absolutely no fault of their own, I find it beyond unconscionable that any employer would not consider unemployed workers for current job openings," Judy Conti, federal advocacy coordinator for the National Employment Law Project, told the Huffington Post. "Increasingly, politicians and policy makers are trying to blame the unemployed for their condition, and to see this shameful propaganda trickle down to hiring decisions is truly sad and despicable."

Make no mistake: Though it's not war, it is financial warfare—and there's an enemy out there that does not wish you well. The bad guys are not firing bullets; they are setting financial traps. Foreclosures continue to surge. Health-care costs are going to continue to skyrocket—even for the insured. And long-term unemployment is going to be a fact of life for the foreseeable future.

The consequences can be far-reaching: A study by researchers at Yale found that "high unemployment rates increase mortality and low unemployment decreases mortality and increases the sense of well being in a community." According to M. Harvey Brenner, one of the study's authors, economic growth is the single biggest factor in life expectancy. "Employment is the essential element of social status and it establishes a person as a contributing member of society and also has very important implications for self-esteem," he says. "When that is taken away, people become susceptible to depression, cardiovascular disease, AIDS and many other illnesses that increase mortality."

So how can we protect ourselves and those close to us? How can we re-create the sense of "unshakable meaning" and "necessariness" Junger describes? How can we create our own bands of brothers—and sisters—in communities all across the country that will give us that sense of purpose and necessariness, and allow us to face down these threats?

The truth is, we are hardwired to seek out unshakable meaning. The longing for necessariness is in our DNA. Fifteen years ago, I wrote a book—*The Fourth Instinct*—about the part of ourselves that compels us all to go beyond our impulses for survival, sex, and power, and drives us to expand the boundaries of our caring beyond our solitary selves to include the world around us: "The call to community is not a hollow protestation of universal brotherhood. It is the call of our Fourth Instinct to make another's pain our own, to expand into our true self through giving. This is not the cold, abstract giving to humanity in general and to no human being in particular. It is concrete, intimate, tangible."

This is what the soldiers Junger wrote about were missing when they left the battlefield. And we can create it in our own lives . . . if we choose to. We must, because it's difficult to face the perils of our new economic landscape alone. Those of us who are under less of a threat need to reach out to those who have already been ensnared. When soldiers talk about being in a foxhole, it's always about who they are in the foxhole with—it's not a place you want to be by yourself. There's not just strength in numbers—there's purpose and meaning if we reach out and connect.

As Pablo Neruda said, "To feel the intimacy of brothers is a marvelous thing in life. To feel the love of people whom we love is a fire that feeds our life. But to feel the affection that comes from those whom we do not know, from those unknown to us, who are watching over our sleep and solitude, over our dangers and weaknesses—that is something still greater and more beautiful because it widens out the boundaries of our being, and unites all living things."

THOMAS JEFFERSON WASN'T SUGGESTING WE PURSUE HAPPY HOURS OR HAPPY MEALS

From the beginning, America has been dedicated to "Life, Liberty, and the pursuit of Happiness." But the signers of the Declaration of Independence assumed that some truths did not have to be proven; they were, to borrow a phrase, self-evident. It was self-evident, for example, that the happiness that was to be pursued was not the buzz of a shopping spree high. It was the happiness of the book of Proverbs: "Happy is he that has mercy on the poor." It was the happiness that comes from feeling good by doing good.

But, in a spiritual fire sale, too often over the past fifty years, happiness has been reduced to instant gratification. We search for "happy hours" that leave us stumbling through life; we devour "Happy Meals" that barely nourish the body. We buy into ads that tell us that there is a pill for every ill and that happiness is just a tablet away.

Faced with hard times, more and more Americans are now choosing to redefine the pursuit of happiness in ways much closer to the original Jeffersonian concept. The widening holes in America's social safety net make a commitment to service even more urgent. We've seen the American people rise to the call of service time and again in times of national tragedy—witness the outpouring of money and volunteerism in the wake of disasters such as Hurricane Katrina, the earthquake in Haiti, or the 9/11 attacks. After 9/11, Americans showed they were eager to work for the common good, to be called to that higher purpose. It was the best of times amid the worst of times.

President Obama doesn't need to convince the American people of the value of service; his challenge is finding a way to direct that national impulse into an ongoing effort to deal with the dark days we find ourselves in. He's got the right words: "When you serve," he said during a commencement speech at Notre Dame, "it doesn't just improve your community, it makes you a part of your community. It breaks down walls. It fosters cooperation. And when that happens—when people set aside their differences, even for a moment, to work in common effort toward a common goal; when they struggle together, and sacrifice together, and learn from one another—then all things are possible."

But it is going to take more than soaring rhetoric. Every president pays lip service to service. In the immediate aftermath of 9/11, President Bush declared, "We have much to do, and much to ask of the American people." A month later he echoed that theme, saying simply: "America is sacrifice." Of course, the sum total of his idea of sacrifice turned out to be shopping, going to Disney World, and offering tax cuts to the wealthiest Americans.

And President Obama has yet to turn his words into action and follow through on his promise to emulate FDR's Civilian Conservation Corps, JFK's Peace Corps, and LBJ's Volunteers in Service to America (VISTA). The role that service can—and must—play in addressing the urgent needs our country faces is all the more important among the nation's young people who were so galvanized by the '08 campaign, but who will now find it increasingly hard to get a job or to afford to stay in school.

And the demand among young people is growing. In 2009, for example, Teach for America received 35,000 applications for 4,100 positions. In 2008, 75,000 AmeriCorps members mobilized and led 2.2 million community volunteers. The Serve America Act, introduced by Ted Kennedy and Orrin Hatch, will increase the number of full-time service positions (based on the AmeriCorps model) from 75,000 to 250,000. These jobs can have an exponential impact on the recruitment of volunteers.

Among our senior citizens, the payoff from service has also been remarkable. Approximately 280,000 special needs children were mentored by 30,000 Senior Corps "Foster Grandparents" in 2007. Eighty-one percent of the children helped by the Foster Grandparents program showed improved academic performance, 90 percent showed improved self-image, and 59 percent reported a reduction in risky behavior. And students working with an Experience Corps tutor showed a 60 percent improvement in reading skills over students who were not in the program. These volunteers use their skills to help others even while they're dealing with their own harsh economic realities.

"FIND YOUR OWN CALCUTTA"

When people used to offer to join Mother Teresa in her "wonderful work in Calcutta," she would often respond: "Find your own Calcutta." That is, care for those in need where you are. Thousands are doing this—finding their own Calcuttas—all across America.

Geoffrey Canada provides a template of how to do it. Ever since he returned to Harlem with a master's from Harvard and a third-degree black belt, he's been fighting a block-by-block and child-by-child battle against poverty, drugs, gangs, and indifference. Through the Harlem Children's Zone, he's turned around lives while reminding America that we have, in too many ways, and in too many places, failed our children.

The nonprofit serves a ninety-seven-block section of Harlem, providing the guidance and personal support that the children there have been missing. Visiting his projects is like going from one healing outpost to another, including a baby college (where the parents of infants are taught the value of reading to their children and of avoiding corporal punishment), a technology center, and an employment center.

A front-line soldier in the battle to save our children, Canada says, "The problem cannot be solved from afar with a media campaign or other safe solutions operating from a distance. The only way we're going to make a difference is placing well-trained and caring adults in the middle of what can only be called free-fire zones in our poorest communities."

In 2004, he launched the Promise Academy, the Children's Zone's own charter school. As reported by *Metro*, "In 2008, 97 percent of its eighth-graders scored at or above grade level, compared to only 46 percent of students in area public schools."

Canada summed up his "If not us, who? If not now, when?" approach in a poem he wrote in response to Davis Guggenheim's documentary on the failure of America's schools. He titled it "Waiting for Whom?":

If you asked me where it all went wrong,
And why we find today
That certain children's lives are ruined,
Broken dreams just tossed away,
I would tell you a tale so sad to hear
You might not believe it's true.
It's true, it's sad, and terribly bad.
The question is: what will you do?

It seems that it is not a crime,
And not against the law,
To miseducate millions of children
As long as they are poor.
You can fail them year after year,
And no one will give a damn.
That is, no one except you and me,
But we're quiet and injustice stands.

In fact, adults seem to have the right
To get paid while doing harm.
Even if they have slapped and cursed,
And pinched those little arms.
And some do worse, lest we forget,
Those who punch, demean, molest,

And they get to stay, can't be sent away.
Who supports this system anyway?

I ask who created this broken system,
Where for decades poor children have failed?
And why can't we change such dysfunction
Where for most, failed schools lead to jail?
And who in the hell defends such a thing,
Where the evidence is clear and true?
I, for one, have said enough is enough,
I hope I can count on you too.

Our children are waiting for someone,
A hero who's ready to fight.
To end decades of injustice,
To know and to do what is right.
And what I am saying is shocking,
But what I am saying is true.
The hero children are waiting for,
That hero, it's me and it's you.

Susie Buffett offers another shining example of finding your own Calcutta. Operating in her own backyard of Omaha, Nebraska, the daughter of Warren Buffett has dedicated her Sherwood Foundation—named after the forest of Robin Hood folklore—to caring for those in need in her hometown. Working out of the same building that has housed her father's company, Berkshire Hathaway, for more than forty years, Susie Buffett has launched multiple initiatives that have had a profound impact on the community. Among them are: neighborhood redevelopment, after-school programming, financial literacy, and a gang-violence intervention program that brings former gang members back to the street to talk to current gang members. It also works with schools to prevent and address school-based violence and gang recruitment.

Susie Buffett started working in her own community as a young girl. "My mother and I," she remembers, "were stopped by the police more than once for 'driving while white' in the housing projects. I was a Head Start volunteer in the sixties (my mother started Head Start in Omaha in our living room—it was the second site in the country), and I taught sewing in the housing projects when I was in high school."

Buffett's foundation is also working closely with Omaha's public schools: updating book collections and improving online databases at every school library in the district; keeping school libraries open during the summer; providing grants for students in grades seven to nine to enroll in summer school; and making it possible for many math and English teachers to augment their teaching skills at conferences and summer seminars.

The Buffett Early Childhood Fund focuses on ensuring "a more level playing field for all children as they enter kindergarten" with the goal of redefining education in America to encompass the first five years of life. "When my parents set up the three foundations for my brothers and me in late 1999, I decided that I wanted to work with the Omaha Public Schools," Buffett told me. "I went to see Dr. Mackiel, the superintendent, and told him that I had this money and wanted him to think about what we could do with it. He said, 'Don't give it to me. Figure out who is doing the best work in early childhood and do something for the poorest kids so that they enter kindergarten prepared.'" The result, Building Bright Futures, is a nonprofit seeking to "improve academic performance, raise graduation rates, increase civic and community responsibility and ensure that all students are prepared for post-secondary education by developing partnerships with existing providers and creating new evidence-based programs to develop a comprehensive, community-based network of services."

As we struggle to return our economy to full capacity, we also need to make sure that our communities are operating at full capacity: Our full capacity of giving. Our full capacity of service. Our full capacity of compassion.

EMPATHY FOR THE (BE)DEVIL(ED)

In *The Empathic Civilization*, Jeremy Rifkin describes empathy as "the willingness of an observer to become part of another's experience, to share the feeling of that experience."

Unlike sympathy, which is passive, empathy is active, engaged, and dynamic. New scientific data tells us that empathy is not a quaint behavior trotted out during intermittent visits to a food bank or during a heart-tugging telethon. Instead, it lies at the very core of human existence.

Since the economic crisis, the role empathy plays in our lives has only grown more important. In fact, in this time of economic hardship, political instability, and rapid technological change, empathy is the one quality we most need if we're going to flourish in the twenty-first century. "An individual," said Martin Luther King, "has not started living until he can rise above the narrow confines of his own individualistic concerns to the broader concerns of all humanity."

In the fall of 2009, the Huffington Post published a story

about Monique Zimmerman-Stein, a mother who suffers from Stickler syndrome, a rare genetic condition that leads to blindness. Though almost completely blind, she abandoned the treatments that might have saved her eyesight so that she and her husband could afford medical care for their two daughters, who were also diagnosed with the disorder. The regular injections Monique needed cost $380 each, even after the family's insurance paid its share, and she and her husband were already drowning in medical debt. Sacrificing her own treatment, she said, was "a choice any mom would make."

The Stein family's story struck a chord with readers, many of whom wrote asking how they could help. In response, we designed a fund-raising widget, providing readers who wanted to contribute to the Steins a quick and easy way to give. Within a week, we had raised more than $30,000 to help the family pay down its medical bills. "I was flabbergasted, overwhelmed, overcome," Monique said of the donations. "So many people are having a hard time. The fact that they would give something to us is an amazing gift." Gary, Monique's husband, echoed her gratitude. "We'll do whatever we can to pay it forward," he said.

"We are on the cusp of an epic shift," writes Jeremy Rifkin. "The Age of Reason is being eclipsed by the Age of Empathy." He makes the case that as technology is increasingly connecting us to one another, we need to understand what the goal of all this connectivity is. "Seven billion individual connections," he says, "absent any overall unifying purpose, seem a colossal waste of human energy."

That sense of purpose, which must include expanding the narrow confines of our own concerns, can have powerful social implications. Dr. King showed that for a social movement to become broad-based enough to produce real change, it must be fueled by empathy.

In his 1963 work "Letter from a Birmingham Jail," King lamented the failure of "the white moderate" to "understand that the present tension in the South is a necessary phase of the transition from an obnoxious negative peace, in which the Negro passively accepted his unjust plight, to a substantive and positive peace, in which all men will respect the dignity and worth of human personality."

King understood that he needed to tap into the empathy of whole constituencies that would not themselves be the direct beneficiaries of the civil rights movement. He set about making a compelling moral case by forcing many in white America to see for the first time that millions of their fellow citizens were effectively living in a different world—a different America—than they were. He created pathways for empathy and then used them to create a better country for everybody.

Conservative commentator Tony Blankley once remarked—only half-seriously—that "evolution, cruel as it is, determined that empathy is not a survival trait." If you've been paying attention to the actions of many of our CEOs—from those running big banks to those running Massey Energy and BP—you would be inclined to agree. But if we are to continue as a thriving democratic society, we will need all the empathy we can get. Without it, we'll never be able to create the kind of national consensus required to tackle the enormous problems that face us, rescue the middle class, and stop our descent into Third World America.

As America's Misery Index soars, so must our Empathy Index.

THE EMPATHY INDEX: FROM THE LOCAL TO THE VIRTUAL

"We have to lean on one another and look out for one another and love one another and pray for one another," Barack Obama said when he delivered the eulogy for the fallen West Virginia miners in April 2010. This is a call that transcends left and right political divisions.

David Brooks has written about the need to replace our "atomized, segmented society" with a society "oriented around relationships and associations"—an approach advocated by conservative British writer Phillip Blond in his book *Red Tory*. "Volunteering, especially among professional classes and the young," Blond wrote, "has doubled in recent months"—proof, he suggests, that "the wish to make a difference is a common and rising aspiration."

Those who are working to address the devastation in their own communities are willing to experiment, try many things, fail, and try again, the way you do when you really care. And there is extraordinary creativity in local philanthropy.

In 2002 in San Francisco's Mission district, author Dave Eggers and teacher Nínive Calegari opened 826 Valencia, a writing lab that provides free tutoring to local kids and has attracted hundreds of skilled volunteer instructors. Offering drop-in, one-on-one instruction with a focus on the creative and fun aspects of writing, as well as other learning programs including field trips and in-class learning, 826 Valencia has since fanned out across the country, opening chapters—and enlisting volunteer tutors—in Los Angeles, New York City, Michigan, Seattle, Chicago, and Boston.

In Brooklyn, New York, FEAST (Funding Emerging Art

with Sustainable Tactics) hosts volunteer-prepared dinner parties in a church basement, where locals are invited to pitch ideas for community art and improvement projects. The 250+ dinner-goers pay ten to twenty dollars to attend the fetes, where they feast on local food, listen to live music, socialize, and vote on their favorite proposals. At the end of the dinner, FEAST organizers present the winner with the prize money, raised from that night's admission proceeds, for the implementation of the project.

Matthew Bishop, U.S. business editor for the *Economist,* in his book *Philanthrocapitalism,* explored how this moment of crisis for capitalism and philanthropy could be used to transform both—how capitalism could be imbued with a social mission, and philanthropy could be reinvigorated with the best practices of capitalism. And in seeking to blend the efficiency of enterprise with the benefits of philanthropy, the burgeoning social entrepreneurship movement does precisely that. Social entrepreneurs pinpoint social problems and, rather than waiting for government action, apply market principles to solve them in original ways. Supported by investment funds from organizations such as Echoing Green, Ashoka, and Investors' Circle, trailblazing social ventures are reenvisioning the way social change happens, not only abroad, but here at home, too.

Providing microcredit to small businesses is an innovation for which Muhammad Yunus won the Nobel Peace Prize in 2006. In 2008, Yunus's Grameen Bank opened a branch in New York. In 2010 it opened a branch in Omaha, Nebraska. The Grameen Bank's slogan: "Banking for the unbanked." Hoping to serve one million American entrepreneurs, Grameen America plans to expand into more than fifty cities across the country, including Washington, D.C., and San Francisco. A practice most closely associated with helping struggling Third World countries has now arrived in America. By February 2010, the New York branch had extended loans to 2,500 clients, mostly women. The average loan amount is $1,500 (no collateral necessary) and more than 99 percent of the recipients make their payments on time.

Grameen Bank is not the only organization committed to providing microcredit to small businesses here at home. Since 1991, ACCION USA has lent over $119 million, in the form of more than 19,500 small-business loans, to low- and moderate-income entrepreneurs. Luis Zapeda Alvarez, for example, who was once homeless and out of work, now runs his own business delivering baked goods to New York City restaurants and delis—in large part due to the assistance he received. After banks refused to lend him start-up capital, Alvarez approached ACCION and borrowed enough money to buy the delivery truck he needed to get his business off the ground. When his truck needed new insulation, ACCION USA helped him secure a $5,600 loan to make the improvements. Alvarez's business has expanded to three daily delivery routes—he's now so busy that he had to hire a part-time employee—and his success as an entrepreneur has helped cement his relationship with his children.

Another New Yorker, Lyn Genet Recitas, opened Neighborhood Holistic, a yoga studio and spa, in Harlem with the help of a microloan from ACCION USA. Within a year, the studio was profitable, and Recitas expanded her venture, bringing on twelve part-time employees and providing yoga scholarships for low-income community members.

Some of the most exciting social advocacy and "citizen philanthropy" is happening on the Web. DonorsChoose.org, for example, invites public school teachers from around the country to post funding proposals for classroom needs. Users browse the listings—for things such as notebooks and pencils, LCD projectors for math instruction, or mirrors so that art students can practice drawing self-portraits—and donate however much they'd like to their chosen projects. By May 2010, just a decade after the site was started by Bronx high school social studies teacher Charles Best, DonorsChoose.org had raised over $52 million across more than 130,000 different proposals.

In Connecticut, Web developer Ben Berkowitz has launched SeeClickFix.com, which invites users to post nonemergency problems in their neighborhoods, such as a broken streetlamp or a potholed road. Other community members are encouraged to chime in with solutions; sometimes neighbors reply with fixes within minutes. With SeeClickFix.com, citizens can more rapidly identify and repair local problems to improve their neighborhoods and, by extension, the entire country.

Using the backbone of social networking to help people connect and find service opportunities that fit their specific abilities and aspirations is the idea behind All for Good, launched in 2009 by Google engineers (using the company's "20 percent" philosophy that allows employees to spend one day a week working on passion projects). The goal was to apply the power of the search engine to service and volunteerism and put social media—including Facebook Connect and Google Friend Connect—at the service of service. Among the initiatives is Cities of Service, which makes it easier for mayors across America to use the Web to promote volunteerism opportunities in their communities.

Social media sites are also being used to create a sense of

community to see us through these dark economic times and help us transcend feelings of being victimized and powerless. At sites such as Recessionwire.com, LayoffSupportNetwork .com, LayoffSpace.com, HowIGotLaidOff.com, and The 405Club.com, job seekers share tips about finding work and getting by, and safely voice anxieties and fears about the future. Others have reported landing jobs by using Web stalwarts such as Facebook and Twitter to informally network with friends and associates.

When television journalist Andrea McCarren was abruptly laid off from her job at ABC affiliate WJLA-TV in Washington, D.C., her first move was to update her Facebook status. "Andrea McCarren was just laid off, and is enormously grateful for her 26-year run in television news," she wrote. Her friends and former colleagues were immediately made aware of her job loss—and they responded with an outpouring of support, spreading the news via Twitter. "Social media, I learned that day, was like a wildfire, spreading rapidly across the Internet, with little possibility of containment," McCarren wrote in a March 2010 piece for *Nieman Reports*. "My Facebook posting immediately led to a flood of phone calls, condolence e-mails, and job leads. A Facebook friend I'd met in person just one time introduced me to a high-profile CEO and entrepreneur who flew me to California for a job interview the next week. Former colleagues and even several interns I'd mentored in the past spoke to their bosses and paved my way into their news operations within days. No one was hiring but it boosted my spirits to make so many contacts." McCarren and her husband, "awed by the compassion and kindness of Americans who wrote," were inspired to launch Project

Bounce Back, an online community centered around stories of resilience in times of economic hardship. The project eventually sent the McCarrens and their three children on the road, traveling around the country and chronicling tales of American hope and vitality.

Taken together, these efforts, and thousands of others like them, are helping turn the country around. And it would be great if more of America's super affluent—the wealthiest 1 percent, who hold 35 percent of the nation's wealth—also tapped into their reserves of empathy and acted on Andrew Carnegie's assertion that "he who dies rich dies disgraced."

That's a sentiment that Bill Gates and Warren Buffett clearly share. The pair has launched The Giving Pledge, a campaign to convince the world's billionaires to give at least 50 percent of their money away. Buffett has promised to give 99 percent of his roughly $46 billion to charity; Gates has made a similar pledge. And others are starting to join in, including Michael Bloomberg, who, echoing Carnegie, says: "I am a big believer in giving it all away and have always said that the best financial planning ends with bouncing the check to the undertaker." If The Giving Pledge catches on, Gates and Buffett believe they can generate $600 billion for philanthropic causes.

At the tail end of the last Gilded Age, the opulently rich—men like Andrew Carnegie, Cornelius Vanderbilt, John D. Rockefeller and Andrew W. Mellon—led a nationwide wave of philanthropy. If Buffett and Gates are successful, as our own Gilded Age nears its end, a second great wave of giving is coming. And it couldn't be more timely.

HOPE 2.0

The 2008 election was all about "hope." But just hoping that our leaders in Washington will somehow miraculously start doing the right thing—especially when they are locked inside a system with overwhelmingly powerful incentives to do the wrong thing—simply won't cut it.

What we need is Hope 2.0: the realization that our system is too broken to be fixed by politicians operating within the status quo, however well intentioned. Change is going to have to come from outside Washington. But no fundamental political change can be accomplished without a movement demanding it. As Frederick Douglass put it, "Power concedes nothing without a demand; it never did and it never will."

The perfect example of this came in March 1965. In an effort to push for voting rights legislation, Martin Luther King met with President Lyndon Johnson. But LBJ was convinced he didn't have the votes needed for passage. King left the meeting certain that the votes would never be found in Washington until he turned up the heat in the rest of the country. And that's what he set out to do: produce the votes in Washington by getting the people to demand it. Two days later, the "Bloody Sunday" confrontation in Selma—in which marchers were met with tear gas and truncheons—captured the conscience of the nation. Five months after that, on August 6, LBJ signed the National Voting Rights Act into law, with King and Rosa Parks by his side.

At that March meeting, LBJ didn't think the conditions for change were there. So King went out and changed the conditions.

Similarly, before the start of WWII, legendary labor leader

A. Philip Randolph, president of the Brotherhood of Sleeping Car Porters, lobbied FDR to promote equal employment opportunities in the defense industry. Roosevelt was sympathetic but made no promises. Randolph responded by taking his cause to the American people, organizing a massive march on Washington. Concerned about the impact the march would have on the country's wartime morale, Roosevelt got Randolph to call it off by issuing an executive order banning discrimination in defense industries and creating the Fair Employment Practices Committee to watch over hiring practices.

In recent decades the system has gotten only more rigged and the powers that be more entrenched. The ability of special interests to thwart meaningful change has never been stronger. And the reason we are given—time after time after time—for why we can't have fundamental reform? What else: The votes just aren't there!

That's where Hope 2.0 comes in. If the votes aren't there, the people need to create them. If politicians put their finger in the wind to see which way it's blowing before deciding what to do, well, let's change the direction of the wind.

In the early days of the financial crisis, as I looked at the tone-deaf response of Wall Street, including former Merrill Lynch CEO John Thain and his now infamous $1.2 million office redecoration in the midst of the economic collapse, I thought of Thain and his Big Banking brethren as the Marie Antoinettes of the meltdown. They just didn't get it.

Little did I realize just how small-scale Thain's outrages would seem and how much worse things would get in the ensuing months. Goldman Sachs's Lloyd "Doing God's Work" Blankfein, BP's Tony "I'd Like My Life Back" Hayward, and their fellow too-big-to-fail CEOs—with their utter cluelessness about the public's anger over what they've done and continue to do—take "not getting it" to a whole other level.

Luckily for them, society has evolved, and we express our anger differently than we did in Marie Antoinette's day. "Off with their bonuses" is a lot less painful than "off with their heads." But the question is, can the American people's righteous—and entirely justifiable—rage be productively channeled to produce a real movement for reform, or will it be hijacked by dangerous demagogues, with whatever is left over co-opted by agents of the status quo in Washington?

In 2004, hope was ignited by an unknown state senator standing up and proclaiming that we are not blue states and red states, but one people who can only solve our problems together.

In 2008, hope was about crossing our fingers and electing leaders who we thought would enact the change we so desperately need.

Hope 2.0 is about creating the conditions that give them no other choice.

THE CHOICE IS OURS

Clearly, we all have a lot of work to do—both on ourselves and on our country. The good news: Real change, fundamental change, is possible, but only if we recognize that democracy is not a spectator sport—and get busy.

President Obama has said that we find ourselves at "a rare inflection point in history where the size and scope of the challenges before us require that we remake our world to renew its promise."

So, as we stand at this inflection point and gradually move

from what Jonas Salk called Epoch A (our survival-focused past) to Epoch B (our meaning-focused future), we have to ask ourselves what this remade world will look like.

Will it be a place where economic opportunity is once again real for everyone, not just the economic elite?

Will it be a place where greed and selfishness are no longer rewarded and "the least among us" are given a helping hand, rather than the back of it?

Will it be a place where bridges are fixed before they collapse, and students aren't allowed to founder in failing schools?

Will it be a place where the public interest once again trumps the special interests, and public policy is no longer auctioned off to the highest bidder?

Will it be a place where transparency reigns and backroom deals are banished from the halls of power?

Will it be a place where Main Street replaces Wall Street as the center of the economic universe?

Will it be a place where the middle class no longer has a bull's-eye on its back and the American Dream is more than just a hallucination or a distant memory seen only in our nation's rearview mirror?

The choices we make—both as individuals and as a society—will determine whether America becomes a Third World country or the "more perfect union" our founding fathers envisioned.

The moment to act is now. Inflection points in history don't come along very often.

NEXT STEPS?
CLICK HERE

*Few will have the greatness to bend history itself, but each
of us can work to change a small portion of events and in
the total of all those acts will be written the history of this
generation.*

ROBERT F. KENNEDY

So often, our desire to take action gets derailed by our uncertainty over exactly what action to take, and how to best make a difference. To bridge the gap between intention and involvement, we've created a section on the Huffington Post where you can find out more about what *you* can do to help make sure we never find ourselves living in Third World America. Go to www .huffingtonpost.com/ThirdWorldAmerica—and get involved.

ACKNOWLEDGMENTS

After finishing my twelfth book, I asked my daughters and close friends to do an intervention if I ever decided to write another one. "No more books" I promised them—and myself. No more juggling the demands of writing a book and the demands of HuffPost (now a tireless and rambunctious five-year-old that never takes a nap).

And then Richard Pine, my wonderful agent and friend, called. "Roger Scholl wants you to write a book for Crown about—" Politely but firmly, I stopped him. "I don't want to know," I said. "I don't want to be tempted." A few days later he called back and before I could stop him he told me that Roger had been reading what I'd been writing about the decline of America's middle class and wanted me to write a book about it. The decline of the middle class was, in fact, a subject I had become obsessed with, both in my own writing and in HuffPost's coverage of the economic crisis. We had even dedicated one of our reporters, Arthur Delaney, to the beat—putting flesh and blood on the gloomy statistics. We considered calling him our "economic suffering correspondent" but that sounded too lugubrious, so we settled on our "economic impact correspondent."

So I went from "never again" to "how soon could we bring it out?" As for that intervention thing, I just didn't tell my daughters or my friends what I was doing until I'd already finished the first draft. So, first of all, thank you to Michael Palgon, the deputy publisher at the Crown Publishing Group, and Editorial Director Roger Scholl for the idea—and to Michael Palgon for the book title. And thanks for all of Roger's brilliant editing along the way.

And thank you to Katie Flynn, Nour Akkad, Anna Almendrala, Alex Amend, and Michael Spies for all their help with research, fact-checking, and source notes. My gratitude goes to HuffPost's editor Roy Sekoff, who read the first draft and vastly improved it, to Stephen Sherrill, for all his great editorial suggestions, and to Grace Kiser and Kerstin Picht, who brought extraordinary dedication and commitment both to the subject and to the process of getting the book to press.

My gratitude also goes to Nick Penniman, Dan Froomkin, Adam Rose, Ryan Grim, Shahien Nasiripour, Marcus Baram, Alex Leo, Ryan McCarthy, Brian Sirgutz, and Mario Ruiz, who read the galleys and offered many improvements and suggestions.

Very special thanks to Brenda Carter, Johnny Parker, Matt Stagliano, Linda D. Wilson, Dean Blackburn, Ron Bednar, Mary McCurnin, Kimberly Rios, Faye Harris, Ricky Macoy, Heather Tanner, Amy Brisendine, Rajiv Narayan, Janet H., Patty C., Henry Chalian, Jim Laman, Troy Renault, Rebecca Admire, Monique Zimmerman-Stein, Gary Stein, H. Lee Grove, and Lesa Deason Crowe for sharing their stories of struggle and resilience.

Many thanks also to Jeff Swafford and Patty Elvey, who kept the rest of my life humming. And thanks to the great team at Crown, including Tricia Wygal, art director Whitney Cookman, who designed the powerful cover, and Rachel Rokicki in publicity and Meredith McGinnis in marketing, who were responsible for bringing the book to the world.

Finally, deep thanks to my daughters, Christina and Isabella, and my sister, Agapi—always an incredible source of love and support. This book is dedicated to the millions of middle-class Americans fighting to keep the American Dream alive.

NOTES

Preface

ix *The Italian journalist Luigi Barzini:* Luigi Barzini, *The Europeans* (New York: Penguin, 1983), 14, 234.

x *"America," Winston Churchill reportedly said:* William Antholis, "The Good, the Bad, and the Ugly: EU-U.S. Cooperation on Climate Change," 19 Jun. 2009, www.brookings.edu.

PART 1: THIRD WORLD AMERICA

4 *"The middle class has been . . .":* Barack Obama, remarks by the president and vice president at Middle Class Task Force Meeting, 25 Jan. 2010, www.whitehouse.gov.

4 *During the 2008 campaign:* David Plouffe, interviewed by the author in Washington, D.C., 31 Oct. 2009.

5 *According to Plouffe, Obama and his team:* David Plouffe, *The Audacity to Win* (New York: Viking, 2009), 9.

5 *Just how bad things have:* Elizabeth Warren, "America Without a Middle Class," 3 Dec. 2009, www.huffingtonpost.com.

6 *In April 2010, the shot heard:* Joshua Gallu and Christine Harper, "Goldman Sachs Sued by SEC for Fraud Tied to CDOs," 16 Apr. 2010, www.bloomberg.com.

9 *In November 2008, as the initial:* David Brooks, "The Formerly Middle Class," 18 Nov. 2010, www.nytimes.com.

9 *In a 2010 strategy paper:* "From Recession to Recovery to Renewal," 20 Apr. 2010, www.brookings.edu.

10 *At least forty-five states:* Center on Budget and Policy Priorities, "An Update on State Budget Cuts," 19 Apr. 2010, www.cbpp.org.

10 *According to a report by:* Ibid.

10 *America's states faced:* Center on Budget and Policy Priorities, "Recession Continues to Batter State Budgets; State Responses Could Slow Recovery," 25 Feb. 2010, www.cbpp.org.

10 *These are massive numbers:* Brady Dennis, "AIG Plans Millions More in Bonuses," 11 Jul. 2010, www.washingtonpost.com.

10 *$12.9 billion of which:* Christine Harper, "Taxpayers Help Goldman Reach Height of Profit in New Skyscraper," 21 Dec. 2008, www.bloomberg.com.

10 *Toss in the $45 billion:* Shahien Nasiripour, "Bank of America TARP Repayment Premature, Analyst Says," 4 Dec. 2010, www.huffingtonpost.com.

10 *and the $45 billion:* Malden Read, "Citigroup: TARP Loans Near $45 billion Mark," Associated Press, 12 May 2009.

11 *California is eliminating CalWORKS:* Judy Lin, "Schwarzenegger Lays Out Bleak California Budget," Associated Press, 14 May 2010.

11   *Minnesota has eliminated a program:* Center on Budget and Policy Priorities, "An Update on State Budget Cuts," 19 Apr. 2010, www.cbpp.org.

12   *Perhaps the reason can:* Center for Labor Market Studies, Northeastern University, "Labor Underutilization Problems of U.S. Workers Across Household Income Groups at the End of the Great Recession," Feb. 2010, www.clms.neu.edu.

13   *These numbers, according to:* Robert Frank, "High Unemployment? Not for the Affluent," 12 Feb. 2010, www.wsj.com.

13   *"These are the kinds . . .":* Bob Herbert, "The Worst of the Pain," 9 Feb. 2010, www.nytimes.com.

16   *In the last chapter of:* Michael Herr, *Dispatches,* 5th ed. (New York: Knopf, 2009), 201.

16   *And Tom Wolfe:* Tom Wolfe, "The Birth of 'The New Journalism': Eyewitness Report by Tom Wolfe," *New York* magazine, 14 Feb. 1972, 38.

16   *So, in 1845, he wrote:* Benjamin Disraeli, *Sybil, or the Two Nations* (London: Macmillan, 1895), 74.

17   *Forty years ago, top executives:* Kenneth Dodge, "Make CEOs Help the Little Guy," *Pittsburgh Post-Gazette,* 7 Feb. 2010, www.post-gazette.com.

18   *Between 2007 and 2008, more than:* Derek Douglas and Almas Sayeed, "An Ever Increasing Divide," Center for American Progress, 1 Sep. 2006, www.americanprogress.org.

18   *In 2005, households:* Ibid.

18   *In 2007, the top 10 percent:* Henry Blodget, "The Rich Get Richer and the Poor Get . . . Fired," 13 Aug. 2010, www.businessinsider.com.

18   *Between 2000 and 2008, the poverty rate:* "The Suburbanization of Poverty: Trends in Metropolitan America, 2000 to 2008," 20 Jan. 2010, www.brookings.edu.

19   *Almost one hundred million Americans:* Matt Miller, "The Upside of Downward Mobility," 29 Dec. 2010, www.money.cnn.com.

19   *The percentage of Americans:* Economic Mobility Project, "Getting Ahead or Losing Ground: Economic Mobility in America," Feb. 2010, www.economicmobility.org.

19   *If you were born:* Ibid.

19   *In a study of economic mobility:* Isabel Sawhill and John E. Morton, "Economic Mobility: Is the American Dream Alive and Well?" May 2007, www.economicmobility.org.

20   *Since the recession began:* Darlene Superville, "Obama: Jobs Bill Will Help Small Business Owners," 13 Mar. 2010, www.huffingtonpost.com.

20   *Over 2 million of those:* Christopher Rugaber, "Millions of Jobs That Were Cut Won't Likely Return," 13 May 2010, www.bostonglobe.com.

20   *We lost 1.2 million:* Diana Furchtgott-Roth, Irwin Stelzer, and John Weicher, "Hudson Institute Economic Report," 8 Jan. 2010, www.hudson.org.

20   *In 1950, manufacturing accounted:* Richard Florida, "How the Crash Will Reshape America," Mar. 2009, www.theatlantic.com.

20   *Indeed, one-third of all:* Richard McCormack, "The Plight of American Manufacturing," 21 Dec. 2009, www.prospect.org.

21   *According to Thomas Philippon:* Thomas Philippon, "The Future of the Financial Industry," 16 Oct. 2008, www.sternfinance.blogspot.com.

21   *As MIT professor Simon Johnson recounted:* Simon Johnson, "The Quiet Coup," May 2009, www.theatlantic.com.

21   *That's right—over 40:* Ibid.

21   *James Kwak, coauthor of:* James Kwak, "'13 Bankers' in 4 Pictures: Why Wall Street Profits Are Out of Whack," 15 Apr. 2010, www.huffingtonpost.com.

21   *According to New York Times columnist Paul Krugman:* Paul Krugman, "Don't Cry for Wall Street," 22 Apr. 2010, www.nytimes.com.

22   *But the data points:* Sandra Pianalto, Federal Reserve Bank of Cleveland, "Forecasting in Uncertain Times," 18 May 2010, www.clevelandfed.org.

23   *Her conclusion: "Many people . . .":* Ibid.

23 *At a D.C. jobs fair:* Laura Bassett, "D.C. Career Fair for Older Workers Attracts Thousands," 12 May 2010, www.huffingtonpost.com.

23 *According to* BusinessWeek: Mike Dorning, "College Grads Flood U.S. Labor Market with Diminished Prospects," 19 May 2010, www.businessweek.com.

24 *And many workers who have managed:* Laura Bassett, "Same Job, Less Pay: Employees Learn to Swallow Their Demotions," 7 May 2010, www.huffingtonpost.com.

24 *Adding insult to injury, a growing number:* Peter S. Goodman, "Cuts to Child Care Subsidy Thwart More Job Seekers," 23 May 2010, www.nytimes.com.

24 *And kids were left scrambling:* Heather Hollingsworth, "Cash-Strapped Districts Cutting Summer School," Associated Press, 23 May 2010.

24 *As the* Los Angeles Times's *Don Lee put it:* Don Lee, "Consumer Spending Trend Is a Shaky Foundation for Economic Recovery," 16 May 2010, www.latimes.com.

24 *According to the Federal Reserve:* Board of Governors of the Federal Reserve System, "H.8 Assets and Liabilities of Commercial Banks in the United States," 23 Jun. 2010, www.research.stlouisfed.org.

25 *Senator Sheldon Whitehouse's amendment:* "Senate Rejects Credit Card Interest Rate Measure," Associated Press, 19 May 2010.

25 *Or how about payday lending:* Gary Rivlin, "The Payday Lenders Confront Their Mortality," 17 May 2010, www.huffingtonpost.com.

25 *It was killed without a vote:* Kay Hagan, "Republicans Object to Considering Hagan Payday Lending Amendment," 18 May 2010, www.hagan.senate.gov.

25 *Then there is the Merkley-Levin amendment:* Simon Johnson, "Focus on This: Merkley-Levin Did Not Get a Vote," 21 May 2010, www.huffingtonpost.com.

26 *A recent study by Duha Tore Altindag and Naci H. Mocan:* Duha Tore Altindag and Naci H. Mocan, "Joblessness and Perceptions About the Effectiveness of Democracy," National Bureau of Economic Research, working paper no. 15994, May 2010, www.nber.org.

26 *especially since one out of every six:* Molly Line, "Job Hunt: Blue Collar Workers Struggle Most," 23 Mar. 2010, www.foxnews.com.

26 *Andrew Sum, director of the:* Ibid.

27 *Economist Jeff Madrick doesn't think so:* Jeff Madrick, "Should We Still Make Things?" 11 Mar. 2009, www.dissentmagazine.org.

27 *According to the Hackett Group:* Patrick Thibodeau, "Survey: One in Four IT Jobs Moving Offshore," 9 Dec. 2010, www.computerworld.com.

27 *Linda Levine of the Congressional Research Service:* Linda Levine, "Offshoring (a.k.a. Offshore Outsourcing) and Job Insecurity Among U.S. Workers," 2 May 2005, www.fpc.state.gov.

27 *And in a 2006 study:* Booz Allen Hamilton, "The Globalization of White-Collar Work: The Facts and Fallout of Next-Generation Offshoring," 2006, www.booz.com.

28 *Accenture now employs:* Julia Hanna, "How Many U.S. Jobs are 'Offshorable'?" Harvard Business School, 1 Dec. 2008, www.hbswk.hbs.edu.

28 *A June 2008 Harvard Business School study:* Ibid.

28 *Even more troubling:* Booz Allen Hamilton, "The Globalization of White-Collar Work: The Facts and Fallout of Next-Generation Offshoring," 2006, www.booz.com.

29 *"The financial sector," wrote Martin Wolf:* Martin Wolf, "The Challenge of Halting the Financial Doomsday Machine," 20 Apr. 2010, www.ft.com.

29 *By 2020, interest alone:* David Brooks, "The Ecstasy of Fiscal Policy," 1 Apr. 2010, www.nytimes.com.

29 *That same year, five segments:* Douglas W. Elmendorf, "The Economic and Budget Outlook," Congressional Budget Office, 13 May 2010, www.cbo.gov.

30 *A recent report:* John Mauldin, "The Future of the Global Public Debt Explosion," 2 May 2010, www.businessinsider.com.

30   *For instance, in Greece:* Bank for International Settlements, "The Future of Public Debt Prospects and Implications," Mar. 2010, www.bis.org.

30   *"While fiscal problems need . . .":* Ibid.

30   *As Mauldin says:* John Mauldin, "The Future of the Global Public Debt Explosion," 2 May 2010, www.businessinsider.com.

31   *Mauldin goes on to:* Ibid.

31   *Princeton economist Alan Blinder:* Alan Blinder, "Opening Remarks and Consequences of Current Fiscal Trajectory," 8 Oct. 2009, www.americanprogress.org.

32   *Historian Arnold Toynbee believed that:* Arnold Toynbee, *A Study of History* (New York: Oxford University Press, 1946), 273.

32   *Partisanship pop quiz time:* Dwight D. Eisenhower, "The Chance for Peace," speech before the American Society of Newspaper Editors, 16 Apr. 1953, www.eisenhower.archives .gov.

32   *No, it was that unrepentant lefty:* "Civilian Unemployment Rate," Federal Reserve Bank of St. Louis, 4 Jun. 2010, www.research.stlouisfed.org.

32   *Yet today, while America's economy:* Bureau of Labor Statistics, "Alternative Measures of Labor Underutilization," Table A-15, 7 May 2010, www.bls.gov.

32   *We hear endless talk:* Anne Gearan and Anne Flaherty, "War Cost: Obama Wants $33 Billion More for Afghanistan, Iraq," 12 Jan. 2010, www.huffingtonpost.com.

33   *Indeed, during his State of the Union speech:* Jackie Calmes, "Obama to Seek Spending Freeze to Trim Deficits," 25 Jan. 2010, www.nytimes.com.

33   *According to defense analyst Lawrence Korb:* Lawrence Korb, "Spending Freeze Must Include Defense," 27 Jan. 2010, www.thinkprogress.org.

33   *In fact, as Katherine McIntire Peters reported:* Katherine McIntire Peters, "Defense Budget Portends Difficult Trade-offs," 12 Aug. 2009, www.govexec.com.

33   *To quote then Illinois:* Barack Obama, "Against Going to War with Iraq," 2 Oct. 2002, www.barackobama.com.

33   *fewer than one hundred members:* Joshua Partlow, "In Afghanistan, Taliban Surpasses Al-Qaeda," 11 Nov. 2009, www.washingtonpost.com.

34   *According to the Los Angeles Times:* Doyle McManus, "The Kandahar Gambit," 4 Apr. 2010, www.latimes.com.

34   *Berkeley professor Ananya Roy:* Robert Greenwald, "Rethink Afghanistan," video, 21 Apr. 2010, www.huffingtonpost.com.

34   *And Representative Barney Frank:* Diane Francis, "Knife Military Spending: Kill the Deficit," 4 Feb. 2010, www.huffingtonpost.com.

35   *For example, according to the NPP:* National Priorities Project, "Federal Budget Trade-Offs," www.nationalpriorities.org.

PART 2: NIGHTMARE ON MAIN STREET

44   *As Newsweek's Nancy Cook pointed out:* Nancy Cook, "Foreclosures Spread to Middle Class," 28 Oct. 2009, www.newsweek.com.

45   *"Amongst the novel objects . . .":* Alexis de Tocqueville, *Democracy in America*, 8th ed., trans. Henry Reeve (Cambridge: 1848), 1.

45   *"Democratic laws," he noted:* Ibid., 241.

47   *"I know it when I see it":* Jacobellis v. Ohio, 378 U.S. 184 (U.S. Sup. Ct. 1964).

47   *"Is a $30,000-a-year doctor . . .":* Testimony of Paul Taylor, executive vice president, Pew Research Center, to the Senate Finance Committee, 26 Mar. 2009, www.pewre search.org.

47   *According to the Pew Research Center:* Pew Research Center, "Inside the Middle Class: Bad Times Hit the Good Life," 9 Apr. 2008, www.pewsocialtrends.org.

47   *But behind this assertion:* Ibid.

48   *At the same time, a third of those:* Ibid.

48   *For purposes of its research, Pew defined:* Ibid.

48   *In dollars and cents, that meant:* Ibid.

48   *From 1945 to the 1970s:* Claudia Goldin and Lawrence F. Katz, "Long-Run Changes in the Wage Structure: Narrowing, Widening, Polarizing," 2007, www.brookings.edu.

48   *From factory employees to chief executives:* John Cassidy, "Who Killed the Middle Class?" 16 Oct. 1995, www.newyorker.com.

48   *By the end of the 1980s:* Paul Krugman, "The Great Wealth Transfer," *Rolling Stone,* 30 Nov. 2006.

48   *They had, but rather than Ponce de León:* Ibid.

50   *Alfred Marshall, one of the founding fathers:* Alfred Marshall, "Some Aspects of Competition: The Address of the President of Economic Science and Statistics of the British Association," *Nature* XLII (1890): 497.

50   *There is a reason Adam Smith's:* Amartya Sen, "The Economist Manifesto," 23 Apr. 2010, www.newstatesman.com.

51   *Given how close we were in 2008:* David Herszenhorn, "Senate Acts on Credit-Rating Agencies," 13 May 2010, www.nytimes.com.

51   *"[The Bush] administration made . . .":* Jo Becker, Sheryl Gay Stolberg, and Stephen Labaton, "White House Philosophy Stoked Mortgage Bonfire," 20 Dec. 2008, www.nytimes .com.

51   *Even Alan Greenspan:* Andrew Clark and Jill Treanor, "Greenspan—I Was Wrong About the Economy. Sort Of," 24 Oct. 2008, www.guardian.co.uk.

52   *"Wall Street got drunk":* Jo Becker, Sheryl Gay Stolberg, and Stephen Labaton, "White House Philosophy Stoked Mortgage Bonfire," 20 Dec. 2008, www.nytimes.com.

52   *stubbornly refused to dip below thirty-two million:* U.S. Census Bureau, "Table 23 People in Poverty by Nativity: 1993 to 2008," www.census.gov.

52   *soup kitchen or food bank hit twenty-six million:* "Who Are the Hungry?" *California Agriculture* 48, 7 (Dec. 1994), www.californiaagriculture.ucanr.org.

52   *with more homeless children:* National Center on Family Homelessness, "Homeless Children: America's New Outcasts," 2009, www.homelesschildrenamerica.org.

52   *In early 1996, after forty thousand AT&T workers:* James Cramer, "Let Them Eat Stocks," *New Republic,* 29 Apr. 1996, 24–25.

52   *their corporate cronies from Enron and Halliburton:* Frank Rich, "All the President's Enrons," 5 Jul. 2002, www.nytimes.com.

53   *"From 1980 to around 1987 . . .":* Claudia Goldin and Lawrence F. Katz, "Long-Run Changes in the Wage Structure: Narrowing, Widening, Polarizing," 2007, www.brookings .edu.

53   *In 1995, the midway point:* John Cassidy, "Who Killed the Middle Class?" 16 Oct. 1995, www.newyorker.com.

54   *In contrast, the nation's top 5 percent:* Ibid.

54   *According to a report compiled by Elizabeth Warren:* Testimony of Elizabeth Warren, Committee on Banking, Housing and Urban Affairs, U.S. Senate, 25 Jan. 2007, www .banking.senate.gov.

54   *Over the same period, the top 1 percent:* Emmanuel Saez, "Striking It Richer: The Evolution of Top Incomes in the United States (Update with 2007 Estimates)," *Pathways Magazine,* Stanford Center for the Study of Poverty and Inequality, Winter 2008, 6–7.

54   *And according to a report released in May 2010:* "The State of Metropolitan America," 9 May 2010, www.brookings.edu.

54   *Indeed, in a 2008 Pew survey:* Pew Research Center, "Inside the Middle Class: Bad Times Hit the Good Life," 9 Apr. 2008, www.pewsocialtrends.org.

54   *It was, according to Pew:* Ibid.

55   *In a revised take on the original Misery Index:* Marcus Baram, "The Real Misery Index April 2010: Underemployment Woes Lead to Two-Tier Economy," 12 May 2010, www .huffingtonpost.com.

56   *One of the most glaring examples:* Gretchen Morgenson, "Death of a Loophole, and Swiss Banks Will Mourn," 26 Mar. 2010, www.nytimes.com.

56   *According to the White House:* Office of the Press Secretary, "Leveling the Playing Field: Curbing Tax Havens and Removing Tax Incentives for Shifting Jobs Overseas," 4 May 2009, www.whitehouse.gov.

56   *In December 2008, the Government Accountability Office:* United States Government Accountability Office, "International Taxation: Large U.S. Corporations and Federal Contractors with Subsidiaries in Jurisdictions Listed as Tax Havens or Financial Privacy Jurisdictions," Dec. 2008, www.gao.gov.

56   *Even more egregiously:* Ibid.

56   *It's as easy as opening up:* Michael Brostek, "Cayman Islands: Business Advantages and Tax Minimization Attract U.S. Persons and Enforcement Challenges Exist," United States Government Accountability Office, 24 Jul. 2010, www.gao.gov.

57   *At the time of the GAO report:* United States Government Accountability Office, "International Taxation: Large U.S. Corporations and Federal Contractors with Subsidiaries in Jurisdictions Listed as Tax Havens or Financial Privacy Jurisdictions," Dec. 2008, www.gao.gov.

57   *The company got billions from U.S. taxpayers:* Farah Stockman, "Top Iraq Contractor Skirts US Taxes Offshore," 6 Mar. 2008, www.bostonglobe.com.

57   *In 2008, KBR listed 10,500 Americans:* Ibid.

58   *Indeed, back in 2002, to call attention:* Arianna Huffington, "Tax Avoidance and a Tan: Why I'm Thinking of Moving This Column to Bermuda," 15 May 2002, ariannaonline .huffingtonpost.com.

58   *Washington has been trying:* Stephen Ohlemacher, "Obama Cracking Down on Tax Havens," Associated Press, 4 May 2009.

58   *The latest tax-reform bills are far from perfect:* Gretchen Morgenson, "Death of a Loophole, and Swiss Banks Will Mourn," 26 Mar. 2010, www.nytimes.com.

59   *As the law stands now:* Pat Garofalo, "Baucus and Orszag See 'Growing Sense of Inevitability' for Ending Hedge Fund Manager Tax Break," 13 May 2010, www.thinkprogress.org.

59   *According to former labor secretary Robert Reich, in 2009:* Robert Reich, "Closing Tax Loopholes for Billionaires," 23 May 2010, www.huffingtonpost.com.

59   *Closing this outrageous loophole:* Ibid.

59   *Indeed, the double standard was famously ridiculed:* Tomoeh Murakami Tse, "Buffett Slams Tax System Disparities," 27 Jun. 2007, www.washingtonpost.com.

59   *A more accurate snapshot:* Nan Mooney, *Not Keeping Up with Our Parents: The Decline of the Professional Middle Class* (Boston: Beacon Press, 2008), 3–6.

61   *the jobless rate is almost 10 percent:* Bureau of Labor Statistics, "Alternative Measures of Labor Underutilization," 2 Apr. 2010, www.bls.gov.

61   *and twenty-six million people:* Rex Nutting, "GDP to Show More Balanced Growth, Survey Says," 29 Apr. 2010, www.marketwatch.com.

61   *Troy Renault is one of them:* Laura Bassett, "Middle Class No More, Families Struggle to Fight Off Homelessness," 4 Feb. 2010, www.huffingtonpost.com.

61   *Says Troy: "You wind up starting to think . . .":* Ibid.

61   *Rebecca Admire is another:* Ibid.

61   *Mount Airy, North Carolina, for example:* Paul Wiseman, "When the Textile Mill Goes, So Does a Way of Life," 11 Mar. 2010, www.usatoday.com.

62   *And in Mount Airy—the city where Andy Griffith grew up:* Ibid.

62   *"We were not prepared":* Ibid.

63   *By the end of 2009, the unemployment rate:* Dion Hoynes, "Blacks Hit Hard by Economy's Punch," 24 Nov. 2009, www.washingtonpost.com.

63   *And 19.7 percent of all American men:* Floyd Norris, "In Global Unemployment, a Sea of Young Faces," 16 Apr. 2010, www.nytimes.com.

63   *"Every downturn pushes some people . . .":* Peter S. Goodman, "Despite Signs of Recovery, Chronic Joblessness Rises," 20 Feb. 2010, www.nytimes.com.

64   *For a century, from the mid-1890s:* Dean Baker, "The Great Recession Didn't Have to Happen," 25 Jan. 2010, www.cepr.net.

65   *By 2005, subprime mortgages had skyrocketed:* Gene Sperling, "Subprime Market—Isolated or a Tipping Point?" 14 Mar. 2007, www.bloomberg.com.

65   *Fueling the boom was the development:* Jim Puzzanghera, "Senators Grapple with Derivatives Rules in Financial Overhaul," 19 May 2010, www.latimes.com.

65   *"The Federal Reserve Board completely failed . . .":* Dean Baker, "The Great Recession Didn't Have to Happen," 25 Jan. 2010, www.cepr.net.

65   *Even after a spate of accounting scandals:* Charles W. Caolmiris and Peter J. Wallison, "Blame Fannie Mae and Congress for the Credit Mess," 23 Sep. 2008, www.wsj.com.

65   *Between 2004 and 2007, Fannie and Freddie:* Ibid.

65   *George W. Bush and the GOP also helped:* George W. Bush, Second Inaugural Address, 20 Jan. 2005, georgewbush-whitehouse.archives.gov.

66   *By 2006, 62 percent of all new mortgages:* Dan Dorfman, "Liars' Loans Could Make Many Moan," 20 Dec. 2006, www.nysun.com.

66   *Among the findings:* Sewell Chan, "Memos Show Risky Lending at WaMu," 12 Apr. 2010, www.nytimes.com.

67   *Enter the bankruptcy bill:* Jeanne Sahadi, "President Signs Bankruptcy Bill," 20 Apr. 2005, www.money.cnn.com.

68   *They even rejected an amendment:* U.S. Senate, "S. 256, the Bankruptcy Reform Bill," *Congressional Record*, 109th Cong., 1st Sess., vol. 151, no. 26, 8 Mar. 2005, www.senate.gov.

68   *According to the Institute for Financial Literacy:* Institute for Financial Literacy, "2009 Annual Consumer Bankruptcy Demographics Report: The American Debtor in the Great Recession," Jun. 2010, www.financiallit.org.

68   *The Institute's executive director, Leslie Linfield:* Leslie Linfield, in an email communication with the author, 19 May 2010.

68   *In fact, a 2009 study by researchers at Harvard:* Catherine Arnst, "Study Links Medical Costs and Personal Bankruptcy," 4 Jun. 2009, www.businessweek.com.

69   *Using that rate, roughly:* American Bankruptcy Institute, "Annual Business and Nonbusiness Filings by State (2007–09)," www.abiworld.org.

69   *Here's another: 78 percent of the so-called:* Catherine Arnst, "Study Links Medical Costs and Personal Bankruptcy," 4 Jun. 2009, www.businessweek.com.

69   *Barry Bosworth and Rosanna Smart of the Brookings Institution:* Barry Bosworth and Rosanna Smart, "The Wealth of Older Americans and the Sub-Prime Debacle," Nov. 2009, crr.bc.edu.

69   *We are facing nothing less than:* Lynn Adler, "U.S. 2009 Foreclosures Shatter Record Despite Aid," 14 Jan. 2010, www.reuters.com.

69   *and an estimated 3 million more are expected:* Dan Levy, "U.S. Foreclosures May Rise to 3 Million This Year," 14 Jan. 2010, www.bloomberg.com.

70   *Currently, mortgages are exempt from bankruptcy proceedings:* Wenli Li, Michelle J. White, and Ning Zhu, "Did Bankruptcy Reform Cause Mortgage Default Rates to Rise?" Apr. 2010, www.philadelphiafed.org.

70   *Subsequent court battles eventually eliminated their use:* Doris Dungey, "Just Say Yes to Cram Downs," 7 Oct. 2007, www.calculatedriskblog.com.

70   *The banks scored a lopsided victory:* Ryan Grim, "Banks Beat Homeowners: Foreclosure Bill Killed in Senate," 31 May 2009, www.huffingtonpost.com.

70   *There had already been more than eight hundred thousand:* Julianne Peitone, "Foreclosure Filings Jump 24%," 16 Apr. 2009, www.money.cnn.com.

70　*But even after major concessions:* Ryan Grim, "Banks Beat Homeowners: Foreclosure Bill Killed in Senate," 31 May 2009, www.huffingtonpost.com.

70　*the Mortgage Bankers Association:* Margaret Chadbourn, "Senate Defeats Mortgage 'Cram-Down' as Democrats Balk (Update 2)," 30 Apr. 2010, www.bloomberg.com.

70　*As ProPublica's Paul Kiel reported:* Paul Kiel, "Disorganization at Banks Causing Mistaken Foreclosures," 4 May 2010, www.propublica.org.

71　*According to a study by the Brennan Center:* Melanca Clark and Maggie Baron, "Foreclosures: A Crisis in Legal Representation," Brennan Center for Justice 6 Oct. 2009, www.brennancenter.org.

71　*In New York's Nassau County:* Ibid.

71　*Having legal help can be the difference:* Ibid.

71　*In 1996, the budget for the Legal Services Corporation:* Ibid.

71　*At this point, to match:* Ibid.

72　*The second barrier is that restrictions:* Ibid.

72　*The $789 billion stimulus plan:* "After the Stimulus," 12 Feb. 2009, www.nytimes.com.

72　*Almost forty-one million homes:* Pew Charitable Trusts, "Defaulting on the Dream: States Respond to America's Foreclosure Crisis," Apr. 2008, www.pewtrusts.org.

72　*The value of these homes:* Ibid.

72　*This translates into a total property value loss:* Ibid.

73　*A 1 percent increase in foreclosures:* Dan Immergluck and Geoff Smith, "The Impact of Single-Family Mortgage Foreclosures on Neighborhood Crime," *Housing Studies* 21, 6 (Nov. 2006): 851–66.

73　*A September 2009 New York Times story:* Erik Eckholm, "Surge in Homeless Pupils Strains Schools," 5 Sep. 2009, www.nytimes.com.

73　*The National Center on Family Homelessness:* National Center on Family Homelessness, "America's Youngest Outcasts: State Report Card on Child Homelessness," 2009, www.homelesschildrenamerica.org.

73　*San Antonio, for example, enrolled:* Erik Eckholm, "Surge in Homeless Pupils Strains Schools," 5 Sep. 2009, www.nytimes.com.

73　*homeless children are four times as likely:* National Center on Family Homelessness, "Annual Report: Working to End Family Homelessness," 2009, www.homelesschildren america.org.

73　*twice as likely to have learning:* National Center on Family Homelessness, "Homeless Children: America's New Outcasts," 1999, www.homelesschildrenamerica.org.

73　*"We see eight-year-olds telling Mom . . .":* Erik Eckholm, "Surge in Homeless Pupils Strains Schools," 5 Sep. 2009, www.nytimes.com.

74　*Banks don't want to adjust nonperforming mortgages:* Melanca Clark and Maggie Baron, "Foreclosures: A Crisis in Legal Representation," Brennan Center for Justice, 6 Oct. 2009, www.brennancenter.org.

74　*The four largest banks:* "Miller, Ellison Introduce Bill to Address Conflict of Interest in Mortgage Companies," 1 Apr. 2010, www.bradmiller.house.gov.

74　*These banks collectively hold:* Mike Konczal, "Principal Writedowns and the Fake Stress Test," 9 Mar. 2010, www.rortybomb.wordpress.com.

74　*"The banks are too big to fail":* Matthew Karnitschnig, Deborah Solomon, Liam Pleven, and Jon E. Hilsenrath, "U.S. to Take over AIG in $85 Billion Bailout; Central Banks Inject Cash as Credit Dries Up," 16 Sep. 2008, www.wsj.com.

75　*As of January 2010, U.S. consumers:* Jeremy M. Simon, "Consumer Credit Card Balances Fall for 16th Straight Month," 5 Mar. 2010, www.creditcards.com.

75　*98 percent of which is credit card debt:* Ben Woolsey and Matt Schulz, "Credit Card Statistics, Industry Facts, Debt Statistics," 13 May 2010, www.creditcards.com.

75　*There are more than 576 million credit cards:* Ibid.

75　*The average credit cardholder has 3.5 cards:* Ibid.

75 *"For much of America," says Elizabeth Warren:* "Elizabeth Warren on Credit Card 'Tricks and Traps,'" *NOW*, 2 Jan. 2009, www.pbs.org.

75 *In fact, in 2007, even before the economic crisis began:* National Association for the Advancement of Colored People, "Usury: The Impact of Credit Card Debt and High Interest Rates on African American Wealth," 4 Sep. 2009, www.naacp.org.

76 *In 1958, American Express pioneered:* Ben Woolsey and Matt Schulz, "Credit Card Statistics, Industry Facts, Debt Statistics," 13 May 2010, www.creditcards.com.

76 *But the modern credit card industry: Marquette Nat. Bank v. First of Omaha Corp.*, 439 U.S. 299 (1978).

76 *Hoping to lure banks' business:* Robin Stein, "The Ascendancy of the Credit Card Industry," *Frontline*, 23 Nov. 2004, www.pbs.org.

76 *"In 1980, the typical credit card contract . . .":* "Elizabeth Warren on Credit Card 'Tricks and Traps,'" *NOW*, 2 Jan. 2009, www.pbs.org.

76 *Fees now account for 39 percent of card issuers' revenue:* Steven Gray and Michael Peltier, "Exposing the Credit-Card Fine Print," 21 Feb. 2008, www.time.com.

76 *In fact, last year, lenders collected more than $20 billion:* Robin Sidel, "Banks Roll Out New Check, Card Fees," 2 Jan. 2010, www.wsj.com.

77 *"inactivity fee" for not using their card!:* Brad Tuttle, "Credit Card Fee Watch: Now There's a Fee for NOT Buying Stuff," 6 Aug. 2009, www.time.com.

77 *As a result, according to CreditCards.com:* Ben Woolsey and Matt Schultz, "Credit Card Statistics, Industry Facts, Debt Statistics," 26 Mar. 2010, www.creditcards.com.

77 *Half of all college undergraduates:* Ibid.

77 *According to FinAid, 66 percent of college graduates:* "Student Loans," FinAid: The Smart-Student Guide to Financial Aid, www.finaid.org.

79 *In 2008, securities backed by credit card debt:* Jessica Silver-Greenberg, "The Next Meltdown: Credit-Card Debt," 9 Oct. 2008, www.businessweek.com.

79 *could be the knockout blow:* "Elizabeth Warren on Credit Card 'Tricks and Traps,'" interview with David Brancaccio, *NOW*, 2 Jan. 2009, www.pbs.org.

80 *In March 2010, a FOX News poll found that 79 percent:* Dana Blanton, "Fox News Poll: 79% Say U.S. Economy Could Collapse," 23 Mar. 2010, www.foxnews.com.

80 *An April 2010 Gallup poll revealed:* Jeffrey M. Jones, "Americans Remain Down About Their Financial Situations," 22 Apr. 2010, www.gallup.com.

80 *And 21 percent of workers think:* Dennis Jacobe, "One In Five Americans Fear Job Loss in Next 12 Months," 23 Apr. 2010, www.gallup.com.

80 *As reported by Don Peck:* Don Peck, "How a New Jobless Era Will Transform America," Mar. 2010, www.theatlantic.com.

80 *Researchers at Rutgers University interviewed:* Arthur Delaney, "Long-Term Unemployment: 80 Percent of People Jobless Last Summer Still Out of Work," 4 May 2010, www.huffingtonpost.com.

80 *"The cushion's completely gone":* Ibid.

82 *came word that an Oklahoma Tea Party group:* Sean Murphy and Tim Talley, "Oklahoma Tea Party Plans to Form Armed Militia," Associated Press, 12 Apr. 2010.

82 *The FBI was investigating an antigovernment extremist group:* Michael Winter, "Anti-Government Group Tells Governors to Resign or Be Removed," 2 Apr. 2010, www.usatoday.com.

82 *This followed the arrests of members:* Brett Michael Dykes, "Who are the Christian Militia 'Hutaree' and Why Was the FBI Targeting Them?" 29 Mar. 2010, www.yahoo.com.

83 *When Tea Party members gathered for tax-day protests:* Nick Wing and Jeremy Binckes, "Tea Parties Protest Tax Day 2010," 17 Apr. 2010, www.huffingtonpost.com.

83 *Sarah Palin urged her supporters to "reload":* Ron Fournier, "Sarah Palin Tells GOP 'Don't Retreat—Reload' at Southern Republican Leadership Conference," Associated Press, 9 Apr. 2010.

83   *Michele Bachmann said she wants her constituents:* Rachel Weiner, "Michele Bachmann: I Want People 'Armed and Dangerous' over Obama Tax Plan," 23 Mar. 2009, www.huffingtonpost.com.

83   *According to* Rage on the Right: Mark Potok, *Rage on the Right: The Year in Hate and Extremism,* Southern Poverty Law Center Intelligence Report No. 137, Spring 2010, www.splcenter.org.

83   *"Discontent with the present and apprehension . . .":* Tim Rutten, "The Winter of America's Discontent," 5 Feb. 2010, www.latimes.com.

83   *"There are times—they mark the danger point for a political system . . .":* Ian Kershaw, *Hitler: A Biography* (New York: W. W. Norton, 2008), 206.

84   *For example, in the 1880s, as the post–Civil War Gilded Age:* Rebecca Edwards, *Angels in the Machinery* (New York: Oxford University Press, 1997), 111.

84   *The Chinese Exclusion Act of 1882:* John Findlay, "Industrialization, Class and Race: Chinese and Anti-Chinese Movement in the Late 19th Century Northwest," Center for the Study of the Pacific Northwest, University of Washington, 1998, www.washington.edu.

84   *One newspaperman captured the mood:* Ibid.

84   *Then, as now, the agitation resulted in the formation:* Richard Hofstadter, *The Age of Reform* (New York: Random House, 1955), 62.

85   *Conspiracy theories were rampant:* Ibid., 70.

85   *during the Great Depression, the United States:* Wendy Koch, "U.S. Urged to Apologize for 1930s Deportations," 5 Apr. 2006, www.usatoday.com.

85   *In 1935, for example, many shops:* Hasia R. Diner, *The Jews of the United States, 1654 to 2000* (Los Angeles: University of California Press, 2004), 211.

85   *And, of course, the flames of bigotry:* Social Security Administration, "Social Security History: Father Charles Coughlin," www.ssa.gov.

85   *In 1969, Pete Hamill published:* Pete Hamill, "The Revolt of the White Lower Middle Class," *New York,* 14 Apr. 1969, 24–29.

86   *and 92 percent of Tea Partiers:* Kate Zernike and Megan Thee-Brenan, "Poll Finds Tea Party Backers Wealthier and More Educated," 14 Apr. 2010, www.nytimes.com.

86   *A Harris poll in March 2010:* "'Wingnuts' and President Obama," 24 Mar. 2010, www.harrisinteractive.com.

86   *But then again, according to psychologist Michael Bader, paranoia:* Michael Bader, "We Need to Have Empathy for Tea Partiers," 5 Mar. 2010, www.psychologytoday.com.

PART 3: AMERICA THE ~~BEAUTIFUL~~ DILAPIDATED

93   *George Washington knew that:* Robert Fishman, "Beyond Motor City, 1808–1908–2008: National Planning for America," 23 Jan. 2010, www.america2050.org.

94   *The nation's overall infrastructure grade:* American Society of Civil Engineers, *2009 Report Card for America's Infrastructure,* www.infrastructurereportcard.org.

94   *downward trend since 2005:* American Society of Civil Engineers, *2005 Report Card for America's Infrastructure,* www.asce.org.

94   *"It's the kind of report card you . . .":* Katherine Harmon, "U.S. Infrastructure Crumbling," 28 Jan. 2009, www.scientificamerican.com.

94   *According to the ASCE:* American Society of Civil Engineers, *2009 Report Card for America's Infrastructure,* www.infrastructurereportcard.org.

94   *But we've only budgeted $975 billion:* Ibid.

95   *America's population is expected to reach:* Jeffrey Passel and D'Vera Cohn, "Immigration to Play Lead Role in Future U.S. Growth," 11 Feb. 2008, www.pewresearch.org.

95   *We invest just 2.4 percent of gross domestic product:* "The Cracks Are Showing," 28 Jun. 2008, www.economist.com.

95 *China is busy building the most up-to-date:* "Rushing on by Road, Rail and Air," 14 Feb. 2008, www.economist.com.

96 *For example, from 2006 through 2009, China spent:* Keith Bradsher, "China Sees Growth Engine in a Web of Fast Trains," 12 Feb. 2010, www.nytimes.com.

96 *World Bank officials have described as:* "Rushing on by Road, Rail and Air," 14 Feb. 2008, www.economist.com.

96 *And by 2020 China plans to construct:* Andrew Peaple, "China's Infrastructure Still on Rails," 3 Mar. 2010, www.wsj.com.

96 *In 2009 China built over 230,000 miles:* "China's Rural Road Length Hits 3.3 Million Kilometers; Most Villages, Towns Connected: Official," People's Daily Online, 22 Feb. 2010, www.english.peopledaily.com.

96 *and announced plans to build ninety-seven airports:* "Rushing on by Road, Rail and Air," 14 Feb. 2008, www.economist.com.

96 *In a column headlined "Time to Reboot America":* Thomas Friedman, "Time to Reboot America," 23 Dec. 2008, www.nytimes.com.

96 *Armando Carbonell, chairman of the Department of Planning:* "Are 'Mega-Regions' the Future of Transportation?" 29 Jun. 2008, www.npr.org.

96 *Felix Rohatyn, author of* Bold Endeavors: Felix Rohatyn, *Bold Endeavors: How Our Government Built America, and Why It Must Rebuild Now* (New York: Simon & Schuster, 2009), 2, 3.

97 *Building America's Future (BAF):* www.bafuture.org/about.

97 *"deliver a message to Washington . . .":* "Pa.'s Rendell Urging Fix for Bridges, Roads," 29 Jun. 2008, www.npr.org.

97 *"If we don't do something quickly . . .":* "The Next American Economy: Transforming Energy and Infrastructure Investment," 3 Feb. 2010, www.brookings.edu.

98 *According to Department of Transportation estimates:* American Society of Civil Engineers, "National Fact Sheet," 2005, www.asce.org.

98 *In addition, it could also produce what Rendell:* "Pa.'s Rendell Urging Fix for Bridges, Roads," 29 Jun. 2008, www.npr.org.

98 *As the debate over the stimulus began:* Thomas Friedman, "Time to Reboot America," 23 Dec. 2008, www.nytimes.com.

98 *The result was a bill Jeffrey Sachs:* Jeffrey Sachs, "A Fiscal Straitjacket," 27 Jan. 2009, www.ft.com.

98 *In the end, the $787 billion American Recovery and Reinvestment Act:* Ed O'Keefe, "Eye Opener: April 14, 2009," www.washingtonpost.com.

98 *"I fear that we may soon look back and say . . .":* Van Jones, in conversation with the author, 2 Feb. 2009.

99 *Faced with an even more devastating economic crisis:* Alan Brinkley, "Roosevelt, Franklin Delano," Feb. 2000, www.fdrheritage.org.

100 *Among them is Steven Solomon:* "Will the Next War Be Fought over Water?" 3 Jan. 2010, www.npr.org.

100 *Despite the indispensable nature:* Jeanne M. VanBriesen, "The Nation's Big Water Repair Bill," 11 Apr. 2010, www.nytimes.com.

100 *Indeed, some of the nation's tap water:* Charles Duhigg, "Saving U.S. Water and Sewer Systems Would Be Costly," 14 Mar. 2010, www.nytimes.com.

100 *As a result of leaking pipes, we lose:* American Society of Civil Engineers, "Infrastructure Report Card Fact Sheet: Drinking Water," 2009, www.infrastructurereportcard.org.

100 *According to a* New York Times *analysis of data:* Charles Duhigg, "Saving U.S. Water and Sewer Systems Would Be Costly," 14 Mar. 2010, www.nytimes.com.

100 *Washington, D.C., averages a water line break:* Ibid.

100 *"We have about two million miles of pipe . . .":* "Liquid Assets: The Story of Our Water Infrastructure," 19 Oct. 2009, www.infrastructureusa.org.

101 *Even now, our tap water is becoming:* Testimony of Judy Treml, House Committee on Transportation and Infrastructure, 15 Oct. 2009, www.transportation.house.gov.

101 *"Older systems are plagued by chronic overflows . . ."*: American Society of Civil Engineers, "America's Infrastructure Report Card Fact Sheet: Wastewater," 2009, www.infrastructurereportcard.org.

101 *While demand for electricity has risen:* Thomas J. Donohue, "Rebuilding America—the Time Is Now," U.S. Chamber of Commerce, 10 Aug. 2007, www.uschamber.com.

102 *Since we need all the power:* American Society of Civil Engineers, "America's Infrastructure Report Card Fact Sheet: Energy," 2009, www.infrastructurereportcard.org.

102 *These ongoing brownouts and blackouts:* U.S. Department of Energy, "Smart Grid System Report," Jul. 2009, www.energy.gov.

102 *The ASCE estimates that it could take:* American Society of Civil Engineers, "America's Infrastructure Report Card Fact Sheet: Energy," 2009, www.infrastructurereportcard.org. *

102 *On August 14, 2003, we got a glimpse:* Allan J. DeBlasio et al., "Learning from the 2003 Blackout," U.S. Department of Transportation, Federal Highway Administration, Sep./Oct. 2004, www.tfhrc.gov.

102 *What happened? Power lines, heavy from:* "U.S.-Canada Power System Outage Task Force: Final Report on the August 14th Blackout in the United States and Canada," 61, 93, www.energy.gov.

102 *America's roads are also in miserable shape:* American Society of Civil Engineers, "America's Infrastructure Report Card: Roads," 2009, www.infrastructurereportcard.org.

102 *From 1980 to 2005, the miles traveled by cars:* Ibid.

103 *Americans spend 4.2 billion hours a year:* Ibid.

103 *City drivers have it particularly bad:* Ted R. Miller and Eduard Zaloshnja, "On a Crash Course: The Dangers and Health Costs of Deficient Roadways," Apr. 2009, www.pire.org.

103 *Transportation Construction Coalition (TCC) determined:* Ibid.

103 *53 percent of the forty-two thousand road fatalities:* Ibid.

103 *We are currently spending $70 billion annually:* American Society of Civil Engineers, "America's Infrastructure Report Card: Roads," 2009, www.infrastructurereportcard.org.

104 *By the year 2000, each day, 3.5 million:* Nick Paumgarten, "There and Back Again: The Soul of the Commuter," 16 Apr. 2007, www.newyorker.com.

104 *One in eight workers—17.5 million Americans:* Hope Yen, "Recession's Impact: Census Data Show Longer Commutes, Delayed Marriage, Fewer Immigrants," Associated Press, 21 Sep. 2009.

104 *Robert Putnam, a Harvard political scientist:* Nick Paumgarten, "There and Back Again: The Soul of the Commuter," 16 Apr. 2007, www.newyorker.com.

104 *A study by Swiss economists:* Alois Stutzer and Bruno S. Frey, "Stress That Doesn't Pay: The Commuting Paradox," Institute for the Study of Labor (IZA), Discussion Paper No. 1278, Aug. 2004, www.iew.unizh.ch

104 *America's railway system is speeding down the tracks:* Tom Vanderbilt, "Stop This Train!" 15 May 2009, www.slate.com.

105 *At the moment, the only high-speed train:* Chris Dolmetsch, "Amtrak Cuts Acela Train Fares to Attract More Leisure Travelers," 17 Feb. 2009, www.bloomberg.com.

105 *While in theory the trains:* Nicole C. Wong, "Will Stimulus Funds Put Rail on the Fast Track?" 25 Feb. 2009, www.bostonglobe.com.

105 *Meanwhile, countries such as Japan, France, and Italy:* Mark Reutler, "How America Led, and Lost, the High-Speed Rail Race," 31 Mar. 2010, www.progressivefix.com.

105 *For example, the six-hundred-mile ride:* Randy James, "A Brief History of High-Speed Rail," 20 Apr. 2010, www.time.com.

105 *The stimulus bill included $8 billion:* "Obama Wants Nationwide High-Speed Rail System," 28 Jan. 2010, www.cnn.com.

105 *$1.25 billion going to a high-speed rail corridor:* Michael Cooper, "Stimulus Plan for Rail Line Shows System of Weak Links," 22 Mar. 2010, www.nytimes.com.

105 *Of course, high-speed rail systems:* Matt Van Hattem, "High Speed Rail in the Northeast: Beyond the Corridor, Slow Trains Get Some Help," *Trains Magazine,* 28 Jan. 2010, www.trains.com.

106 *So while this new investment is a start:* Tom Vanderbilt, "Stop This Train!" 15 May 2009, www.slate.com.

106 *According to the Department of Transportation:* American Society of Civil Engineers, "America's Infrastructure Report Card for 2009: Bridges," 2009, www.infrastructurereportcard.org.

106 *The problem is pretty basic: The average bridge:* Ibid.

106 *It was May 2002, and Webbers Falls:* Tim Tally, "Up to 12 Feared Dead in Bridge Collapse," 27 May 2002, www.bgdailynews.com.

107 *Down in the river, towboat captain William Joe Dedmon: Magnolia Marine Transport Company v. State of Oklahoma,* U.S. Court of Appeals (10th Cir. 2004).

107 *Up above, a six-hundred-foot section:* "Divers Find 3 Victims from Bridge Collapse," 27 May 2002, www.cnn.com.

107 *In an instant, the Arkansas River turned:* Kris Glenn, "Oklahoma Faces Bridge Tragedy," 29 May 2002, www.oudaily.com.

107 *"Officials set up a morgue inside city hall":* Tim Tally, "Up to 12 Feared Dead in Bridge Collapse," 27 May 2002, www.bgdailynews.com.

107 *Indeed, the state had the dubious distinction:* Justin Juozapavicius, "Nearly a Quarter of Oklahoma Bridges Need Overhaul or Replacement," Associated Press, 25 May 2008.

107 *In August 2007, the Interstate 35W:* Steve Karnowski, "Contractor Settles with State in 35W Bridge Collapse," 19 Mar. 2010, www.minnesota.publicradio.org.

107 *The bridge had been inspected:* Elizabeth Stawicki, "Why Did the Bridge Collapse?" 2 Aug. 2007, www.minnesota.publicradio.org.

108 *On March 16, 2006, the Ka Loko Dam in Kilauea, Hawaii:* Craig Gima, "Ka Loko Settlement Is Reached," 30 Oct. 2009, www.starbulletin.com.

108 *The breach created an ecological disaster:* Diane Leone, "State Keeps Eye on Dams," 16 Mar. 2006, www.starbulletin.com.

108 *According to Hawaii congresswoman Mazie Hirono, it was not:* Joint Hearing on National Levee and Dam Safety Programs, House Committee on Transportation and Infrastructure, 8 May 2007.

108 *There are more than 85,000 dams in America:* American Society of Civil Engineers, *2009 Report Card for America's Infrastructure,* www.infrastructurereportcard.org.

109 *It would take $12.5 billion over the next five years:* Ibid.

109 *Plus, of our 85,000 dams, the federal government regulates:* Ibid.

109 *In 2007, during congressional testimony:* Joint Hearing on National Levee and Dam Safety Programs, House Committee on Transportation and Infrastructure, 8 May 2007.

110 *Like any number of agencies charged with protecting:* Harry Shearer, "Fixing the Responder, Ignoring the Cause," 25 Nov. 2008, www.huffingtonpost.com.

110 *Instead of fulfilling its responsibility to build:* Harry Shearer, "New Orleans: Where Accountability Failed, Liability Follows," 19 Nov. 2009, www.huffingtonpost.com.

111 *The American Society of Civil Engineers estimates:* American Society of Civil Engineers, *2009 Report Card for America's Infrastructure,* www.infrastructurereportcard.org.

111 *Over the next ten years, there will be a five-hundredfold:* "Fixing America's Crumbling Infrastructure," *Free Enterprise: News and Views from the U.S. Chamber of Commerce,* Jul. 2008, www.uschambermagazine.com.

112 *Federal Communications Commission chair Julius Genachowski explains:* "National Broadband Plan: Consumer Survey Results Are In," 23 Feb. 2010, www.brookings.edu.

112 *In a study of 120 countries, researchers found:* Iain Morris, "Resilience Amid Turmoil: Benchmarking IT Industry Competitiveness 2009," Sept. 2009, www.economist.com.

112 *Even a farmer these days needs high-speed Internet:* "National Broadband Plan: Consumer Survey Results Are In," 23 Feb. 2010, www.brookings.edu.

112 *In 2001, the United States ranked fourth among:* Jerome Cukier, "Internet Penetration— Who's Online?" OECD Factblog, 12 Feb. 2010, www.oecd.org.

112 *Over one hundred million Americans still:* Julius Genachowski, "America's 2020 Broadband Vision," 18 Feb. 2010, www.huffingtonpost.com.

112 *And while 83 percent of college graduates:* John Horrigan, "Home Broadband Adoption 2009," Pew Research Center, Jun. 2009, www.pewinternet.org.

113 *To help close the widening gap:* Tony Romm, "FCC Unveils Executive Summary of National Broadband Plan," 15 Mar. 2010, www.thehill.com.

113 *although the National Education Association estimates:* American Society of Civil Engineers, *2009 Report Card for America's Infrastructure,* www.infrastructurereportcard.org.

114 *Among thirty developed countries ranked:* Alliance for Excellent Education, "How Does the United States Stack Up? International Comparisons of Academic Achievement," www .all4ed.org.

114 *Even the top 10 percent:* Stéphane Baldi et al., "Highlights from PISA 2006: Performance of U.S. 15-Year-Old Students in Science and Mathematics Literacy in an International Context," National Center for Education Statistics, 4 Dec. 2007, www.nces.ed .gov.

114 *A National Assessment of Educational Progress report found:* National Assessment of Educational Progress, "The Nation's Report Card," 2009, www.nationsreportcard.gov.

114 *In 2001, amid much fanfare:* Robert Schlesinger, "Senate OK's Education Bill, Win for Bush; New Spending, Required Testing," 15 Jun. 2001, www.bostonglobe.com.

114 *But it turned out to be reform in name only:* National Assessment of Educational Progress, "The Nation's Report Card," 2009, www.nationsreportcard.gov.

114 *"Education," said President Obama:* Remarks by the President at Hampton University Commencement, 19 May 2010, www.whitehouse.gov.

115 *"Jobs today often require at least a bachelor's degree":* Ibid.

115 *But rather than rising "to meet the challenges of a changing world":* Stacy Teicher Khadaroo, "US High School Graduation Rate Climbs to 69.2 Percent," 9 Jun. 2009, www.csmonitor.com.

115 *And even those who do graduate:* "Measuring College and Career Readiness," 2009 ACT National Profile Report, www.act.org.

116 *Ramon Quintero:* Robert Greenwald, "Rethink Afghanistan," 21 Apr. 2010, www.huffing tonpost.com.

116 *Patsy Ramirez:* Ibid.

116 *Amy Brisendine:* Ibid.

117 *The result is his film,* **Waiting for Superman:** Scott Weinberg, "Sundance Review: Waiting for Superman," 24 Jan. 2010, www.cinematical.com.

117 *He turns a particularly withering spotlight:* *Waiting for Superman,* directed by Davis Guggenheim, written by Billy Kimball and Davis Guggenheim, release date: Sept. 2010.

117 *By way of example, he cites the state of Illinois:* Ibid.

118 *In New York, tenured teachers awaiting disciplinary:* Ibid.

118 *On average, they remain in this well-paid limbo:* Erin Einhorn, "Teachers in Trouble Spending Years in 'Rubber Room' Limbo That Costs $65M," 4 May 2010, www.nydaily news.com.

118 *"we could just eliminate the bottom six to ten percent . . .":* *Waiting for Superman,* directed by Davis Guggenheim, written by Billy Kimball and Davis Guggenheim, release date: Sept. 2010.

118 *The film charts the connection:* Center for Responsive Politics, Federal Election Commission Data, 16 May 2010, www.opensecrets.org.

118 *Andrew Coulson of the Cato Institute points out:* Andrew J. Coulson, "The Effects of Teachers Unions on American Education," *Cato Journal* 30, 1 (Winter 2010): 162.

118 *"Since 1971, educational spending . . .":* *Waiting for Superman*, directed by Davis Guggenheim, written by Billy Kimball and Davis Guggenheim, release date: Sept. 2010.

119 *Based on the Prussian educational model:* Ann O'Connell, "Are We Teaching American Citizens or Training Prussian Serfs?" May 1998, nj.npri.org.

119 *Plus, as President Obama pointed out:* Association of American Colleges and Universities, Greater Expectations Initiative, www.aacu.org.

119 *In the 1950s, only 20 percent of high-school graduates:* Diane Ravitch, *Left Back: A Century of Failed School Reforms* (New York: Simon & Schuster, 2000), 328–330.

119 *"The problem is," says Guggenheim:* *Waiting for Superman*, directed by davis Guggenheim, written by Billy Kimball and Davis Guggenheim, release date: Sept. 2010.

119 *"Once again, it's a question of priorities:* Pew Center on the States, "One in 31: The Long Reach of American Corrections," Mar. 2009, www.pewcenteronthestates.org.

119 *and the number of people living behind bars:* U.S. Department of Justice, "Prison Inmates at Midyear 2008," 31 Mar. 2009, www.ojp.usdoj.gov.

119 *In fact, America has more people living behind bars:* International Centre for Prison Studies, "Prison Brief," Kings College London, www.kcl.ac.uk.

119 *Sadly, in that prison population:* "Don't Teach Our Children Crime," 3 Jul. 2008, www.nytimes.com.

120 *Bill Clinton started his second term vowing:* Bill Clinton, State of the Union Address, 4 Feb. 1997, clinton2.nara.gov.

120 *But as of 1999, America's:* U.S. National Center for Education Statistics, "Trends in International Mathematics and Science Study (TIMSS)," Dec. 2000, www.nces.ed.gov.

120 *"By the year 2000," Bush 41 vowed:* George H. W. Bush, State of the Union Address, 31 Jan. 1990, www.cspan.org.

120 *But 2000 arrived:* National Center for Education Statistics, "Program for International Student Assessment (PISA)," Dec. 2001, www.nces.ed.gov.

121 *What Abraham Lincoln said:* *Collected Works of Abraham Lincoln,* comp. Roy P. Basler (New Brunswick, NJ: Rutgers University Press, 1955), 537.

PART 4: CSI USA: WHO KILLED THE AMERICAN DREAM?

129 *Since 1964 the American National Election Studies:* American National Election Studies, "The ANES Guide to Public Opinion and Electoral Behavior," 27 Nov. 2005, www.electionstudies.org.

129 *In the mid-1960s, only 29 percent:* Ibid.

129 *And in 2008, 80 percent of Americans surveyed:* "World Publics Say Governments Should Be More Responsive to the Will of the People," 12 May 2008, www.worldpublicopinion.org.

129 *In 2009, more than 13,700 registered lobbyists:* Dave Levinthal, "Federal Lobbying Climbs in 2009 as Lawmakers Execute Aggressive Congressional Agenda," 12 Feb. 2010, www.opensecrets.org.

129 *double the amount lobbyists spent:* Center for Responsive Politics, "Lobbying Database," 25 Apr. 2010, www.opensecrets.com.

130 *From 1974 to 2008 the average amount:* Alan R. Grant, *The American Political Process,* 7th ed. (New York: Routledge, 2004), 252.

130 *to more than 1.3 million:* Center for Responsive Politics, "Big Picture: Price of Admission," www.opensecrets.org.

130 *For an example of how special interests took advantage:* Simon Johnson and James Kwak, "Too Big for Us to Fail," 26 Apr. 2010, www.prospect.org.

130 *According to Simon Johnson and James Kwak in their book:* Simon Johnson and James Kwak, *13 Bankers: The Wall Street Takeover and the Next Financial Meltdown* (New York: Pantheon, 2010), 91.

130 *And the money was, of course, targeted:* Ibid.

130 *Over the course of the debate:* Brian Wingfield, "Wall Street Overhaul Not So Bad for Wall Street," 17 May 2010, www.forbes.com.

131 *For instance, when the Senate was crafting its financial reform bill:* "Fannie, Freddie Need to Be Part of Reform: Corker," 18 May 2010, www.cnbc.com.

131 *This despite the fact that in just the first quarter of 2010:* Gretchen Morgenson, "Ignoring the Elephant in the Bailout," 7 May 2010, www.nytimes.com.

131 *As of May 2010, according to Morgenson:* Ibid.

131 *"I don't understand why people are not talking about it":* Ibid.

131 *And why would they do that:* Ibid.

133 *Indeed, as far back as 1910, Teddy Roosevelt warned:* Theodore Roosevelt, *The New Nationalism* (New York: The Outlook Company, 1910), 13.

133 *Teddy Roosevelt must have been spinning in his grave:* Adam Liptak, "Justices, 5–4, Reject Corporate Spending Limit," 21 Jan. 2010, www.nytimes.com.

133 *President Obama called the decision "a major victory . . .":* Ibid.

135 *Or the chemical industry's long-term cover-up:* Dan Agin, "More than Genes III: Pregnancy, Toxic Environments, and Fetal Vulnerability," 1 Dec. 2009, www.huffingtonpost.com.

135 *Or the way Big Tobacco has fought tooth and nail:* American Cancer Society, "Cigarette Smoking," 24 Nov. 2009, www.cancer.org.

135 *Or the outrageous ripping off of the American taxpayer:* Kimberly Hefling, "Iraq Contracts Have Cost Taxpayers at Least $85 Billion Since Invasion," Associated Press, 12 Aug. 2008.

136 *Days after the Upper Big Branch disaster:* Michael Cooper, Gardiner Harris, and Eric Lipton, "In Mine Safety, a Meek Watchdog," 10 Apr. 2010, www.nytimes.com.

136 *In an eerie echo, in the wake of the Deepwater Horizon:* Russell Gold and Stephen Power, "Oil Regulator Ceded Oversight to Drillers," 7 May 2010, www.wsj.com.

136 *Florida senator Bill Nelson summed it up:* Ibid.

136 *Chris Oynes, the Interior Department's top official:* Carol E. Lee, "Oynes to Resign in Wake of Oil Leak," 17 May 2010, www.politico.com.

137 *Elizabeth Birnbaum, the head of MMS, was forced out:* Tom Raum and Jennifer Loven, "Elizabeth Birnbaum Quits Under Pressure: MMS Director Is Pushed Out After Gulf Spill," Associated Press, 27 May 2010.

137 *Indeed, a federal inspector was at the Upper Big Branch mine:* Michael Cooper, Gardiner Harris, and Eric Lipton, "In Mine Safety, a Meek Watchdog," 10 Apr. 2010, www.nytimes.com.

137 *Similarly, there are plenty of financial regulatory agencies:* Craig Torres, "Fed Says Capital at Some Major Banks Is 'Substantially Reduced,'" 24 Apr. 2009, www.bloomberg.com.

137 *Fannie Mae and Freddie Mac had the Office of Federal Housing Enterprise Oversight:* Jonathan J. Miller, "The Federal Housing Finance Agency: Regulators Awaken!" 19 Nov. 2008, www.nytimes.com.

137 *And, after Bear Stearns crashed, the New York Fed:* Andrew Ross Sorkin, "At Lehman, Watchdogs Saw It All," 15 Mar. 2010, www.nytimes.com.

137 *Regulations are "very difficult to comply with":* Jason Linkins, "Massey CEO Blankenship Has Complained About 'Nonsensical' Regulation," 9 Apr. 2010, www.huffingtonpost.com.

137 *The Wall Street Journal cites the arguments:* Russell Gold and Stephen Power, "Oil Regulator Ceded Oversight to Drillers," 7 May 2010, www.wsj.com.

137 *"There has been a very good record in deep water [drilling]":* Ibid.

138 *Similarly, the reason the financial industry can't be regulated:* Shahien Nasiripour and Ryan McGarthy, "Greenspan Testifies to Financial Crisis Commission, Blames Fannie, Freddie for Subprime Crisis," 7 Apr. 2010, www.huffingtonpost.com.

138 *Massey offers a textbook—and in this case tragic—example:* Michael Hupp, "Reports Critical of Massey, Other Mining Operations," 22 Apr. 2010, www.statejournal.com.

138 *In 2009, its Upper Big Branch mine was ordered:* Daniel Malloy, "Upper Big Branch Mine Forced to Shut Before," 9 Apr. 2010, www.post-gazette.com.

138 *That same year, the mine was cited for 515 violations:* "Miners' Families Cling to 'Sliver of Hope,'" Associated Press, 7 Apr. 2010.

138 *In 2010, by the time of the explosion:* Emily C. Dooley, "Safety Violations Posted at Massey Mine," 7 Apr. 2010, www.timesdispatch.com.

138 *What's more, in the ten years before:* Kim Bobo, "Psalm 20 and the Massey Mining Disaster," 19 May 2010, www.huffingtonpost.com.

138 *So how did Massey escape greater oversight:* Steven Mufson, Kimberly Kindy, and Ed O'Keefe, "West Virginia Mine Has Years of Serious Violations, Officials Say," 9 Apr. 2010, www.washingtonpost.com.

139 *At the time of the explosion, Massey was contesting:* Ibid.

139 *According to another loophole in the law:* Thomas Frank, "Mines Carry Backlog of $90M in Violations," 8 Apr. 2010, www.usatoday.com.

139 *Only $8 million of $113 million:* Ibid.

139 *The BP disaster has a similar story line:* Marcus Baram, "Big Oil Fought Off New Safety Rules Before Rig Explosion," 26 Apr. 2010, www.huffingtonpost.com.

139 *Over the last decade the Minerals Management Service:* Eric Lipton and John M. Broder, "Regulator Deferred to Oil Industry on Rig Safety," 7 May 2010, www.nytimes.com.

139 *The piece of equipment that the industry resisted:* Russell Gold, Ben Casselman, and Guy Chazan, "Leaking Oil Well Lacked Safeguard Device," 28 Apr. 2010, www.wsj.com.

139 *The replacement value of the Deepwater Horizon platform:* Ibid.

139 *As for fines for safety violations:* Marian Wang, "Oil Companies Pay a Pittance in Penalties to Offshore Drilling Regulator," 4 May 2010, www.propublica.org.

140 *between 1998 and 2007, BP racked up a dozen:* Ibid.

140 *Even after the Gulf catastrophe, oil companies:* Ian Urbina, "Despite Moratorium, Drilling Projects Move Ahead," 23 May 2010, www.nytimes.com.

140 *one of the exempted projects was run by BP:* Marian Wang, "After Spill, More Gulf Drilling Plans Got Environmental Exemptions," 11 May 2010, www.propublica.org.

140 *Not content with controlling politicians and kneecapping:* Linda Keenan and Janine R. Wedel, "Shadow Elite: Think BP's the Bad Guy? Think Bigger, Way Bigger," 13 May 2010, www.huffingtonpost.com.

141 *The names of the Wall Streeters:* Matthew Vadum, "Goldman Sachs Government," 16 Oct. 2008, www.spectator.org.

141 *The finance industry has 70 former members of Congress:* Public Citizen, "Stop Congress' Revolving Door of Corruption," www.citizen.org.

141 *This includes 33 chiefs of staff, 54 staffers of the House:* Arthur Delaney, "Big Bank Takeover: Report Blames Revolving Door for 'Too Big to Fail,'" 11 May 2010, www.huffingtonpost.com.

141 *Five of Senate Banking Committee chair Chris Dodd's:* Kevin Connor, "Big Bank Takeover: How Too-Big-to-Fail's Army of Lobbyists Has Captured Washington," Institute for America's Future, 11 May 2010, www.ourfuture.org.

141 *Of course, the revolving door spins both ways:* Arthur Delaney, "Big Bank Takeover: Report Blames Revolving Door for 'Too Big to Fail,'" 11 May 2010, www.huffingtonpost.com.

141 *On the mining front, former Massey chief operating officer:* Brad Johnson, "Don Blankenship's Record of Profits Over Safety: 'Coal Pays the Bills,'" 8 Apr. 2010, www.thinkprogress.org.

141 *At the time of the Upper Big Branch accident he was:* Ibid.

141 *And President Bush named Massey executive Richard Stickler:* Ibid.

142 *Stickler had such a lousy safety record:* Ibid.

142 *That's what happened when Bush put Edwin Foulke:* Stephen Labaton, "OSHA Leaves Worker Safety in Hands of Industry," 25 Apr. 2007, www.nytimes.com.

142 *Earlier in his career, while serving as chairman:* Ibid.

142 *Then there was Bush's choice of Mary Sheila Gall:* "Mary Sheila Gall Named to Chair CPSC," 20 Apr. 2001, www.consumeraffairs.com.

142 *In her ten years on the commission:* Lizette Alvarez, "Consumer Product Safety Chief Sets Deadline to Resign," 9 Aug. 2001, www.nytimes.com.

142 *She even adopted a "Let them eat marbles" stance:* Hearing on the nomination of Mary Sheila Gall to chair the Consumer Product Safety Commission before the Committee on Commerce, Science, and Transportation, U.S. Senate, 25 Jul. 2001, www.gpo.gov.

143 *And while I'm all for slapping warnings:* Matthew Robinson and Daniel Murphy, *Greed Is Good: Maximization and Elite Deviance in America* (Lanham, MD: Rowman & Littlefield, 2009), 94–95.

143 *Thankfully, the Senate refused to confirm Gall:* Caroline E. Mayer, "Senate Panel Rejects Bush's Choice for Consumer Job," 3 Aug. 2001, www.sfgate.com.

143 *Undeterred, Bush filled the slot with Harold Stratton:* Daphne Eviatar, "Toy Story," 3 Jan. 2008, www.thenation.com.

143 *Following the money once again:* Center for Responsive Politics, "Pharmaceuticals/ Health Products: Long-Term Contribution Trends," 1990–2010, www.opensecrets.org.

143 *In return, the Bush administration served up:* Marc Kaufman, "Former FDA Chief Illegally Held Stocks," 17 Oct. 2006, www.washingtonpost.com.

143 *And, if you want to see "overly cozy" run amok:* Charlie Savage, "Sex, Drug Use and Graft Cited in Interior Department," 10 Sep. 2008, www.nytimes.com.

144 *We saw how all those former Senate and House staffers:* Brian Beutler, "Do Baucus' Ties to Health Care Industry Compromise His Reform Efforts?" 6 Jul. 2009, www.talking pointsmemo.com.

144 *Among those lobbying Baucus were two of his former chiefs of staff:* Dan Eggen and Kimberly Kindy, "Familiar Players in Health Bill Lobbying," 6 Jul. 2009, www.washingtonpost. com.

144 *And among those on his staff being lobbied:* Peter Dreier, "Citizens Confront WellPoint: Poster Child for Health Insurance Reform," 22 Sep. 2009, www.huffingtonpost.com.

144 *We got an unsettling glimpse of what this:* Sam Stein, "Dodd: Treasury Officials Insisted on Weakening Bonus Provision," 2 Apr. 2009, www.huffingtonpost.com.

145 *Think about that: Even after having been bailed out:* Congressional Oversight Panel, "The AIG Rescue, Its Impact on Markets, and the Government's Exit Strategy," 10 Jun. 2010, www.cop.senate.gov.

145 *It's the same kind of inside juice that allowed:* Raymond J. Learsy, "The Key Question No One Asked About Goldman's Role in the AIG Bailout," 20 Nov. 2009, www.huffingtonpost .com.

145 *a fate that would have a multibillion-dollar impact:* Ibid.

145 *The crooked firm's chairman, Kenneth Lay:* Dan Ackman, "Enron Shifts Cash to Democrats," 27 Dec. 2001, www.forbes.com.

145 *Enron also spent $3.45 million lobbying Congress:* Public Citizen, "Blind Faith: How Deregulation and Enron's Influence over Government Looted Billions from Americans," Dec. 2001, www.citizen.org.

145 *"Kenny Boy" Lay was known to boast about his "friends at the White House":* Interviews with Ken Lay, *Frontline*, 27 Mar. 2001, 22 May 2001, www.pbs.org.

145 *friends who helped him engineer the replacement:* Robert Scheer, "Connect the Enron Dots to Bush," 24 Dec. 2001, www.thenation.com.

146 *He also had a lot of input on energy policy:* "Enron Had Cheney's Ear," 8 Jan. 2002, www .cbsnews.com.

146 *including two with Lay:* Michael Abramowitz and Steven Mufson, "Papers Detail Industry's Role in Cheney's Energy Report," 18 Jul. 2007, www.washingtonpost.com.

146 *The last of those meetings took place six days:* "Enron Had Cheney's Ear," 8 Jan. 2002, www.cbsnews.com.

146 *Back in 2000, Massey was responsible for a coal:* Brad Johnson, "Don Blankenship's Record of Profits over Safety: 'Coal Pays the Bills,'" 8 Apr. 2010, www.thinkprogress.com.

146 *The company very successfully limited the damage:* "Two for the Money," 20 Oct. 2006, www.kentucky.com.

146 *According to Jack Spadaro:* Ibid.

146 *And you can't get any cozier than Linda Daschle:* Doug Ireland, "I'm Linda, Fly Me," 23 Jan. 2003, www.laweekly.com.

146 *But there is no need to worry about familial:* Paul Blumenthal, "Daschle, Dole Release Health Care Plan, Forget to Mention They Are Health Care Lobbyists," 18 Jun. 2009, www.huffingtonpost.com.

147 *Daschle, you'll recall, came within a few:* Jeff Zeleny, "Daschle Ends Bid for Post; Obama Concedes Mistake," 3 Feb. 2009, www.nytimes.com.

147 *Daschle has also bolstered his personal bottom line:* Linda Keenan and Janine R. Wedel, "Shadow Elite: Think BP's the Bad Guy? Think Bigger, Way Bigger," 13 May 2010, www.huffingtonpost.com.

147 *Hopefully he wasn't the one who advised BP:* Tim Webb, "BP Boss Admits Job on the Line over Gulf Oil Spill," 14 May 2010, www.guardian.co.uk.

147 *Tom Daschle is a senator:* Arthur Delaney, "How Tom Daschle Lobbies in Secret: Influence Laundering," 25 Nov. 2009, www.huffingtonpost.com.

147 *Robert Rubin is co-chairman of Goldman Sachs:* Eric Dash and Louise Story, "Rubin Leaving Citigroup; Smith Barney for Sale," 9 Jan. 2009, www.nytimes.com.

147 *Dick Cheney is a congressman:* Dan Froomkin, "Halliburton's Return: Oil Spill Puts Symbol of Cronyism and Corruption Back in the News," 11 May 2010, www.huffingtonpost.com.

148 *You thought Halliburton had been eradicated:* Ibid.

148 *You thought it was over when the Justice Department:* Ibid.

148 *You thought reports that Halliburton had allowed:* Ibid.

148 *Well, they're baaa-aaack! And their work sealing:* Charlie Cray, "Time to Drill Down into Halliburton's Role in Big Oil Spill," 30 Apr. 2010, www.huffingtonpost.com.

148 *Doing a segment on Halliburton's involvement:* Robert F. Kennedy, "Sex, Lies and Oil Spills," 5 May 2010, www.huffingtonpost.com.

148 *MSNBC's Chris Matthews couldn't contain his indignation:* Hardball with Chris Matthews, 11 May 2010, www.msnbc.com.

149 *Janine Wedel calls them "flexians":* Linda Keenan and Janine R. Wedel, "Shadow Elite: Think BP's the Bad Guy? Think Bigger, Way Bigger," 13 May 2010, www.huffingtonpost.com.

149 *His résumé is the personification:* Robert Rubin: Executive Profile and Biography, www.businessweek.com.

150 *Early in 2010, he penned a lengthy essay in* Newsweek: Robert E. Rubin, "Getting the Economy Back on Track," 29 Dec. 2009, www.newsweek.com.

150 *What grabbed my attention was not the 2,500-word piece:* Ibid.

150 *Given that the piece is about the:* Jonathan Stempel and Dan Wilchins, "Robert Rubin Quits Citigroup Amid Criticism," 9 Jan. 2009, www.reuters.com.

150 *But that's how our system "works":* Robert E. Rubin, "Getting the Economy Back on Track," 29 Dec. 2009, www.newsweek.com.

150 *This from the man who, as Bill Clinton's Treasury secretary:* Timothy A. Canova, "The Legacy of the Clinton Bubble," *Dissent* Summer 2008, www.dissentmagazine.org.

150 *and who lobbied the Treasury during the Bush years:* Mark Lewis, "Rubin Red-Faced over Enron? Not in the *Times*," 11 Feb. 2002, www.forbes.com.

151 *"Politics is like sales":* Simon Johnson and James Kwak, *13 Bankers: The Wall Street Takeover and the Next Financial Meltdown* (New York: Pantheon, 2010), 104.

152 *Just as Ptolemy was convinced:* Owen Gingerich and James R. Voelkel, "Tycho and Kepler: Solid Myth Versus Subtle Truth," *Social Research* 72, 1 (22 Mar. 2005).

152 *Writing about the "grand book" that is the universe:* Galileo Galilei, *Discoveries and Opinions of Galileo*, trans. and notes by Stillman Drake (New York: Doubleday, 1957), 237–238.

153 *"The struggle of man against power . . .":* Milan Kundera, *The Book of Laughter and Forgetting*, trans. Aaron Asher (New York: Harper Perennial, 1996), 4.

153 *Until the Securities and Exchange Commission sued Goldman Sachs:* Shahien Nasiripour, "Goldman Sachs Fraud Charges Could Be Just the Beginning, Say Analysts," 16 Apr. 2010, www.huffingtonpost.com.

153 *Six months earlier, the SEC arranged a settlement:* Martin Z. Braun and William Selway, "JPMorgan Ends SEC Alabama Swap Probe for $722 Million," 4 Nov. 2009, www.bloomberg.com.

153 *As part of the settlement, JPMorgan:* William Selway and Martin Z. Braun, "JPMorgan Arranging Alabama Swaps Provided Payoffs, SEC Shows," 5 Nov. 2009, www.bloomberg.com.

154 *We saw the same dynamic played out:* Michael J. Merced and Louise Story, "Nearly 700 at Merrill in Million-Dollar Club," Feb. 2009, www.nytimes.com.

154 *Bank of America executives failed to inform:* Ibid.

154 *Bank of America agreed to pay a $33 million fine:* Stephen Bernard, "Judge Overturns Bank of America-SEC Settlement over Merrill Bonuses," Associated Press, 14 Sep. 2009.

154 *A heroic U.S. district judge, Jed Rakoff:* Larry Neumeister, "Federal Judge Approves $150 Million Bank of America, SEC Settlement, but Calls It 'Half-Baked Justice,'" Associated Press, 22 Feb. 2010.

154 *The SEC and Bank of America came back:* Ibid.

154 *The judge said he was forced by judicial restraint:* Ibid.

154 *The total amount of fines levied by the SEC:* Jonathan Stempel and Rachelle Younglai, "SEC May Wield Stronger Hand After BofA Bonus Case," 26 Aug. 2009, www.reuters.com.

155 *Three weeks after the Deepwater Horizon:* Associated Press, "BP Oil Spill Underwater Video Shows Oil Gushing Like Steam from Geyser," 13 May 2010.

156 *Within a week, Obama administration officials:* "Ken Salazar Calls Gulf Coast Disaster a 'Grave Scenario' and 'Very Catastrophic,'" Associated Press, 2 May 2010.

156 *Katrina looked like it could be bad but:* Joby Warrick, "White House Got Early Warning on Katrina," 24 Jan. 2006, www.washingtonpost.com.

156 *Even though we now know that people in the Fed were forecasting:* Ryan Grim, "Greenspan Wanted Housing-Bubble Dissent Kept Secret," 3 May 2010, www.huffingtonpost.com.

156 *But the government promised to protect homeowners:* Dan Levy, "U.S. Foreclosure Filings Rise 16% as Bank Seizures Set Record," 15 Apr. 2010, www.businessweek.com.

157 *In October 2009, the unemployment rate hit 10.2 percent:* Peter S. Goodman, "U.S. Unemployment Rate Hits 10.2%, Highest in 26 Years," 6 Nov. 2009, www.nytimes.com.

157 *When BP first applied to operate the Deepwater Horizon:* Marian Wang, "After Spill, More Gulf Drilling Plans Got Environmental Exemptions," 11 May 2010, www.propublica.org.

158 *Let's start with Iraq, an unnecessary war:* Margaret Griffis, "Casualties in Iraq: The Human Cost of Occupation," 8 May 2010, www.antiwar.com.

158 *and American taxpayers three-quarters of a trillion:* Matthew Duss, Peter Juul, and Brian Katulis, "The Iraq War Ledger: A Tabulation of the Human, Financial, and Strategic Costs," Center for American Progress, 6 May 2010, www.americanprogress.org.

158 *And for what? As the Center for American Progress:* Ibid.

158 *In the run-up to the war, General Eric Shinseki:* Eric Schmitt, "Threats and Responses: Military Spending; Pentagon Contradicts General On Iraq Occupation Force's Size," 28 Feb. 2003, www.nytimes.com.

159 *U.S. deputy secretary of defense Paul Wolfowitz told Congress:* House Committee on the Budget, Hearing on FY 2004 Defense Budget, 27 Feb. 2003.

159 *The Bush administration also told the public:* Andrew Natsios, *Nightline*, 1 Oct. 2003, www.abcnews.com.

159 *To say the administration massively underestimated:* James Glanz and T. Christian Miller, "Official History Spotlights Iraq Rebuilding Blunders," 13 Dec. 2008, www.nytimes.com.

159 *The New York Times described our reconstruction efforts:* Ibid.

159 *In late 2002, Charles Prince was put in charge:* Eric Dash and Julie Creswell, "Citigroup Saw No Red Flags Even as It Made Bolder Bets," 22 Nov. 2008, www.nytimes.com.

159 *The banking giant was already knee-deep:* Ibid.

159 *According to a former Citigroup executive:* Ibid.

160 *"I've thought a lot about that," Rubin said:* Ibid.

160 *Former Fannie Mae CEO Franklin Raines:* Marcus Baram, "Fannie Mae, Freddie Mac Hearing," 9 Dec. 2009, www.huffingtonpost.com.

160 *We saw a familiar insistence on ignoring all warnings:* Diana B. Henriques and Alex Berenson, "The 17th Floor, Where Wealth Went to Vanish," 14 Dec. 2008, www.nytimes.com.

160 *Well, financial fraud investigator Harry Markopolos, for one:* Gregory Zuckerman, "Fees, Even Returns and Auditor All Raised Flags," 13 Dec. 2008, www.wsj.com.

161 *In the wake of 9/11, Condoleezza Rice assured us:* Dan Collins, "'99 Report Warned of Suicide Hijacking," Associated Press, 17 May 2002.

161 *Except, of course, the 1999 government report:* Ibid.

161 *After Katrina, the Bush White House read:* Joby Warrick, "White House Got Early Warning on Katrina," 24 Jan. 2006, www.washingtonpost.com.

161 *Then there is the high priest of "Who Could Have Known?":* Neil Irwin and Amit R. Paley, "Greenspan Says He Was Wrong on Regulation," 24 Oct. 2008, www.washingtonpost.com.

PART 5: SAVING OURSELVES FROM A THIRD WORLD FUTURE

170 *But just three years later, as John Kao points out:* John Kao, *Innovation Nation* (New York: Simon & Schuster, 2007), 4.

170 *We had a similar reaction to the Soviets' launch of Sputnik:* Ibid., 6.

170 *President Obama captured this essential part:* Barack Obama, "Remarks by the President on the 'Education to Innovate' Campaign," 23 Nov. 2009, www.whitehouse.gov.

171 *America is rich with resources:* Thomas Friedman, "Advice from Grandma," 21 Nov. 2009, www.nytimes.com.

171 *"You can't cross a chasm in two small jumps":* Frederick Lewis Schuman and George D. Brodsky, *Design For Power: The Struggle For the World* (New York: A.A. Knopf, 1942), 200.

171 *Instead, we have to reconnect with:* Barack Obama, "Remarks by the President on the 'Education to Innovate' Campaign," 23 Nov. 2009, www.whitehouse.gov.

172 *Among those working to make this happen:* Fix Congress First!, www.fixcongressfirst.org.

173 *"We must," says Lessig:* Lawrence Lessig, "Why I'm Calling for a Constitutional Amendment," 27 Jan. 2010, www.fixcongressfirst.org.

173 *As the Fix Congress First! founders put it:* Fix Congress First!, www.fixcongressfirst.org.

173 *In March 2010, on his seventy-first birthday:* Ted Kaufman, "The Rule of Law and Wall Street," 15 Mar. 2010, www.kaufman.senate.gov.

174 *"Sunlight," Justice Louis Brandeis famously said:* Louis D. Brandeis, *Other People's Money—and How Bankers Use It* (New York: Frederick A. Stokes, 1914), 92.

175 *A great early iteration of this:* John Brewer, "Sunlight on Health Care Summit," 25 Feb. 2010, www.huffingtonpost.com.

176 *He describes Government 2.0 as:* Tim O'Reilly, "Gov 2.0: It's All About the Platform," 4 Sep. 2009, techcrunch.com.

176 *Many of the most interesting experiments:* Betsy Kraat, "Mayor Cory Booker Serves as Keynote Speaker for Social Media Conference," 31 Mar. 2010, www.njand.com.

177 *We are reminded on a daily basis:* Tim O' Reilly, "Gov 2.0: The Promise of Innovation," 10 Aug. 2009, www.forbes.com.

178 *Teacher effectiveness is the single most:* William L. Sanders and June C. Rivers, "Cumulative and Residual Effects of Teachers on Future Student Academic Achievement," University of Tennessee Value-Added Research and Assessment Center, Nov. 1996, www .mccsc.edu.

178 *And cash-strapped states inevitably:* Pauline Vu, "Do State Tests Make the Grade?" 17 Jan. 2008, www.stateline.org.

180 *In January 2010, during his State of the Union:* Barack Obama, State of the Union Address, 27 Jan. 2010, www.whitehouse.gov.

181 *But we need to move beyond the lofty rhetoric:* Bureau of Labor Statistics, "Alternative Measures of Labor Underutilization," Table A-15, 7 May 2010, www.bls.gov.

181 *Since August 2008, more than 150,000 state and local jobs:* "How Not to Write a Jobs Bill," 11 Feb. 2010, www.nytimes.com.

181 *states' combined budget gap for fiscal 2010:* Center on Budget and Policy Priorities, "An Update on State Budget Cuts," 19 Apr. 2010, www.cbpp.org.

181 *which would, in turn, lead to the loss of another 900,000 jobs next year:* Ibid.

181 *This is why the Economic Policy Institute (EPI):* Economic Policy Institute, "American Jobs Plan: A Five-Point Plan to Stem the U.S. Jobs Crisis," Dec. 2009, www.epi.org.

181 *"The federal government could provide jobs by . . .":* Paul Krugman, "The Jobs Imperative," 29 Nov. 2009, www.nytimes.com.

182 *In fact, the EPI estimates that one million jobs:* Economic Policy Institute, "American Jobs Plan: A Five-Point Plan to Stem the U.S. Jobs Crisis," Dec. 2009, www.epi.org.

182 *This approach is also favored by Princeton's Alan Blinder:* Alan Blinder, "How Washington Can Create Jobs," 15 Nov. 2009, www.wsj.com.

182 *One way to finance the massive rebuilding:* Josh Voorhees, "White House Budget Seeks $4B for Transportation Infrastructure Bank," 1 Feb. 2010, www.nytimes.com.

182 *Modeled after the European Investment Bank:* "About the EIB," European Investment Bank, www.eib.org.

182 *An investment of $25 billion in government funds:* Testimony of Rosa L. DeLauro on the National Infrastructure Development Bank Act, Ways and Means Subcommittee on Select Revenue Measures, 13 May 2010, www.waysandmeans.house.gov.

182 *That won't cover the $2.2 trillion needed:* American Society of Civil Engineers, *2009 Report Card for America's Infrastructure*, www.infrastructurereportcard.org.

182 *Washington needs to get its act together:* United States Senate, 110th Cong., 1st Sess., S. 1926, introduced 1 Aug. 2007, www.gpo.gov.

183 *To take just one example, as the rest of the economy:* John Collins Rudolf, "Renewables Industry Promotes Its Potential," 10 Feb. 2010, www.nytimes.com.

183 *The Solar Energy Industries Association estimates:* Solar Energy Industries Association, "New Study: Solar Industry Poised to Create 200,000 Jobs with Key Tax Policies," 19 May 2010, www.seia.org.

183 *Another way of promoting the green economy:* John D. Podesta and Karen Kornbluh, "The Green Bank: Financing the Transition to a Low-Carbon Economy Requires Targeted Financing to Encourage Private-Sector Participation," 21 May 2009, www.american progress.org.

184 *Reed Hundt, the Federal Communications Commission chair:* Reed Hundt, in conversation with the author, 20 Mar. 2010.

184 *According to Hundt, a green bank would create:* Reed Hundt, www.coalitionforgreen capital.com.

184 *According to a May 2010 report by the Congressional Oversight Panel:* Congressional Oversight Panel, "May Oversight Report: The Small Business Credit Crunch and the Impact of the TARP," 13 May 2010, www.cop.senate.gov.

184 *Even more important than helping small businesses:* Barbara Kiviat, "The Workforce: Where Will the New Jobs Come From?" 19 Mar. 2010, www.time.com.

185 *Right now, the United States has an immigration limit:* Jonathan Ortmans, "In the National Interest: High-Skill Immigration Reform," 31 Aug. 2009, www.entrepreneurship.org.

185 *The people behind StartupVisa.com:* Douglas MacMillan, "Visas for Foreign Entrepreneurs," 11 Mar. 2010, www.businessweek.com.

185 *Our current law allows foreign investors to get a visa:* Brad Feld, "StartUp Visa Act Introduced by Senators Kerry and Lugar," 24 Feb. 2010, www.businessinsider.com.

186 *The proposal, the StartUp Visa Act of 2010:* John Kerry and Dick Lugar, "Visa for Startups Will Keep Innovation and Jobs in the U.S," 18 Mar. 2010, www.mercurynews.com.

186 *As Kerry put it, "This bill is a small . . .":* Douglas MacMillan, "Visas for Foreign Entrepreneurs," 11 Mar. 2010, www.businessweek.com.

187 *But they never seem to have the same reaction:* Office of Management and Budget, Updated Summary Tables, Budget of the U.S. Government, Fiscal Year 2010, May 2009, www.whitehouse.gov.

187 *when it's time to sign the next check:* Anne Gearan and Anne Flaherty, "War Cost: Obama Wants $33 Billion More for Afghanistan, Iraq," 12 Jan. 2010, www.huffingtonpost.com.

187 *A perfect example of this came:* Stephen Ohlemacher and Andrew Taylor, "Senate OKs War Funding; House to Cut Spending Bill," Associated Press, 28 May 2010.

187 *For example, we are planning:* Office of the Undersecretary of Defense, Program Acquisition Costs by Weapons System, 1 Feb. 2010, www.comptroller.defense.gov.

187 *For the same amount:* National Priorities Project, "Federal Budget Trade-Offs," www.nationalpriorities.org.

188 *Representative Barney Frank suggests a good place:* Barney Frank, in conversation with the author, 21 Feb. 2010.

188 *Targeting Defense Department waste:* Sam Stein, "Obama Deficit Commission Member Calls for Pentagon Audit," 26 May 2010, www.huffingtonpost.com.

188 *Not exactly the description you want to hear:* Office of Management and Budget, Updated Summary Tables, Budget of the U.S. Government, Fiscal Year 2010, May 2009, www.whitehouse.gov.

188 *Even after cutting billions, defense spending:* Lawrence J. Korb, "Ten Myths About the Defense Budget," 2 Apr. 2001, www.inthesetimes.com.

189 *America cannot survive as "a muscle-bound . . .":* Robert Gates, speech at the Dwight D. Eisenhower Presidential Library, Abilene, Kansas, 8 May 2010, www.defense.gov.

189 *Cramdown legislation, facing intense opposition:* Arthur Delaney, "Durbin Considers Cramdown-Related Amendment as Part of Wall Street Reform," 17 May 2010, www.huffingtonpost.com.

189 *Some, including Bank of America and Citigroup:* Shahien Nasiripour, "Bank of America Now Supports Cramdown, Giving Judges Authority to Modify Home Mortgages," 13 Apr. 2010, www.huffingtonpost.com.

189 *We should also make it mandatory that homeowners and lenders:* Arlen Specter, "Nation's Economic Repairs Must Include Homeowners," 24 Oct. 2008, www.philly.com/inquirer.

190 *Currently, many homeowners don't even talk:* Margo Irvin, "Homeowners Seeking 'Making Home Afforable' Loan Modifications Frustrated by Inefficiency," 22 Jun. 2009, www.huffingtonpost.com.

190 *"I've been to the City Hall courtroom where the mediation . . .":* Bob Casey, in conversation with the author, 16 Feb. 2009.

190 *Judge Annette Rizzo, who has been working hard:* Dan Geringer, "The Miracle of Courtroom 676: Saving Lives, One Address at a Time," 28 Jan. 2009, www.philly.com/dailynews.

190 *The foreclosure prevention program has worked:* Ibid.

190 *Until we do, we'll need to rely on officials:* Michael Powell, "A 'Little Judge' Who Rejects Foreclosures, Brooklyn Style," 30 Aug. 2009, www.nytimes.com.

191 *For example, the new law still allows promotional teaser:* Max Alexander, "Credit Card Tricks and Traps," Mar. 2010, www.readersdigest.com.

191 *As Elizabeth Warren sees it: "That's exactly . . .":* "Elizabeth Warren on Credit Card 'Tricks and Traps,'" *NOW*, 2 Jan. 2009, www.pbs.org.

191 *According to the new law, the credit card issuer:* Max Alexander, "Credit Card Tricks and Traps," Mar. 2010, www.readersdigest.com.

192 *Because fees account for 39 percent:* Ibid.

192 *And the new law doesn't prevent:* Ibid.

192 *Senator Bernie Sanders, whose attempts at capping:* Jeff Plungis, "Senate Nears Completing Credit Card Bill, Blocks 15% Rate Cap," 14 May 2009, www.bloomberg.com.

192 *Aristotle called usury the "sordid love of gain":* Aristotle, *Nicomachean Ethics* (Minneapolis: Filiquarian, 2007), 87.

192 *Thomas Aquinas said it was "contrary to justice":* St. Thomas Aquinas, *Summa Theologica*, trans. by Fathers of the English Dominican Province (London: R. T. Washburne, Ltd., 1918), 330.

192 *In* The Divine Comedy, *Dante assigned:* Dante Alighieri, *The Divine Comedy of Dante Alighieri: Hell, Purgatory, Paradise,* trans. by Henry F. Cary (New York: P.F. Collier & Son, 1909–14), 49.

193 *Right after President Obama's election, Rahm Emanuel famously declared:* Jeff Zeleny, "Obama Weighs Quick Undoing of Bush Policy," 9 Nov. 2010, www.nytimes.com.

194 *Even Alan Greenspan, the oracle of free markets:* Council on Foreign Relations, "Peter McColough Series on International Economics: The Global Financial Crisis: Causes and Consequences," transcript, 15 Oct. 2009, www.cfr.org.

194 *Discussing the economic crisis, Michael Lynton:* Michael Lynton, in conversation with the author, 31 Jan. 2009.

194 *The answer was no. Likewise: PBS NewsHour,* "Greenspan Admits 'Flaw' to Congress, Predicts More Economic Problems," 23 Oct. 2008, www.pbs.org.

195 *In 1967, speaking at:* Robert F. Kennedy, campaign speech at University of Kansas, 18 Mar. 1967, www.jfklibrary.org.

196 *As Justice Potter Stewart wrote of the Pentagon Papers: New York Times Co. v. United States,* Supreme Court of the United States, No. 1873, Stewart, J., Concurring Opinion (1971).

196 *The media is also addicted: Real Time with Bill Maher,* HBO, 7 Mar. 2008, www.hbo.com.

197 *What if we could repurpose some of that concern:* The National Center on Family Homelessness, "America's Youngest Outcasts: State Report Card on Child Homelessness," 2009, www.homelesschildrenamerica.org.

197 *or the 51 percent of homeless children who are under the age of six:* Ibid.

197 *How about some attention to the 75 to 100 percent increase:* Erik Eckholm, "Surge in Homeless Pupils Strains Schools," 5 Sept. 2009, www.nytimes.com.

197 *Or the 14 million American children living in poverty:* Vanessa R. Wight, Michelle Chau, and Yumiko Aratani, "Who Are America's Poor Children? The Official Story," National Center for Children in Poverty, Jan. 2010, www.nccp.org.

197 *"People work for justice . . .":* Paul Loeb, "'Soul of a Citizen': Stories of Impact Will Push Us to Fix the Oil Spill, Homelessness, and Other Big Problems," 27 May 2010, www .huffingtonpost.com.

200 *Tip O'Neill said, "All politics is local":* Tip O'Neill and Gary Hymel, *All Politics Is Local, and Other Rules of the Game* (Holbrook: Bob Adams Inc., 1994), xii.

201 *The concept was simple: If enough people who had money:* Colin Barr, "Big Banks Mint Money Again: $18.7 Billion," 21 Apr. 2010, www.money.cnn.com.

201 *And since deposit insurance at small banks:* Kara McGuire, "'Move your Money' Campaign Wants to Sock It to Big Banks," 14 Mar. 2010, www.startribune.com.

201 *We launched the Move Your Money campaign:* Ibid.

201 *Bill Maher compared moving your money to ending:* Bill Maher, "Stop the Abuse: It's Time to Break Up with Your Big Bank," 13 Jan. 2010, www.huffingtonpost.com.

202 *About 2 million people, in every region:* Dennis Santiago, "For Bigger Banks, Deposits Remain Sticky," 10 May 2010, www.huffingtonpost.com.

202 *One of them, H. Lee Grove, wrote:* Comment by H. Lee Grove in the Huffington Post, 7 Jan. 2010.

203 *Consumer credit unions are not owned by shareholders:* Bob Trebilcock, "Bye, Bye, Banks: Time to Join a Credit Union," CBS Money Watch, 12 Jan. 2010, www.bnet .com.

203 *Since their goal is not to maximize short-term profit:* Péralte C. Paul, "Credit Unions Fare Better in Banking Downturn," 14 May 2010, www.ajc.com.

203 *Nearly ninety million Americans belong to credit unions:* John Hielscher, "Region's Credit Unions Weather Downturn," 31 May 2010, www.heraldtribune.com.

203 *Around 70 percent of credit union mortgages:* Frank Michael, testimony before the Committee on Banking, Housing, and Urban Affairs, United States Senate, 8 Jul. 2009, www.banking.senate.gov.

204 *(The exceptions are corporate credit unions . . .):* Mark Maremont, "U.S. Moves to Bail Out Credit Union Network," 29 Jan. 2009, www.wsj.com.

204 *"A credit union saved me from Bank of America":* Joe McKesson, in response to a Face-book and Twitter request from the author, spring 2009.

204 *"All I can say is that nothing beats the personal . . .":* Consuelo Flores, in response to a Facebook and Twitter request from the author, spring 2009.

204 *Deborah Bohn's nineteen-year-old daughter:* Deborah Bohn, in response to a Facebook and Twitter request from the author, spring 2009.

204 *20 percent of households can afford:* "Hello Wallet: Our Story," www.hellowallet.com.

204 *Witness HelloWallet.com, a start-up:* Keith Epstein. "Will HelloWallet Transform On-line Financial Advice?" 29 Sep. 2009, www.businessweek.com.

205 *The site will automatically find:* www.hellowallet.com.

205 *Best of all, the site is:* "HelloWallet: We make banks work for you," www.hellowallet.com.

205 *Another good online tool is:* Virginia Heffernan, "Home Economics," 21 May 2009, www .nytimes.com.

205 *And it's important to keep track of your credit report:* Liz Pulliam Weston, "Raise Your Credit Score to 740," 10 Mar. 2010, www.moneycentral.msn.com.

206 *In April 2010, President Obama issued a proclamation:* Barack Obama, presidential proclamation on Financial Literacy Month, 2 Apr. 2010, www.whitehouse.gov.

206 *I was reading* Consumer Reports *and came across:* "The New Money Rules," May 2009, www.consumerreports.org.

207 *Or, as Suze Orman puts it, "No Blame, No Shame . . .":* Suze Orman, "Suze Orman's 10 Tips for a Fresh Financial Start," 16 Dec. 2008, www.oprah.com.

207 *Karen Reivich and Andrew Shatté:* Karen Reivich and Andrew Shatté, *The Resilience Factor* (New York: Broadway Books, 2002), 1, 3–4.

208 *Dominique Browning, who lost her job as editor in chief:* Dominique Browning, "Losing It," 22 Mar. 2010, www.nytimes.com.

208 *Indeed, after being fired she went through:* Dominique Browning, *Slow Love* (New York: Atlas, 2010), 148.

208 *But slowly, she began:* Ibid., 23.

209 *Eventually, things turned around for her:* Ibid., 5, 165.

213 *Take the case of Annette Arca:* Lynnette Curtis, "Jobless Volunteer Has Time to Spare," 16 Nov. 2010, www.lvrj.com.

214 *Then there's Seth Reams, who lost his job as a concierge:* Nancy Wood, "After Losing His Job, Portland Man Founds a New Nonprofit," 6 May 2009, www.komonews.com.

214 *More projects soon followed:* Seth Reams, "People Call Us with Tales of Hunger, Home

Loss, Job Loss, Personal Loss, and Myriad Difficulties," 6 May 2010, www.wevegottimetohelp
.blogspot.com.

214 *"The ultimate measure of a man or woman"*: Martin Luther King Jr., *Strength to Love*
(Philadelphia: Fortress, 1963), 35.

215 *After spending months embedded*: Sebastian Junger on *Real Time with Bill Maher*, 14
May 2010, www.hbo.com.

215 *But twenty-six million people are unemployed or underemployed*: Rex Nutting, "GDP to
Show More Balanced Growth, Survey Says," 29 Apr. 2010, www.marketwatch.com.

215 *over 4 percent of U.S. workers have been unemployed*: Kevin Drum, "Who Are the
Long-Term Unemployed?" 13 May 2010, www.motherjones.com.

216 *And more and more people are entering the ranks of "the 99ers"*: Arthur Delaney, "Tier
5: The Despair of the 99ers," 28 May 2010, www.huffingtonpost.com.

216 *Of course, a third of America's unemployed*: Jay Bookman, "Do Jobless Checks Subsidize
Laziness? Research Shows . . . ," 21 Apr. 2010, www.ajc.com.

216 *Making matters worse, there is a growing*: Laura Bassett, "Disturbing Job Ads: 'The Unemployed Will Not Be Considered,'" 4 Jun. 2010, www.huffingtonpost.com.

216 *A study by researchers at Yale*: "Rising Unemployment Causes Higher Death Rates, New
Study by Yale Researcher Shows," 23 May 2002, www.yale.edu.

217 *Fifteen years ago, I wrote a book—The Fourth Instinct*: Arianna Huffington, *The Fourth
Instinct: The Call of the Soul* (New York: Simon & Schuster, 1994), 147–148.

218 *As Pablo Neruda said: "To feel the intimacy of brothers . . ."*: "Childhood and Poetry,"
Neruda and Vallejo: Selected Poems, Robert Bly, ed. (Boston: Beacon, 1993), 12.

218 *It was the happiness*: Prov. 14:21 (King James edition).

219 *He's got the right words: "When you serve"*: Barack Obama, commencement address at
the University of Notre Dame, 17 Mar. 2009, www.whitehouse.gov.

219 *In the immediate aftermath of 9/11*: "Bush Says US Will Wage 'Long and Unrelenting
War,'" Associated Press, 15 Sept. 2001.

219 *A month later he echoed that theme*: George W. Bush, press conference, 11 Oct. 2001,
www.georgewbush-whitehouse.archives.gov.

220 *Of course, the sum total of his idea of sacrifice*: Andrew J. Bacevich, "He Told Us to Go
Shopping. Now the Bill Is Due," 5 Oct. 2008, www.washingtonpost.com.

220 *In 2009, for example, Teach for America received 35,000 applications*: Associated
Press, "Teach for America Applications Soar," 28 May 2009.

220 *In 2008, 75,000 AmeriCorps members*: Alan Silverleib, "Hope in Cedar Rapids as Washington Pushes Volunteerism," 22 Oct. 2010, www.cnn.com.

220 *The Serve America Act, introduced by Ted Kennedy*: "S. 277, the Serve America Act,"
Democratic Policy Institute Legislative Bulletin, 23 Mar. 2009, www.dpc.senate.gov.

220 *Approximately 280,000 special needs children*: USA Freedom Corps, "Answering the
Call to Service," Sept. 2008, 19.

220 *Eighty-one percent of the children*: "Independent Research Shows National Service Program Enlisting Tutors over Age 55 Produces Big Gains in Student Learning," 7 Apr. 2009,
www.experiencecorps.org.

220 *And students working with an Experience Corps tutor*: Nancy Morrow-Howell et al.,
"Evaluation of Experience Corps," Washington University in St. Louis, Jan. 2009, www
.csd.wustl.edu.

221 *When people used to offer to join*: Susan Conroy, *Mother Teresa's Lessons of Love and Se-
crets of Sanctity* (Huntington, IN: Our Sunday Visitor, 2003), 199.

221 *Geoffrey Canada provides a template*: Dan Collins, "Harlem's Miracle Man," 22 Jan.
2010, www.huffingtonpost.com.

221 *As reported by* Metro: "A Model for Obama," *Metro*, 17 Mar. 2009, www.metro.us.

222 *He titled it "Waiting for Whom?"*: Geoffrey Canada, "Waiting For Whom?" Harlem Children's Zone, www.hcz.org.

223 *Susie Buffett offers another shining example:* Quotes and materials provided by Susie Buffett to the author in conversation and by email, May 2010.

225 *In* The Empathic Civilization, *Jeremy Rifkin:* Jeremy Rifkin, *The Empathic Civilization: The Race to Global Consciousness in a World in Crisis* (New York: Penguin, 2009), 12.

225 *New scientific data tells us:* Ibid., 47.

225 *"An individual," said Martin Luther King:* Martin Luther King Jr., *The Measure of a Man* (Minneapolis: Augsburg Fortress, 2001), 43.

225 *the Huffington Post published a story about Monique Zimmerman-Stein:* Julian Hattem, "Mom Goes Blind So Her Daughters Can See," 28 Sep. 2009, www.huffingtonpost.com.

226 *The Stein family's story struck:* Victoria Fine, "Help the Steins: Mother Who Went Blind to Save Her Children's Sight Struggles with Medical Debt," 13 Oct. 2009, www.huffingtonpost .com.

226 *"We are on the cusp of an epic shift":* Jeremy Rifkin, *The Empathic Civilization: The Race to Global Consciousness in a World in Crisis* (New York: Penguin, 2009), 3.

226 *"Seven billion individual connections":* Ibid., 594.

227 *In his 1963 work "Letter from a Birmingham Jail":* Martin Luther King Jr., "Letter from a Birmingham Jail," www.africa.upenn.edu.

227 *Conservative commentator Tony Blankley: Left, Right and Center,* 15 Jan. 2010, www .kcrw.com.

227 *As America's Misery Index soars:* www.miseryindex.us.

228 *"We have to lean on one another . . .":* Barack Obama, eulogy for West Virginia Miners, 25 Apr. 2010, www.whitehouse.gov.

228 *David Brooks has written about the need:* David Brooks, "The Broken Society," 18 Mar. 2010, www.nytimes.com.

228 *"Volunteering, especially among professional classes and the young":* Philip Blond, "Cameron's 'Big Society,'" 25 Apr. 2010, www.guardian.co.uk.

228 *In 2002 in San Francisco's Mission district:* "About 826," www.826valencia.org.

228 *In Brooklyn, New York, FEAST:* Danny LaChance, "An Idea Grows in Brooklyn," University of Minnesota Alumni Association, spring 2010, www.minnesotaalumni.org.

229 *Matthew Bishop, U.S. business editor for the* Economist: Howard Davies, "A New Take on Giving," 10 Jan. 2009, www.guardian.co.uk.

229 *Social entrepreneurs pinpoint social problems:* Caroline Hsu, "Entrepreneur for Social Change," 31 Oct. 2005, www.usnews.com.

229 *Providing microcredit to small businesses:* Devin Leonard, "Microcredit? To Him, It's Only a Start," 30 Apr. 2010, www.nytimes.com.

229 *In 2008, Yunus's Grameen bank opened a branch in New York:* "About Us," www .grameenamerica.com.

229 *In 2010 it opened a branch in Omaha, Nebraska:* "Grameen America Celebrates Grand Opening of Omaha Branch," 24 Feb. 2010, www.grameenamerica.com.

229 *The Grameen Bank's slogan: "Banking for the unbanked":* Emily Belz, "Recession-Proof Banking?" *World Magazine,* 20 Jun, 2009, www.worldmag.com.

229 *Hoping to serve one million American entrepreneurs:* "About Us," www.grameenamerica .com.

230 *By February 2010, the New York branch had:* Ibid.

230 *The average loan amount is $1,500 (no collateral necessary):* Laura Thompson Osuri, "Coming to America," *American Banker,* Apr. 2010, www.americanbanker.com.

230 *Since 1991, ACCION USA:* "About ACCION USA: Who We Are," www.accionusa.org.

230 *Luis Zapeda Alvarez:* "Meet Our Borrowers: Bakery Delivery Service," www.accionusa.org.

230 *Another New Yorker, Lyn Genet Recitas:* "Meet Our Borrowers: Neighborhood Holistic," ACCION USA, www.accionusa.org.

230 *DonorsChoose.org, for example, invites public school teachers:* "Impact to Date," May 2010, www.donorschoose.org.

231 *In Connecticut, Web developer Ben Berkowitz:* Daniel E. Slotnik, "News Sites Dabble with a Web Tool for Nudging Local Officials," 3 Jan. 2010, www.nytimes.com.

231 *Using the backbone of social networking to help people connect:* Robin Wauters, "Google, Other Tech Heavyweights Back Volunteer Community Service All for Good," 15 Jun. 2009, www.techcrunch.com.

232 *When television journalist Andrea McCarren:* Andrea McCarren, "A Laid-off Journalist Charts a New Course via Social Media," *Nieman Reports,* Winter 2009, www.nieman .harvard.edu.

232 *were inspired to launch Project Bounce Back:* "About This Project," www.projectbounceback .com.

233 *And it would be great if:* Andrew Carnegie, *The Gospel of Wealth and Other Timely Essays* (New York: The Century Co., 1901), 43.

233 *the wealthiest 1 percent:* G. William Domhoff, "Wealth, Income, and Power," Apr. 2010, www.sociology.usc.edu/whorulesamerica.

233 *The pair has launched The Giving Pledge:* Carol J. Loomis, "The $600 Billion Challenge," 16 Jun. 2010, www.fortune.cnn.com.

233 *Buffett has promised to give:* Warren Buffett, "My Philanthropic Pledge," 16 Jun. 2010, www.fortune.cnn.com.

233 *And others are starting to join in:* Dakin Campbell and Katya Kazakina, "Broad, Bloomberg Back Buffett Call for Billionaire Donations," 17 Jun. 2010, www.bloomberg.com.

233 *If The Giving Pledge catches on:* Carol J. Loomis, "The $600 Billion Challenge," 16 Jun. 2010, www.fortune.cnn.com.

234 *As Frederick Douglass put it:* W. D. Wright, *Racism Matters* (Westport, CT: Praeger, 1998), 178.

234 *The perfect example of this came in March 1965:* "The Presidents: LBJ," 1991, www.pbs .org.

234 *LBJ signed the National Voting Rights Act:* E.W. Kenworthy, "Johnson Signs Voting Rights Bill, Orders Immediate Enforcement," 7 Aug. 1965, www.nytimes.com.

234 *Similarly, before the start of WWII, legendary labor leader A. Philip Randolph:* Jervis Anderson, *A. Philip Randolph: A Biographical Portrait* (Berkeley: University of California Press, 1972), 259.

235 *former Merrill Lynch CEO John Thain:* Josh Fineman and David Mildenberg, "Thain Pushed Out at Bank of America After Merrill Loss Widens," 22 Jan. 2009, www.bloomberg .com.

235 *Goldman Sachs's Lloyd "Doing God's Work" Blankfein:* John Arlidge, "I'm Doing 'God's Work.' Meet Mr. Goldman Sachs," 8 Nov. 2009, www.thetimes.co.uk.

235 *BP's Tony "I'd Like My Life Back" Hayward:* Jad Mouawad and Clifford Krauss, "Another Torrent BP Works to Stem: Its CEO," 3 Jun. 2010, www.nytimes.com.

236 *President Obama has said that we find:* Barack Obama, commencement address at the University of Notre Dame, 17 Mar. 2009, www.whitehouse.gov.

236 *So, as we stand at this inflection point:* Jonas Salk, *The Survival of the Wisest* (Harper & Row, 1973), 20.

239 *"Few will have the greatness":* Robert F. Kennedy, "Day of Affirmation Address," 6 Jun. 1966, www.jfklibrary.org.

INDEX